Quotes and Test

"Makes sense of complex organizational change issues in a way that anyone would understand them. Business leaders that don't take time out to sit and read this book will wish to heaven they had."
Jane Ling, Director, Ling Turner

"I find myself agreeing with many of the ideas in this book. Like Kaplan, Tomlin injects ideas but leaves leaders to consider how to apply the learning lessons."
Lowell L. Bryan, McKinsey & Co.

"Plenty to grip the reader. Ian has a writing style that appeals to experienced businesspeople and newcomers to the business world alike."
Dr. Martin Vasey, (Ex-) Director of Global Knowledge, Energy, Chemicals and Utilities, Ernst & Young

"This is a must for the bookshelves of any manager wanting to ensure their organization can survive in the complex adaptive system which is the reality of the business world of today. The book is both insightful and pragmatic: insightful as it redefines business agility and paints a picture of the successful organization of the future, or indeed of today; pragmatic through its "how to" examples and stories of experience which bring the subject to life."
Peter Franklin, CEO, enstra consulting

"This book is the innovation manual to revitalize managerial thinking. It provides a convincing direction and enthusiasm to act beyond what has become conventional. This is a chance to put on a good race with inspiration for a solid game-plan yet with room for lots of creativity. The reward is a gratifying business existence in the new society the emergence of which most of us already sense. Perfect timing. A refresh button for the business world that we take for granted."
Tonis Haamer, Solutions Marketing, Imaging Systems Group, Canon U.S.A., Inc.

"Ian Tomlin's book, Agilization, is original, idealistic and written from the heart. It makes a persuasive case for more agile and sustainable approaches to be adopted in business – as an imperative if western enterprise is not to be overwhelmed by competition from the East. The book contains many practical illustrations and ideas about how to do this. I particularly like the notions of "wind-driven enterprise", "golden threads", "digital DNA" and new (and disappearing) board roles. I commend the chapter on Agile IT to all those who have suffered at the hands of large, inflexible corporate systems. The lessons apply just as much to government and third sector enterprise as to profit-making businesses."

Judith Wainwright, Managing Director, BeeAgile

"Implementing less than half of the lessons in this book would make most corporations leaders in their industry."

John Taylor, PA Consulting

"It's a book that encourages leaders to adopt a more thoughtful, externally focused management philosophy that is coming to define successful corporations."

Mike Clargo, Tesseracts Ltd

"Institutionally, the ability to be agile enough is the gut issue in leading an organization today."

James McNerney, CEO, Boeing

"Many organizations haven't changed the way they think and work in decades. Exposing these issues and finding a route to greater levels of agility is something most corporations can benefit from."

Bob Kiley, Transport for London

"A thought provoking valuable read for any business leader"

Nick Dodds, CEO, CWP Consultants

For a complete list of Management Books 2000 titles
visit our website on http://www.mb2000.com

AGILIZATION

The Regeneration of Competitiveness

Ian Tomlin
with Nick Lawrie

2000

First published in 2008 by Management Books 2000 Ltd
Forge House, Limes Road
Kemble, Cirencester
Gloucestershire, GL7 6AD, UK
Tel: 0044 (0) 1285 771441
Fax: 0044 (0) 1285 771055
Email: info@mb2000.com
Web: www.mb2000.com

British Library Cataloguing in Publication Data is available

ISBN 9781852525576

The Tipping Point

Some time during the last 20 years an event occurred that will change society and the way commercial markets work forever.

Without anyone really noticing, the tears of a new generation fell into the Western world's sea of apathy with its aging political structures, religious models and regimented markets that have formed over time. The tears fell because members of this new generation felt utterly *hope*-less and *disconnected*; **Hope-less** because they had more money, choice, freedom and security, yet less to live for because they felt they could not influence the way the world worked. Everything that humankind could achieve appeared to them as having already been done. Their life-choices, whilst broad, did not excite. Whilst many had parents that loved them, in their souls they felt **disconnected** from a society whose organizational structures and emotional support frameworks had no relevance to them.

Few people noticed this transformation in social consciousness. There was no immediate impact on the way people lived, governments worked and corporations still made their money as they always had.

Then something else happened – the digital revolution.

Members of the new generation became empowered to communicate their unhappiness and assert their individual perspectives. They were becoming a market force to be reckoned with. The very success of new products and services would depend on what they thought, what was communicated in the messages that flowed between these individuals via the linking tissue of blogs, podcasts, emails, text messages and social networking sites.

The single teardrop was growing in energy, becoming a *ripple* on the surface attracting attention to these events. Corporations who enjoyed success during good times and bad times over previous years thought that their substantial assets and money in the bank would always cushion any potential blow and give them time to react to any changes in demand. Why should *they* pay any attention whatsoever to the ramblings of a young generation of no-hopers?

But corporate leaders were missing something extremely important and for some it would be life-threatening to their organizations.

The Internet, email, social networking sites, these are new channels of communication – but there will be more. Technologies of the digital age are turning another corner.

When they do, the single teardrop will become storm force and the opinions of the *hope*-less generation will become something that will keep successive corporate leaders awake at night for the next 100 years of commerce. We have entered the age of **individualism** (more on this in Chapter 3).

And so it was that the **tipping point** that irrevocably changed the way society and markets work forever occurred without anybody really noticing.

This book is about what happens next and what corporations can do about it.

About the Author

Ian Tomlin is a management consultant, marketing strategist and theoretician.

As joint chief executive of NDMC Consulting, co-founded with Nick Lawrie in 2002, he helps organizations to realize their potential through better methods of listening to customers and translating customer insight into simpler communications, better capabilities, products and services. NDMC's clients include some of the world's largest public and private sector organizations.

The team at NDMC invented Encanvas, agile business software that enables corporations to adopt adaptable information systems that respond to the changing demands placed on their organization.

Acknowledgements

It takes many friendships to write a book. Projects of this sort are, by necessity, more of a collaborative event shared by like-minded people rather than one individual's work of art. My thanks go to my family and friends for their unrelenting support. I would also like to thank the contributors below who have helped in providing content:

- **Business planning** – Mike Clargo, CEO of Tesseracts Ltd. Mike is one of those personalities in business that you meet by chance and then wonder why he isn't a household name.
- **Brand** – The team at RLYL.com for their inspirational ideas on brand behaviours and tone of voice management and Dr Rob Waller for his thought-leadership on information design.
- **Followership and workforce** – Jane Ling and Jenny Turner, founders of Ling Turner Ltd, for their most significant contributions towards followership and norms of behaviour.
- **Horizon scanning** – George Guernsey, CEO of Insight Mapping Ltd, for his contributions on horizon scanning approaches.
- **Innovation** – Dr. Alpheus Bingham, Founder of InnoCentive Inc. and winner of the Economic Innovator of the Year award in 2005.
- **Knowledge** – Dr Martin Vasey with his pragmatic contributions in the area of extracting value from knowledge.
- **Operational excellence** – A note here to recognize the contribution Nick Lawrie has made to this book by adding substance to topics in the area of operational excellence born out of his career as one of Europe's finest financial directors.
- **Leadership** – Mr. Bob Kiley is recognised as an international problem solver and leadership advisor for transport systems.
- **Workplace** – Nick Dodds, CEO of CWP Consultants Ltd. It was Nick who first alerted me to the influence of workplace on performance.

Contents

In order to succeed, we must first believe that we can.

Michael Korda

Preface

What underpins business success? A great idea... sourcing funding... getting the timing right... having a world-class organization? How do you find yourself standing at the door when opportunity knocks?

In the 21st century business world, it's about identifying things that customers will pay for and rapidly responding to these opportunities with *best-fit* products and services. This single capability separates market leaders from the chasing pack. I needed a term to describe this new logic of the enterprise and so I created **agilization**. In this regard small companies have an advantage. They are naturally intimate with their customers, understand fully what they are capable of, what they are trying to achieve. As companies get bigger they get more dysfunctional, segregated, inflexible, and can rapidly loose their passion, becoming stale and institutionalized in the way they think and consequently the way they act.

If you are a budding entrepreneur or corporate climber, it's a good time to learn about how business works. Many of the old rules have changed. Attend a management school today and chances are you're going to be educated in methods that just don't apply to today's highly competitive, rapidly-changing, business world. Much of this old thinking has been left behind in the dust-trail of the worldwide web and globalization. My personal real-world experiences told me that current textbooks were out of date. I started writing this book when I couldn't find an idiot's guide that described how leaders and entrepreneurs could find *'the fit'*. There is a wealth of information out there on the Internet. What I wanted was a topic guide with easy-to-read explanations of methods. If that's the sort of book you're looking for, here it is.

I believe every manager, CEO, board director and entrepreneur in the world should read this book. Not because I wrote it, but because an agilized enterprise is what every organization – big or small – aspires to be. To understand how to develop a mindset and behaviour that repeatedly delivers this *best-fit to market demands* I rounded up the best ideas of management practitioners who have graciously shared their thoughts on good practice that I believe collectively create an *agilized* enterprise.

Making sense of how markets *could* or *should* work is my day job. I'm privileged to work with a brilliant business practitioner, Nick Lawrie. By the time I met Nick he had already gone through more corporate life experiences than most people touch in their careers. There was no chance of my ever catching up. So in the spirit of our relationship, when authoring this book, I assembled my thoughts and those of some exceptional business practitioners, and Nick helped me to edit (should I say re-write) many words and replace them with better ones. What's left is this book.

I examine the changing commercial environment that makes agilization such an important topic for businesses. I expose a significant evolution in society that is happening now and its influence on how we, as consumers, want to live. It will influence how we, as consumers, will purchase their goods and services, how we will identify with brands and how this will form a *new deal* between individuals and corporations. These market dynamics require that organizations always find a fit between customer demands and their capabilities. I then describe what organizations can do to become more agile so they can be better than their competitors at acquiring new customers and achieving growth. These capabilities will change the culture, management attitudes and make-up of organizations, and ultimately differentiate the successful enterprise of tomorrow from the archetypal high performing enterprise of today.

Society is changing and with it, the relationship between buyers and sellers. The Internet has introduced a new purity to competition. It means that the supplier best able to deliver customer value wins. Leaders that encourage their organizations to adopt agile behaviours can achieve *first mover advantage* and profit from opportunities as they emerge. They will be the *first* to develop meaningful relationships with the many new types of organizations that will emerge to embrace consumer preferences and self-expression, *first* to develop new business models, *first* to market with products that consumers want to pay for.

These organizations will have the capacity to respond more ably to the needs of stakeholders and create a trusted and valued brand. It will give organizations that adopt these methods a leadership position. Shareholders will make more money. Leaders will be hoisted up on the shoulders of their workforce!

(Did I get carried away there?!)

Introduction

In Western world society we are all dependents of large corporations. Many millions of people are employed by these market juggernauts. Millions more eat the scraps from their tables. Others benefit more indirectly from their presence. They are important to *all* of us. Without corporations the Western world's consumer markets of (almost) free trade, of free-flowing goods, of (relative) plenty, would not exist. They matter to you.

If you were to sit back in an armchair and design the perfect business organization, what would this slick corporate machine look like? How *actually* should a 21st century organization be engineered? Would it have a small centre, harness the skills of specialist individuals and partners to stay small and nimble, be a caring employer and have motivated people, embrace innovation? Would it appear to possess a sixth sense when it comes to knowing which markets to tap into and how best to model itself to exploit opportunities? Be more responsive to markets than competitors?

Agility is so often mentioned today. It has become the new 'black dress' of business. Organizations focus too much on trying to change and too little time thinking about why. It isn't the *degree* of agility that matters. Every now and again organizations appear compelled to meddle with departmental structures, with huge negative impact on staff, but little business benefit.

The ambition of business improvement is no longer to move from one rigid organizational structure to the next. Change is a constant. It necessitates a fluid structure so that organizations are always able to fit profitable markets at any point in time. That's the difference between business agility (the ability of a business to adapt from one state to the next) and an agilized enterprise (the outcome of a mindset and behaviour that results in an organization able to repeatedly fit profitable markets). It demands a new way of thinking about how an organization is structured and how it behaves.

The agilized enterprise rapidly senses and reacts to new sources and forms of demand to then engineer organizational structures and behaviours to meet this demand. With the structure of markets constantly changing, agilization It is the 'X-factor' that differentiates 21st century businesses and ensures success and sustainability.

Being part of a customer-focused, fast changing business is tremendous fun. It is genuinely exciting to be a part of a growing, successful team with people encouraged to be as good as they know they can be, given the *head-room* to try out new things. One person's success motivates another and people are always learning and growing. Visualize a place where people feel they are doing something meaningful with their lives. Agile organizations are great places to be. Profitable. Fun. So why isn't every business agilized?

The core tasks of business don't change. Companies must grow their profitability, manage costs and keep customers happy. In the past, companies could achieve these ambitions by adopting business models that remained more or less the same for years. **This is no longer possible.** The pace of change in global markets is unprecedented. Don't think either that there is a threshold or that at some point the pace of change will slow. It won't. We're entering a new era of social interaction with forms of communication catapulting our society into 'something different' that we cannot comprehend. In response, leaders must challenge assumptions about how they run their businesses and the operating models they choose – not every decade, more like every quarter.

A survey by the Economist Intelligence Unit of 336 senior corporate executives, one quarter of whom were CEOs, found that 47% of respondents anticipated major changes to their business model within three years. Hyper-competitive global markets of the 21st century demand a kind of organization that thinks and behaves differently.

The idea of *business agility* is nothing new. I remember it was big news in the 1980s. I also remember thinking at the time, "It makes sense to me that organizations should be able to flex and change rapidly but how USEFUL is agility? And what does an agile organization look like?"

The commonly-held view of agility in business is that it's about *processes (a series of activities that transform an input into a desired output)*, and how they must flex to respond to changes in business requirements. These business processes are often shaped by inflexible organizational structures and institutionalized behaviours that evolve over time and echo 'static' management thinking, probably formed around priorities that once met a prevailing market need. Agility is about more flexible processes. Many of the traditional elements that have previously defined business excellence, success and sustainability are incorporated into this new formula but they are no longer sufficient to provide a competitive advantage.

Agilization defines an organization that always fits its most profitable markets – formed by a different management mind-set transforming enterprise behaviour from one form, modelled by 20th century corporations focused on automation, to another that meets the competitive imperative of 21st century organizations.

This book answers four important questions:

1. Why is agilization so critical to business success?
2. What is an agilized enterprise?
3. What characteristics make an agilized organization?
4. How can an organization measure its level of agilization?

Agilization is the sum of a number of behavioural characteristics:

'It's about timing'. Some organizations always appear to know *when* to enter a market and *what* customer value they need to deliver when they do. Tesco introduced a catalogue shopping service in the mid 2000's. It meant going toe-to-toe against the UK's king of catalogue retail, Argos. But they did not choose to emulate Argos. Instead they exploited their capabilities in e-commerce, customer insight (through their excellent Club Card customer incentive scheme) and national logistics infrastructure. Combining these capabilities they could provide a value-differentiating service that gave customers the ability to browse through products in a glossy printed catalogue or purchase online, spend Club Card points on new purchases and have goods delivered to local Tesco store with free delivery.

'It's about knowing'. Tesco operates one of the most sophisticated customer insight capture systems in the world which is why the company understands so much about what its customers value and what it needs to deliver when it launches a new business line. Nick and I spend most of our time in meetings with business managers advising them on what matters to their customers – because *we listen* to their customers. You might think it's incredible that any organization could do business *without* understanding how they deliver customer value. Incredibly, many management teams rarely invest time in acquiring customer insight and formalizing how this information cascades through the organization. Tesco knows the strategic value of listening to, and learning from its customers – and embeds this behaviour at both operational and strategic levels. Through this insight it can anticipate where new customer value will come from. Tesco is already *agilized* – it constantly fits profitable markets within its brand reach.

'It's about identifying new opportunities'. The march of technology and pace of market change means that windows of opportunity are smaller than they once were. Advanced warning of new opportunities is shorter. Diminishing reaction times create a demand for technologies that forewarn management teams of weak signals signposting a change in the competitive environment.

'It's about contextualizing information from the outside world and making sense of it'. The Internet has created an information explosion. How much of this information makes a real impact on business opportunity? Data only becomes information when it is timely, and it only becomes insightful when it is contextualized for a purpose.

'It's about *acting*'. It doesn't matter how many 'signals' come from customers and markets unless there's someone paying attention nothing is going to happen. Most organizations do not employ people to listen to what the outside world is telling them.

'It's about being able to act'. How many inventions have failed to reach their market through lack of money or an organization to support them? Corporations fail to act on insight and turn it into shareholder value for many different reasons. Agilization creates an organization that can *roll with the punches*.

A Fortune® magazine study recently found that "Less than 10% of strategies effectively formulated are executed".

Boardroom strategies fail to translate into actionable plans largely because departmental budgets take precedence. Middle managers are remunerated for achieving departmental targets and that is precisely what they do. Most corporations do not act in a coherent, logical way. Creating organizational agility demands that people are motivated to work together in a more inclusive, cohesive way.

To **'agilize'**, leaders must grasp new ways of working and thinking. Thankfully, most of the challenges facing corporations are already understood. Someone, somewhere has already found – or is working on – a solution. This book gathers ideas from practitioners and thought-leaders *at the edge* of innovation in their respective specialist areas.

A new society demands a different way of doing business. A society that is changing rapidly creates a business environment in a constant state of flux. We live in the 24-hour global markets of the digital age. These conditions establish a new dynamic in market behaviours including more fluidity in the structure of markets. In response, operational models are changing ever more rapidly. Sustainable profitability now depends upon the ability of executives to constantly review their methods of operation. Leaders face the discomfort of living in a dynamic business environment they cannot control. Customer demand is no longer without influence on the enterprise, it cannot now be ignored or brushed off. Leaders can ill afford to ignore the influence of changes in the external environment as so many could in the late 20th century. To achieve strategic goals corporate leaders have to reacquaint themselves with the skill of harnessing the prevailing external forces that exert control over their enterprise.

The leaders of organizations in the 21st century find themselves entering a new business climate.

The make-up of society is evolving so quickly with different ethnic groups, characteristics and behaviours that even UK central government recently had to throw away its profiling model. No longer is it possible to accurately split demand into convenient groupings. In the real-world of the 21st century, the market comprises millions of people, all demanding to be treated as individuals.

'**Individualism**' – how individuals choose to assert their personality on their life-course, life-style and buying decisions – is the major driving force behind changes in consumer buying behaviour. Individuals will, in future, leverage their buying power by forming buying syndicates and communities. These will be formed, not synthetically by industry, but organically through changing social patterns and the new technology-driven interactive environments forming the *new tribes* of the 21st century. Individuals will have more say in how products and services are fashioned to meet their discerning requirements. They will invest more time in making sure their suppliers are committed to sustainability policies based on diversity, the environment, charity, investment in community development and social improvement and empowering individuals. There will be many more layers within supply chains providing individuals with a higher degree of personalization and choice. Individuals will choose to buy from brands that honour their social and environmental commitments and have strong ethical policies. We see all of these trends happening in a small way today.

Investors will focus investments in enterprises that promise sustainable profits and that demonstrate an ability to fit those markets producing the highest return. They are likely to shun corporations that appear unwilling to embrace more agile business practices. Why? Because that is how 21st century organizations will need to work in order to sustain their growth. Investors, as empowered individuals, will seek out corporations that honour their own social and environmental commitments and adopt strong ethical policies. A growing number of case histories about corporations that have failed to identify the signs of market change will lead to new demands for leaders to be more vigilant of changing market conditions. Greater emphasis will be placed on management teams being seen to operate business models that are lower geared and more fluid (i.e. employing fewer people directly, embracing external sources of capability, expertise and customer value to achieve higher profit).

Leaders will be measured by their ability to navigate their organization along a course that promises sustainable growth. They will be challenged to focus on the outcomes of strategy and devolve the delivery of processes to a much broader network of individuals contributing towards the success, but no longer employed by, the enterprise.

Managers will spend more of their time looking outwardly at new opportunities and threats and will invest substantially less time in the day-to-day operation of business processes. The overwhelming majority of individuals that contribute to the success of an enterprise will no longer be directly employed through full-time employment contracts. Workers, as individuals, will be expected to develop a specialized skill that they are responsible for keeping updated through sustained learning and training: employers will no longer be expected to be responsible for providing this.

Society will embrace technology in every aspect of life – education and learning, pleasure, shopping, gaming and leisure, politics and work. Everyone will have to accept more responsibility for their personal education, life choices and behaviour. No longer will there be clear distinctions between the life-stages of education, work and retirement that exist today. The idea that we stop education after early years schooling and become workers will be an historical perspective. So too will be the notion of a *job for life*. Workers will not go to work or college every day. They will not retire on a specific birthday or anniversary. There will be variation and fluidity between these life stages and each individual will be challenged to take personal responsibility for developing their own skills and ability to exist within this more liquid state of lifestyle.

Individualism will shape a new social reality that will challenge the behaviour of institutions and the way they define success.

In the 20th century, running an efficient well-oiled corporate machine would guarantee rights of passage. Then, corporate leaders could dismiss the influence of markets as something that happened *beyond their firewall*. As if it would change THEIR world!!!

21st century markets are volatile. Organizations need to think and act differently to survive, bringing their brand values closer to their customers, workforce and shareholders or become sitting ducks. Organizational structures need to embrace this reality and this change won't happen by itself. In the words of Lowell L. Bryan and Claudia Joyce of McKinsey & Co. *"A new organizational model for today's big corporations will not emerge spontaneously from the obsolete legacy structures of the industrial age. Rather, companies must design a new model holistically, using new principles that take into account the way professionals create value."*

In the first section of this book I outline the factors driving the need of organizations to change the way they work. Corporations of the Western world desperately need to learn these lessons and apply new approaches if they are to regenerate their competitiveness.

AGILIZATION is a formula for achieving sustainable profits that can be learnt, applied and benefited from.

In this book I describe the principal factors that will influence the success of tomorrow's world-class organizations; an enterprise that is able to listen and respond to *what matters most* to its customers that can *think and act* faster than its competitors. It creates a driven, outward-looking, loosely coupled organization that is always anticipating what might come next. It is made up of free thinking, high-performing individuals, given the headroom to constantly question norms of behaviour and encouragement to innovate.

What I describe is an enterprise that repeatedly aligns its strengths to meet market opportunities as they arise – to always fit its most profitable market.

Section 1

THE NEXT INDUSTRIAL REVOLUTION

Seek not the favour of the multitude; it is seldom got by honest and lawful means. But seek the testimony of few; and number not voices, but weigh them.

Immanuel Kant

1

How Society is Changing

Individualism describes the different psychological self-determination of new generations – individuals who demand the right to assert their own personal self-identity on the decisions they make in all aspects of daily life.

While *individuality* defines the quality of being individual and the presentation of oneself to the outside world, *individualism* describes an individual's influence on his or her surroundings (i.e. how they assert their personality through their behaviours, ethics and philosophy).

In the previous chapter I mentioned how the industrial revolution highlighted the symbiotic relationship between industry and society. Well, it's happening again. Changes in social values and behaviours are hard to spot. When you're caught up in daily life, it's easy not to notice how the world is changing around you. So many small, iterative changes and no single bound of change. Not like a caterpillar transforming into a butterfly that you can easily spot and say – "Hey Harry, look how that is changing".

Individualism is one of those transitions you don't see the impact of immediately. We will look back on the way society a decade from now and realize how it was irrevocably changed by individualism.

Understanding individualism for what it is

Individualism and technology are symbiotic

Technology alone can cause dramatic changes in our society. Think about the impact of the printing press, when copying and reciting moved up a gear to documenting trillions of new ideas and concepts, feeding the rapid explosion in scientific discovery. Think too about the impact of the telephone in bringing the world closer together. In just a few years people could place a product or service order from thousands of miles away. What *disruptive technology* does is to introduce new ways of doing things *differently* and not just do things *better*. That changes society.

The modern weapons of commerce – the Internet, advertising and brands – are shaping the values and beliefs of individuals. In a chicken-and-egg way, a new vehicle for communication changes society that in turn impacts the way people want to communicate. And so it goes on. The Internet is one of those technologies that have increased the pace of change in the *structure* of society and markets. How long does it take now for people to find out about a major oil spill, a dispute between two governments over the supply of gas, a terrorist attack? The digital age means that in large parts of the Western Hemisphere, individuals have instant access to news through digital TV and radio channels and on the Internet. They are increasingly computer literate.

For consumers, the Internet means they can connect to suppliers anywhere in the world and buy products at any time of the day or night. Within days, a new fashion, the launch of a new technology or a news event can fan the flames of public opinion and change the nature of demand. Fashion outlets now sell trends identified by consumers instead of setting trends, and producers of fashion garments have to be quick to respond. In this way, individuals assert their personality and impose their influence on brands.

Now, with the emergence of participative technologies like blogs and podcasts, they can have even greater influence. We hear expressions today like 'fan-boy' and 'fan-girl' used describe individuals who actively promote products like the Apple® iPhone™ on social networking sites like YouTube™ and Facebook™. These individuals are promoting products not because they are paid to do so, but because THEY CAN. It's their personal choice. The communications tools to make this all happen are now in place and continue to develop (see next chapter for more details). Individuals can send messages that may be read by millions of readers in a matter of hours. Perhaps the author has no credibility, no deep knowledge of the subject. Still, they can air their opinion. Others might believe these opinions to be more truthful than the claims of corporations. The Internet is an obvious platform to carry the opinions of individuals, but that too is changing. New *participative* technologies make social networking more mobile and even more accessible. The combined connecting tissues of communications and computing technologies are casting an ever-more-complete digital web across the planet so that we can always be connected.

Some social commentators see this as the dawn of a new collective consciousness that will spread across the face of the world in a matter of years. Perhaps we will start to establish a common set of values, of behaviours.

The Internet is one of those big events of human history and it is only in its adolescence. We're all still trying to get our head around what we can use it for, what its impact will be. As humans, we are naturally curious. When fed with one tiny new piece of information, we have an insatiable appetite to work out how we can use this new knowledge to do something better or different with it.

This can lead to dramatic changes – such as the invention of concrete, creating the ability to build multi-story buildings, silicone and the ability to protect space vehicles from heat, penicillin, the wheel, the microchip – we can't help ourselves!

It is in these terms that we must consider the power and influence of the Internet. It is a global communications hub bringing communities with common interests and beliefs closer together. It is the equivalent of steam power in the 19th century because it shapes our landscape, our perceptions of space and time. It brings people together through interests they share and a desire to be part of a virtual community.

The digital revolution is extending the shadow of *the Internet* across the planet. Within a matter of a few years most adults will be able to access the Internet. To give an example of this growth, there were 100,000 hosts in 1989 and over 200 million by 2002. By 2010, about 80% of the planet will be on the Internet. The democratization of the Internet is well under way with pilots funded by the public sector to provide free regional wireless networking. On August 2, 2006 the largest wireless broadband network in the UK went live in Norwich. The £1.1 million two-year Norfolk Open Link pilot project offers free mobile Internet access for public sector employees, the business community and the general public.

Think about how you have changed your buying behaviours over the past few years. Perhaps you buy your books and groceries online and have them delivered to your door. Maybe, like my wife, you like to invest some time *Googling* the Internet before making buying decisions on holidays and electrical products. You don't have to wait for things to be in stock. If one store doesn't have it, you can go elsewhere. Most times you can buy whatever you want in a matter of hours, any time of the day. Consumers buy smaller quantities and a richer variety of products, more often. They are more discerning, they have more choice and they are more concerned with work-life balance. The Internet is not just about buying and selling. It influences where products are made, how we learn, share experiences, where we work and how we spend our leisure time. The extent that the Internet influences society has yet to be fully realized.

A tidal wave of new 'participative' technologies will shortly hit our society and its impact is likely to make the rampaging growth of the Internet feel like the calm before the storm.

Successive generations of individuals will place greater value on their differences.

Children today see the Internet as something that has always existed. It is the communications portal to their world of information – their friends, games, shopping and schoolwork. Sure, the Internet is changing society *and* buying behaviours but it isn't the only driver for the changes in society occurring today. It's partly down to where our society has arrived at. Let me explain through some of my personal experiences.

In 2004 I visited a long-standing client, the chief executive of a local authority in the West Midlands. He had previously held a senior position in another rural district council that our company had done some work for. We had helped them to transition into an organization that put its customers first. My client came from a mining family. His father was a coal miner. Mining had been the way the family had made its income for generations. Most of his friends expected to be miners when they left school. But one day, as he reached the end of his schooling, his father said, "You're not going to be a miner. You're going to work up at City Hall. They make better money there and it's a job for life". In my clients' case, his fathers' vision for his future was pretty accurate. The next week, my client applied for a job at his local council and over 30 years later there he was a chief executive – and a very good one!

My own father (now retired) was an engineer and, with few employment options that paid enough to feed a young family, established his own engineering business producing machine parts for Leicester's textiles industry in the early 1960s. I still remember the occasion when it was the turn of my father to present me with my future. I remember anticipating a lecture that would chart my course and leave me with a final outcome. Instead my father simply said, "Just do something that you enjoy. But don't worry, if it doesn't work out you can come and work with me and Mum at the factory." Strangely that little piece of reverse-encouragement was enough to get me motivated! The thought of working in a factory all day, then arriving home late with lacerated fingers, smelling of oil lubricant and covered in black casting dust did not appeal to me. It was enough to power me through my exams and find another path. I had no idea of what I wanted to be, but for sure I wasn't going to be an engineer. For me personally, anything was better than that!

And now today, reading my children their bedtime story, I realize that I am fast approaching the other side of that same life event. What will I say to them? Will it matter what I say?

For the first time in our society we face a new reality. Our children are no longer expected to follow in their father's footsteps. That generation was my father's generation. They do not need our direction to tell them what they are to become (would they listen?). They are a generation with an open book of opportunity. They are not expected to put their family or their community before their career. Our children will decide who they are, what they want to be, what they believe in. And they know that we, their parents, will do everything we can to support them financially and emotionally.

As parents we endeavour to provide the essential building blocks that go to make up 'good people' – social values, empathy, respect, selflessness, charity – but we also encourage individualism, the quality and importance of being an individual. This is not an easy option for our children. When someone offers you unlimited career choices, but you've no experience of them, how can you possibly decide?

A friend of mine in her early twenties one day described the frustrations and apathy of her peers by using the term 'the *hopeless generation*' – a generation without hope. (As a father of two young children it was one of those two-minute conversations that hits hard.)

Individualism is a right of birth that countless generations have fought for. The Suffragettes attaching themselves to the gates of Buckingham Palace to demand voting rights for women, Martin Luther King, Jr. as he campaigned for freedom from racism in the deep southern states of the USA, not to mention countless other acts of selflessness and bravery. Individualism has come about by increased economic freedom, longer life expectancy, greater access to education, equality and a fractured class system. **It is something that will impact all of us and it will change society both significantly and rapidly.**

Individuals are today embracing technology in different ways to find new relationships, share experiences and develop new virtual communities. If you're not convinced visit www.Facebook.com, www.YouTube.com, www.flikr.com, www.myspace.com, www.AIM.org or www.elog.com and you will find thousands of individuals expressing themselves.

It would take some considerable time to describe each of these sites but taking YouTube™ as a case example: www.youtube.com, founded in February 2005, provides a place for people to watch and share original videos worldwide through a web experience. It is a place for people to engage one another in new ways by sharing, commenting on, and viewing videos and has grown into an entertainment destination with people watching more than *70 million videos* on the site daily. This is an online community powered by people. It is visual evidence of a society whose core beliefs and values are on the move.

Institutions are failing to reflect changes in society.

On May 26, 2004, I was driving home from a business trip and tuned into a late night radio talk-show. The subject was a document called *'Cherishing Life in London today'*, published by the Catholic Bishops of England and Wales. It documented their new instructions on how people should live in today's society. The document offered a new set of ground rules, addressing a variety of issues including sex education, abortion, stem cell research, euthanasia, infertility and the importance of marriage.

The panel of notables and its contributing audience found themselves positioned into two camps. One (for now I'll call them the *traditionalists*), made up of clergy and a collection of mature contributors, made the point that bishops are ordained by God to set boundaries of behaviour. They said it was a good thing that the bishops were setting moral values on modern issues because if they didn't, who would?

The other camp, headed by the editor of a major European *men's* magazine (I'll call it the *nouveau* view) argued that as an individual, he set his own moral position on these issues and did not need a group of bigoted old men telling him what his moral values should be. He argued the world would be a much safer and friendlier place if people honoured their own values, respected one another's ways and stopped telling other people how they should lives – especially religious leaders who foster segmentation that leads to friction in society. His argument was quickly interpreted by the 'traditionalists' as being typical of today's selfish generation – people who only think about themselves and do not respect authority.

To me the debate mirrored the way society has shifted towards *individualism*. There was a deeper argument being played out here; that educated individuals living in a multi-cultural society no longer recognise the authority of the traditional institutions. They're not anti-institutional or bad people, they're *individuals* demanding the right to determine their own values of behaviour.

Looking at the reluctance of the new generation to engage with traditional community structures as their parents did before them can be viewed in a negative way. Our children might be seen as a generation of wasters that only care about themselves and don't give anything back to society. I take a more positive outlook. Knowing my children as I do, I know they will want to contribute to their community, to help others, but as *individuals* and not because religious leaders or politicians think that they should.

Ageing organizational command and control structures that were developed to help a minority of educated people to manage the ill-educated majority no longer have the relevance they once did.

The assertion of an individual's right to be different on society and commerce, on life-*course* and life-*style*.

Today, young people are opting out of relationships that do not recognise their individualism. When they don't feel their interests or their opinions make a difference, they elect not to participate. They don't want to mandate a political party, church or association to speak on their behalf, or to buy from a faceless corporation that views them as a *transaction* rather than as an *individual*. **They have the confidence, expectation and ability to make their own choices.**

Individualism is cascading its influence through commerce like a tidal wave. With confidence in a stable international banking and trading environment and the advent of Internet communications extending consumer reach to global markets, new generations have an unsurpassed level of choice in what they buy and where they buy from.

I believe there is a trend in society to not attempt to answer the core life questions of 'Who am I?', 'What do I believe?' and 'Why am I here?', perhaps because religion has less credibility and appears to have less relevance in our lives. As the next generation of consumers shapes their core values, they are likely to be highly influenced by *virtual peers*. These values will determine the characteristics of suppliers they want to buy from and the style of products they buy. The task of marketers is going to get ever more complicated to appeal to these *individuals*.

Is individualism good or bad for society?

New generations of individuals will think differently about who they are and their life choices, how they view their responsibilities and their identity. They will expect to buy at a time, in a way and in a place that suits them. Even more than now, individuals of tomorrow will demand products that satisfy their style and self-image aspirations. These individuals expect to make life choices without interference from parents or ageing social, political and commercial organizations that have failed to reinvent themselves or to keep up with the developing aspirations of young individuals who seek meaning in their lives and not just comfort and security. But the growth of individualism does not mean that human-kind will lose its soul. On December 26, 2004 the Asian Tsunami, one of the most devastating natural disasters of the century, sparked an unprecedented response of selflessness and charity across the world. The power of the *digital age* was demonstrated once more. Within hours of the disaster, pictures were transmitted around the world enabling millions to see the disaster from close up, the suffering faces of mothers, fathers, grandparents and children. Within a matter of hours a major international relief effort was put in place. Humankind has not lost its soul.

Should we treat individualism as an unwanted friend after countless generations have worked to deliver it to their children as a birthright?

Just because the young don't want to be treated as faceless transactions doesn't mean they don't want to buy.

A reluctance to pledge allegiance to a political party or association does not mean young people are not interested in politics or the social privileges of their work colleagues.

Can we blame our children if our systems of capitalism and government fail to keep pace with a change in our social conscience?

Should we be disappointed that the outcome of greater social care, better education, longer life expectancy, the fight to remove inequality and discrimination from our society moulds a generation of people that demand more control over their self-determination and make their own life choices?

In time, individualism might be seen to be the good thing that I believe it is, but it will only become appreciated, and its value assessed, in years to come when social commentators can look over their shoulder and assess its influence on human history.

Is individualism good or bad for commerce?

I think neither – it just creates a new dynamic that all organizations will have to get used to. Individualism will create a layering of loosely-coupled buying communities that will exercise their collective buying power to enforce their preferences and expectations on suppliers. Consumers will expect suppliers to evidence their investment in society and the environment we live in.

Organizations will face the challenges of ever-changing, more fragmented and multi-layered markets leading to tougher competition. As consumers, individuals will demand that products and services reflect their personality. As workers, individuals will want to make sure that employers promote a life-style choice that suits them.

You might well ask – "What does any of this have to do with business in the 21st century?"

It matters because as workers and consumers we are two sides of the same coin. If we work less, we tend to consume more. If we don't have bonding relationships at work, we seek them outside work. If industry is the fuel of capitalism, we as consumers are the oxygen that fans the flames of demand.

Industry and society are on a collision course. This is a fight between the rights of individuals to assert their right to be different versus the mechanistic operation of traditional markets backed by industry that ideally wants every product, service and transaction to be the same.

The influence of individualism on buyer behaviour

With the influence of celebrities on buyer behaviour diminishing, buyers are more liable today to seek out testimonials from real people – individuals – who reflect their personal circumstances, interests and concerns. Even global corporations of the Western world must take the ramblings, comments and opinions of individuals seriously.

Should a housewife publish to her blog a compelling, factual account of her bad experience with a new vacuum cleaner, describe the poor customer service she received when she experienced a problem, within minutes this testimonial might find its way over the Internet into the homes of millions of potential buyers seeking to find a 'lay person's' perspective on the short-list of products they are considering for purchase. Equally, if a student writes about a mobile phone they've just purchased, chances are many more students will be influenced by their comments.

You don't have to be an expert or scientist to exert your influence on buyers.

In summary:

- Individualism describes an assertion of the personality of an individual on their environment.

- It describes a new 'psychology of self' and socio-economic condition that has been created by a cacophony of factors that give new generations the freedom to make their life choices.

- Individualism is not about encouraging individuality, it is not about selfishness. It is a *state of mind* of the young that parents will encourage because they see it to be the birthright of their children.

- It challenges the way society works and how people interact with one another. It directly influences consumer behaviour and places even greater product, environmental and social demands on suppliers.

The factors encouraging individualism are:

- The maturing of a new set of personal values towards self-valuation of what is good, fair – what justice and honour mean.

- Recognition by the young that the earth's resources are being consumed faster than they can be replenished, and of a need to sustain them.

- Failure of the traditional institutions (i.e. government, trades unions, church, etc.) to reflect and embrace the values and expectations of young people who do not feel obliged to follow a particular course.

- The role of technology to create an information-sharing environment (the participative age) where individuals can form new social groups by connecting to one another with device to device communications.

- A transition in markets where new commercial 'organisms' form to support the values and preferences of groupings of individuals.

2

How the Digital Revolution is Driving Societal Change

If you think the Internet has made a big impact on how people live and behave in today's society, just wait until the new wave of sensor networking technologies arrives!

Information technology is the thread that links a rapid globalization of markets to the seismic remodelling of how society will work in the future – the participative age. Technology is the foundation of new social networks that give freedom to individuals to express their opinions and assert their personality on society, markets, corporations and brands. The pace of technological change is truly remarkable. We all think of how personal computers have gained in performance and shrunk in size. And yet principally, the way I have used a personal computer since the mid 1980s has remained the same. Even back then, I was working with a spreadsheet and saved my files to a disk as I still do today. The Internet is not the first technology to instigate a major social change (remember the telegraph?). It won't be the last. Examples of technology facilitating change include:

- E-mail is outpacing postal services. As far back as 1999 – according to Messaging Online – electronic mailboxes grew 83%, amounting to over 569 million. This trend hasn't slowed since.

- Online communities are forming. The Women's Network (www.ivillage.com) launched in early 1999 provides practical solutions and everyday support for women between the ages of 25 and 54. In the first quarter of 2000, there was an average of 155 million monthly page views and revenue exceeded $20 million. These online communities are bringing people closer together.

- Teenagers today communicate with like-minded people who live millions of miles away and yet can meet them in an Internet chat room within minutes of getting home from school. Some surveys suggest that in 2004 there were well over 1,250,000 open and closed chat rooms, with a substantial number outside the EU and North America. In the UK around five million minors of age 9 to 16 use over 10,000 chat rooms each month where they will share opinions on the movie stars they like, the brands they value, the pointlessness of their lives – what happened today.

- Individuals are able to share their ideas and experiences like never before. *Podcasters*, a new group of communicators, record audio content for people to download and listen to later on their iPods and other MP3 audio players. Analyst firm Forrester Research predicts that by 2010 podcasts will reach 12.3 million households. Then we have 'bloggers'. A blog is an individual's journal made available on the web. There were over 55 million blogs on the planet by the end of 2006, and over half were thought to be active. These sites allow bloggers to share their innermost feelings and experiences with millions of others. A survey in 2004 by the Pew Internet & American Life Project found that 7% of U.S. Internet users say they have created blogs and 27% say they read them.

New ways of communicating provide a platform for the emergence of new communities. These communities are forming in cyberspace among individuals with mutual interests but who remain geographically distant. Energized by the Internet they are reshaping society. As yet these new social groups have not translated into buying consortia or vehicles to leverage their influence on product and service quality or selection. That will come. This list of early social networking tools contains examples of participative digital communications technologies that are the foundation of the *participative age*; a new era of society. Since the Millennium, this quiet revolution has slowly started to bring empowerment to individuals who feel an emotional need to 'get connected' to like-minded people with whom they can share their experiences.

New participative technologies

New ways of building social networks are evolving and becoming standardized, enabling individuals to find one another and communicate across the digital airwaves. Whilst the worldwide web continues to reach across the globe, new ad-hoc networking platforms are emerging which mean that in future, individuals are always going to be able to find other like-minded individuals with similar interests and values. The net result of these new innovations is that individuals can always be online. Rather than go looking for information, it can find them. These participative technologies mean that computer users are being liberated from having to understand how to programme computer applications in order to build them.

This liberation from expert skills releases new innovation, new creative ways of sharing:

- **New forms of telecommunications platforms** – Providing the ability to be online and able to communicate at all times, no matter where you are, with or without broadband connectivity.

- **Real world web** – A variety of technologies that make it possible for individuals to interact with their surroundings through sensing and networking capabilities. For example, as you pass an advertisement it might inform you on your mobile where you can get the product being advertised upon entry of a text number.

- **Sensor mesh networking** – A blend of radio frequency, sensing and telecommunications technologies that create ad hoc networks formed by dynamic meshes of peer nodes, each of which includes simple networking, computing and sensing capabilities. In short, sensor mesh networks mean that you can share information between individuals in a local area (something like 100 meters) as the technology enables messages to 'hop' from person to person. In the future, it is conceivable that this message-hopping technology could become so commonplace and effective that a message could pass between 5, 10 or 100 terminals to reach its intended recipient. One could imagine using this technology to empower children in a playground to share a collaborative gaming experience without needing to go online. Because it does not require large amounts of telecommunications infrastructure, this type of technology is likely to find favour in forming play area networks (i.e. public places such as cafes and airport lounges where access to the Web is not free-to-air).

- **Participative and user-created applications** – Sometimes called 'mash-ups', these are tools that liberate the creation of software applications from the hands of programmers to 'consumers'. They enable applications to be created using a single publishing environment by combining 'off-the-shelf' building block components such as databases, tables and spreadsheets, data entry fields and forms components, geographical mapping, report writers, visualization tools, etc that can be instantly brought together along with data feeds into a web, desktop or mobile user interface screen that demands no complicated IT tools, skills or resources. The emergence of mash-ups means that new commercial organization structures (what I call the new 'market *organisms*') can easily establish themselves in the market with trusted IT infrastructure for a fraction of the time and cost it would have taken using traditional software programming tools and applications, leading to rapid market entry in much less time and with much less risk.

And where is the participative technology revolution really likely to start to make an impact on society? I would have to say in the area of participative gaming. In the future children will not be isolated in their bedrooms, cut off from the rest of the planet if they want to play their games and communicate with friends. They could be anywhere. They will always be online. A new generation of participative technologies – computer entertainment and communication technologies – will encourage the rapid formation of new loosely-coupled but highly influential participative social networks.

The computer gaming market that once targeted boys is becoming an industry serving individuals of both genders and of all ages. Innovators such as Nintendo are already establishing a brand footprint for gaming that reaches out to the middle-aged and elderly with specific products for these new gaming communities. We can learn from the experiences of early Internet adoption to recognise that oldies are pretty savvy when it comes to new opportunities to embrace technology. Few marketers in the financial services sector expected so many mature people to take finance online, thinking that online banking was a young person's sport. Wrong!

At the heart of future participative social networks is the mobile (cell) phone. The consumer electronics industry is driving innovation through the perpetual development of mobile phones and by vendors targeting the expansive global market for gaming and entertainments computing products. In future years I expect that telecommunications and gaming will converge even more.

Four key changes are encouraging this innovation to take place:

1. **Technology development trends in video gaming.**
2. **Demand for participative mobile (computer) products.**
3. **The emergence of new communications standards.**
4. **Development of new battery technologies.**

(1) Innovations in video gaming

Gaming console vendors now recognise that participative gaming is the next 'big thing' to hit the computer gaming market. However, the challenge that all vendors face is that a new hardware console requires new games to be authored from software vendors. The success of the Sony PlayStation has been founded on its ability to provide a technically well-documented and open platform that third party software vendors are able to design for.

In the near future, all people will have the ability to share their games, their experiences and/or their political opinions between each other without even necessarily having to connect to the Internet. In this way, innovations in the personal entertainments market can directly influence the way society works. The gaming consoles we will all carry as fashion accessories in future will be able to communicate with each other. They will identify us, they will share our opinions and they will introduce us to others.

It normally takes the vision of one man to change an industry. In the case of the video gaming industry the one man is Nintendo President Satoru Iwata. Mr Iwata observed that increasing numbers of casual gamers were not picking up controllers because whilst complex games with intricate game controls were appealing to avid game enthusiasts, most potential players were not looking for games that required them to invest large amounts of time and energy. Instead most people wanted games they could enjoy periodically at a free moment in their day. Mr Iwata saw that the global opportunity for video gaming could extend beyond the 'young boy, young man' world of highly sophisticated games on expensive computer games consoles. He defined a new strategy that would extend Nintendo's market opportunity for games consoles to the broader household, engaging fathers, mothers, grandparents and ... girls!

From 2004, Nintendo has implemented a strategy to encourage people around the world to play video games regardless of their age, gender or cultural background. Nintendo is turning this vision into reality by designing new portable gaming consoles that are less expensive and better at communicating with one another. Through his vision, Satoru Iwata is shaping the next generation of personal entertainments platforms. Today, with Nintendo Wi-Fi, players can connect and play with other Nintendo DS players across the globe by using the vendor's own collaborative hub with no hidden service fees and no extra equipment. All that players need is the Nintendo DS console and a Wi-Fi ready game. The isolated PlayStation and Gameboy world that our children live with today is changing.

(2) Demand for participative mobile products

The growth of Internet-based platforms for sharing experiences through websites, blogs, chat rooms, video rooms, etc., described in this chapter shows the appetite of people living in the 21st century to bonding with others and share experiences. This need to join together is particularly strong in new generations who are growing up knowing they can always meet others online but are not allowed to venture out to the park. Many children now live in a computer-rich home environment and see computers as their gateway to social interaction.

(3) Emergence of new technology standards

Around the globe today, commerce is investigating new types of networking technologies to make ad hoc person-to-person communication possible by enabling packets of messaging data to hop from one device to the next until messages find their eventual destination (see glossary description of multi-hop packet radio networks). Many of the innovations needed to engender new forms of participative social networking do happen have been around for some time. For example, mesh networking is a way of building a local area network that means 30 people (and maybe more) can share the same information on their computer screens at the same time. Technologists have known about this for several years.

It takes formalized industry standards to kick-start market adoption of technologies used to share data. (Not much point in inventing one phone without another one to talk to!!). Industry standards provide a level playing field by formalizing a set of protocols that manufacturers can adopt in their products. In 1997 the Institute of Electrical and Electronics Engineers, Inc. (IEEE) established the 802.11™ wireless communications standard. This ushered in a stream of new wireless networking hardware and software products in the late 1990s that we now take for granted such as the interface cards that we use today in domestic wireless networks.

In January 2006, the IEEE Standards Association (IEEE-SA) published new high-rate and low-rate personal area network (PAN) standards – IEEE 802.15.3™ and IEEE 802.15.4™.

These new standards of communication have opened the door for consumer electronics manufacturers to develop the new methods of personal collaboration. Without these technology advances, the participative age and deep social networking would not be exploding. Individuals could not themselves vote on political issues time after time, they could not distribute their opinions through podcasts and blogs, they could not easily find like-minded people or social networks.

(4) Development of battery technologies

One area of innovation that has really held back the growth in personal devices has been the challenge of powering portable devices.

Batteries are also one of the largest and heaviest components in portable electronic devices. New breakthroughs are emerging in battery technology every day. Scientists are trying out a wide variety of substrates and configurations to optimize the life, power output, size and weight of batteries. We can expect to see dramatic steps forward in this area over the next few years. For example, in 2005, physicists in Singapore announced the first urine-powered paper battery made of a layer of filter paper steeped in copper chloride, sandwiched between strips of magnesium and copper. This assembly is then laminated within plastic to hold the pieces together, resulting in a battery that is slightly smaller than a credit card. A drop of urine is added to activate the battery, soaking through the sandwiched filter paper, and as the chemicals dissolve, they react to produce electricity. This urine-powered battery has the potential to generate a voltage of about 1.5 volts with a corresponding power of 1.5 micro-watts using 0.2 millilitres of urine. It brings some staggering visual images to mind of how people might supply energy to their mobile phone in future! What these innovations signpost is that scientific endeavour will not stop until batteries are micro-ized to the point of no longer being a design constraint for electronic devices. They will be produced in unimaginable quantities at very low cost.

Who will kick-start the sensor network revolution?

It is likely that industry will be the first to experiment with participative technologies and fund the next generation of technologies through its endeavour to acquire new customer relationships. Already direct marketing experts are talking about sensor networking and participative marketing strategies to embrace new mediums like 'in-game' advertising and sensor network-based advertising tools such as shelf-edge labels that can text your mobile phone with the latest information on the product you're interested in, poster boards that tell you where you can buy the product being advertised, and give-away gifts that update your mobile phone with a walking catalogue of products. Also, imagine your favourite music CD whose outer cover contains a small microchip that offers free mobile phone ring tone downloads and the option of buying more. The possibilities are...well, interesting!

Sensor networking will be upon us within the next few years. How will industry respond? Will we see new business models? New types of organization? New market structures? New market leaders?

Yes.

3

How Individualism Will Change the Way Consumer Markets Work

This chapter describes how changes in society are resetting the balance of power between corporations and consumers

I've described the move towards *individualism*, yet we know as humans we're *natively* tribal. Some academics believe that the human race evolved quicker because of our art, desire to gossip and share stories. Humans have a natural emotional desire to be part of a social group.

There have always been tribes

Those of us born in the Western world of the 20th century are not expected to think of our *tribe* before our *family* or ourselves. Instead, most of us (probably) believe in the right for all people to exist and to live their lives as equals without fear of tyranny. We value our freedom and the right to *choose*. Our children will ASSUME it. We pay politicians, civil servants, armies and policemen to protect these rights. Many of the traditional social support networks our parents took comfort from no longer exist. Our neighbours get into their cars and go to work in a different city. They don't share a common interest in what we do and we do not expect their help if things go wrong.

We might describe our local town as a *community* but for many people living on cramped housing estates with no village centre it has become a dormitory – a place where commuters sleep. In the UK people are likely to feel a closer affinity to fans of the football team we support than neighbours in their community. Generally people do not associate with their neighbours. We don't walk down to the coalmine with these people and each day share the risk of death. Many of us didn't even grow up where we now live. We're not likely to venture next door to help our neighbours give birth to a child. Neither do we expect to be *called up* to stand arm in arm with our neighbours to protect our land.

We rely on commerce, not our community, to deliver our food and wealth – a supporting cast of hundreds of strangers to help us through our lives, educating our children, providing healthcare, policing, insuring us from loss and husbanding our wealth. The power of religion (and other social, non-governmental organizations) to bring communities together has weakened as science continues to explain things away that could not be explained in previous centuries and demanded our faith.

The importance of brands

Brand is not just an identity tag; it represents *values* behind the name of a product, idea, community or company. Major brands you might recognise include Coca-Cola, Xerox, McDonald's, Apple, Sony, Orange, Rolls-Royce, Canon, Hoover, Nestle, IBM, Revlon, Levi's Jeans, Virgin, British Airways, EMI, Disney, Hertz and David Beckham. Companies and individuals invest in their brands because they know over time, and with sufficient promotion, people form a bond of trust with familiar brands that promote values they associate with. In this way, brands are known to increase the value of products and services. When presented with products from two suppliers, a brand that we know and one we don't, we are more likely to choose the familiar one over a name or label that we have no knowledge of, even if the branded product costs more.

We are a brand-conscious society. Today, children as young as 6 or 7 years of age worry over the label on the jeans they wear. As they grow older they will make decisions on the brand of car they are prepared to be seen in, the food they buy. Brand builds communities of interest. Individuals aspire to become like their favourite movie star, footballer, singer or TV celebrity. They are interested in *their* brand values. They want to build an affinity with their mentors to share in this celebrity. This is why singer Jennifer Lopez can sell perfume, footballer David Beckham can sell sunglasses and singer David Bowie can do the same for banking services. However shallow it might be, at some point in our lives we want to be like somebody else whom we acclaim, not normally mom or dad, more commonly a movie star or footballer. We are more likely to see ourselves as the next James Bond or Madonna. These self-determined aspirations form values of our own self image and self worth. It is a very human quality for individuals to want to be seen to exist. We want to assert our personal self-identity on others to impress upon them who we are. It's also very human to feel a closer affinity to other individuals when we find they share the same values we do such as supporting the same football team.

The majority of brands are perceived to be Corporate brands managed by professional brand managers who use a slide rule and database to govern how their brand is to be designed and communicated. This will not always be the case. A brand also provides a visual identity of any entity or group. The British 'Union Jack' flag, the Nazi swastika and the eagle of Napoleon's legions are examples.

Today, we are beginning to see participative technologies encourage the democratization of brands. Corporations are recognizing the benefits of having customers participate in their brand story, to shape the values of a brand in the way that other customers are engaged. Corporations that choose to dictate brand values to consumer market will find themselves significantly disadvantaged.

When Apple's iPhone™ was launched recently, they re-edited and adopted a video produced by a child fan that was published on YouTube™ to promote it. This seed of innovation did not come from within Apple. The company now gets some of its best marketing ideas from consumers and the line between official Apple advertising and consumer productions has blurred so much it is now hard to see. The participative digital world means that the word-of-mouth tree of knowledge has more branches and greater reach than internal marketing teams. Democratizing brands like Apple are likely to continue to dominate the consumer goods market.

In today's markets we have grown more accustomed to commercial supply-side buying groups but we have yet to see consumer-driven brands emerge. Why don't consumers leverage their buying power in a similar way as trading clusters? Couldn't the members of a golf club or trade union combine their buying power to get more value from their suppliers? Commercial attempts to rein together consumer demand have generally been unsuccessful but there are a few notable exceptions to this rule.

- **eBay** is a market-place made up of over 100 million people around the world who buy and sell in the eBay marketplace. It works by enabling anybody to sell anything to anybody else where the goods transacted can be new or used. eBay encourages development of themed buying communities and supports close to 1000 buying groups, many of which are collectors' groups. Imagine what would happen if these buying groups were energized and started to drive procurement for their communities by negotiating with suppliers. This buying power would stand markets on their head!

- The **Freecycle network**, a not-for-profit organization centred on the belief that one person's trash can be another's treasure. The network provides an electronic forum to "recycle" unwanted items. Freecycle was started in May 2003 to promote waste reduction in Tucson's downtown and help save desert landscape from landfill.

- **Quidco**, a web buying community. Quidco charges a £5 per year admin fee to manage the community it serves. The Quidco model works for both the merchant and the buyer where the merchant can reach a large base of motivated savvy buyers and consumers can make big savings by buying from participating merchants.

- The **Pipeline** consumer fuel card is modelled on commercial fuel cards such as ShellCard, fuelserv and dieseldirect that leverage bulk buying to reduce the cost of motor fuel. A similar approach is adopted by the Marmalade Car Club that brings other car-related benefits to employees through company-run schemes.

Industry has failed to synthetically organize consumers into buying communities and I don't personally believe this will happen as the result of businesses 'designing' markets. I believe consumer buying communities will form organically as the result of individuals coming together around their shared values. When they do they will be able to leverage their buying potency and this phenomenon will switch the balance of power in the seller-consumer relationship around in favour of the consumer.

Tribal brands and the consumer

The great irony of today's consumer brand relationship is that the Internet creates consumers that purchase products at a *greater distance* yet feel they need to be *closer* to the *values* that the seller's brand represents. Brands will emerge in the future not just for suppliers and their products, but to define a collection of values or principals that a group of individuals holds dear (what I call *sticky values*) creating virtual communities that individuals can *opt into* – what I call 'tribal brands'.

The next few years will see many consumers in the Western world enjoying 24 hours a day, 7 days a week access to the Internet from anywhere. Participative technologies form the joining tissue that carries the opinions of an individual to many other like-minded people. This encourages like-minded individuals to want to find each other and create social networking communities. Individuals feel an overwhelming sense of need to be 'on the net' and connected with others virtually to overcome the absence of deep emotional support in their communities. Since the Millennium, this quiet revolution has started to bring empowerment. These communities are forming in cyberspace among individuals with mutual interests but who remain geographically distant.

The organic formation of digitally connected communities has the potential to *amplify* the power of the individual. As yet these new social groups have not translated into buying communities able to leverage their influence on product and service quality or selection – but that will come. For product and service suppliers, relationships with these market intermediaries will quickly become (life threateningly) important.

Tribal brands are a new type of consumer 'market organism' born of a common expression of values of loosely coupled (opt-in) virtual communities of individuals manifested in sticky values that are described by their brand. They leverage their buying influence to engineer deals with corporations prepared to meet the specific needs of their communities. Through these tribal brands, individuals can assert their buying power. Corporations will seek to invest in the development of tribal brands because they provide a cost-effective means of reaching buyers with a common set of values (and sometimes interests), better than ageing 20th century direct marketing, advertising and market research methods. Funding from corporations will enable tribal brands to achieve greater market visibility.

I expect tribal brands will employ people to work as customer advocates to help buyers to make decisions, providing a deeper level of emotional support than consumers have previously been accustomed to. For this reason, tribal brands will be more 'trusted' by consumers because their existence depends upon strict adherence to the values they promote.

Tribal brands inherit the following attributes:

1. **Sticky values** – The fundamental start point for a tribal brand is the existence of a set of values within which individuals find a common ground. I expect many of the first tribal brands will be associated with sustainability. New generations of consumers are ever more aware of the scarcity of resources and environmental challenges facing the world. Tribal brands will embrace these values and seek to change supplier behaviours.

2. **Opt-in based organically formed community** – Tribal brands are not likely to set discriminating subscription rules or conditions of entry. They are free for all to join; but given that they promote values that only relate to certain individuals, they are largely self-regulating.

3. **Advocacy support** – A key differentiator to traditional corporations is the 'advocacy model' of relationship management. Tribal brands will provide emotional support to individuals by acting on their behalf. Subscribers are supported by an individual who offers a deep level of emotional support and represents the interests of the individual they serve before the interests of the corporation. Advocacy trades an *investment in time* to support the interests of the individual in exchange for their trust and enduring loyalty. Tribal brands CAN advocate because they are the guardians of the RULES and VALUES that the individual subscribes to.

4. **A 'cool-click' website** – Brands will adopt a friendly persona and web design ethic placing *coolness* above corporate cleanliness. Few teenagers want to be seen buying their iPOD from a guy in a pin-striped suit! Seeing an Apple presenter in a suit and tie these days is as rare as a UK motorway without traffic. Presenters have to be camp and happy if they are to fit the *Apple way*.

5. **Probably co-funded by private sector involvement** – One of the major reasons why organically formed community sites have failed in the past is because they lacked sufficient funding to support the 'organization' needed to achieve a sustainable income. I expect tribal brands will enjoy sponsorship from corporations that want to target new communities of buyers. They will also enjoy the positive 'brand rub-off' that comes from associating with brands that demonstrate an affinity to sustainability and popular culture.

6. **Virtual organizations** – Most tribal brand will operate virtually in that they will be formed by communities of individuals with a small corporate centre. Some are unlikely even to have the head office building we identify with corporations of today.

Growth factors

Consumer tribal brands will be fostered by:

- **Individualism** – Tribal brands are a reflection of the emerging impact of a new generation of individuals repelling the values and attitudes of 20th century organizations that are progressively losing touch with a younger generation more outwardly conscious and energized to act upon its social responsibilities.

- **Cool-click websites** – Younger generations of buyers are actively seeking to move away from procuring products and services from 'pin-stripe-suited', valueless corporations and are seeking more environmentally responsible informal, friendly and personalized relationships with organizations or communities that more accurately reflect their values.

- **Private sector mentoring** – Corporations identify the importance of brand association with websites that attract large numbers of hits. The high cost and lessening impact of other forms of 'push' marketing methods (particularly in encouraging new customer acquisition) will encourage corporations to fund initiatives that bring together communities of buyers with common buying interests.

- **Maturing person-to-person communications technologies** – The growth and development of person-to-person communications technologies in the early 21st century (see comments on sensor networks, motes, etc., in Chapter 4) will make it easier for individuals sharing common interests to find each other and share interests, values and beliefs.

A new layer in the supply-chain

By definition, the emergence of consumer tribal brands creates a more complex and loosely coupled interlayer of product and service providers offering individuals much more variety of choice. As a community-led organization, a tribal brand enjoys an impartial position in the buyer-seller relationship as the organization is a servant of the individual, not an agent of the corporation. Tribal brands will invoke a rebalancing of power in the relationship between consumers and corporations.

The first generation?

The early shoot examples of tribal brands have originated from the efforts of creative capitalists; organizations founded by social entrepreneurs committed to employing capitalism more creatively to improve society and the planet while they make money. Even though they exhibit a soul, tribal brands can be profitable because they are the guardians of customer relationships. Profit comes from sales of products and services through community-led websites whilst avoiding costs of product manufacture and logistics. Tribal brands will only show their real muscle in consumer markets when participative technologies become more widely available. There are however early examples of organizations moving towards being consumer

(PRODUCT)^RED™

tribal brands that provide an interesting glimpse of the future.

(Product) RED™ is an organization created by U2, Bono, Vox, and Bobby Shriver, Chairman of DATA (Debt, AIDS, Trade, Africa) to raise awareness and money for *The Global Fund*. It is an early example of a tribal brand. Bono and Shriver teamed up with a collection of iconic world brands --

American Express, Motorola, Converse, GAP, Giorgio Armani -- to produce RED-branded products. Companies license to sell RED™ branded products and part of the proceeds from the sales go to The Global Fund.

Since its creation in 2002, this public-private partnership has committed in excess of $5.2 billion to life-saving programmes in 131 countries. It accounts for a quarter of the world's funding for AIDS in the developing world, over half for malaria and two-thirds for tuberculosis. This translates as support for nearly half a million people on AIDS treatment.

(Product) RED™ fulfils many of the key criteria of a tribal brand:

- 'Cool-click' persona.
- Opt-in based organically formed community.
- Organization co-funded by private sector involvement.
- Sustainability focused values.

Fairtrade Labelling Organizations International (FLO) has created a worldwide network of organizations actively involved in supporting producers, awareness raising and campaigning for changes in the rules and practices of conventional international trade. Fairtrade-certified products have helped build economic independence and empowerment for Fairtrade-certified small farmer organizations and their members, bringing them economic stability and a higher standard of living. Beyond being paid a fair price (Fairtrade Minimum Price) for their produce, the Fairtrade Premium helps producers to build necessary social infrastructure.

Like (Product) RED™, Fairtrade is in the early stages of becoming a tribal brand. Whilst it has sustainability values, encourages opt-in participation from individuals to support the cause of fair trade and influences product manufacture and buying decisions, it has yet to cause a dynamic shift in market behaviours. Neither RED™ (Products) nor Fairtrade has as yet added eCommerce shopping capabilities to their websites to provide a focal point for buying products. At this time they don't employ advocates to support the development of communities, though there is no reason to believe that these characteristics will not develop in the future.

A number of brands with tribal potential have emerged in recent years but none possess all of the attributes required of a 'super-league' tribal brand and none has created a seismic shift in customer buying behaviour that is the promise of the advocacy-led tribal brands of the future.

Individualism drives tribal brands and vice versa

I believe individualism will prove to be the catalyst that will lead to the emergence of a new type of organizational entity and force in commercial markets that I call 'tribal brands'.

The influence of individualism will transform the concept of brands and brand influence. Brands will play an ever more important role in markets. The appearance of tribal brands will forever change consumer behaviour, buying expectations – and market structures. It's only a matter of time before the ingredients of technology, individualism and corporate self-interest (in encouraging new opt-in customer relationships) lead to the emergence of a major global tribal brand.

The symbiotic relationship between *society* and *commerce* means that changes to one can not help but affect a change in behaviour of the other. The way that society and therefore commerce work is undergoing a fundamental change. Nothing will stop this wheel from turning and it will never go back.

4

How the Business World is Changing

Who will be the economic powers of 2020? Old world economies of the West are facing unprecedented levels of competition from China and India, the emerging industrial powers of the Eastern hemisphere.

It's conceivable that one day almost all of the products we buy will be manufactured in Asia. The major player is China, closely followed by India. China already produces 50% of the world's cameras, 30% of air conditioners and televisions, 25% of washing machines and 20% of refrigerators. One private Chinese company manufactures 40% of all microwave ovens sold in Europe. The Chinese and Indian economies have grown by over 700% and 250% respectively since 1980. By 2010, the world news will be dominated by Asian economic expansion. Consumers in old world countries depend upon the success of these economies. 62% of all shoes and sneakers imported to the United States are made in China. So are 83% of toys and sporting goods. Imagine, without China, there would be basketball without sneakers and many bored children without toys.

Economists in Europe and the USA might take the view that the mature industrialized nations will retain their leadership in knowledge-intensive industries while developing countries in Asia will focus on leveraging their competitive advantage of lower labour costs. It isn't realistic to think that Asian business will settle for an economy based on low labour costs forever. Indian companies are now producing world-class goods and services at ridiculously low prices, from $50 air flights to $2,200 cars. Most of the world's retail banks now operate outsourcing centres in Asia. Even if labour rates in India and China do eventually start to rise, fuelled by economic success, why would anyone expect corporations to move elsewhere? There comes a point when infrastructure and competency becomes so embedded that moving location becomes too great a risk.

In a survey of Chinese and U.S. manufacturers by Industry Week, 54% of Chinese companies cited innovation as one of their top objectives, compared with only 26% of U.S. respondents. Today, Chinese companies spend more on worker training and enterprise management software than their Western counterparts.

What does this have to do with Western world corporations? At one time it wouldn't have meant much at all but the interconnected world created by the worldwide web means any product or service launched today faces immediate and aggressive competition from companies around the world.

Successful leaders know that if you want to make money from a great idea today you need a world-class organization.

The pace of competition has nudged up a gear. Executives report an accelerating pace of change in an increasingly competitive business environment, driven by knowledge and information trends and the forces of globalization. The success and ultimate survival of many Western world corporations depends upon their ability to *reshape* themselves and fit profitable markets. In March 2006, the McKinsey Quarterly conducted a survey and received 3,470 responses from a worldwide representative sample of business executives, 44% of whom were CEOs or other C-level executives. Some 85% of respondents described the business environment in which their companies operate as "more competitive" (45%) or "much more competitive" (40%) than it was five years ago.

The intensity of competition has increased for small as well as big companies, and in all industries.

Market structures are changing rapidly. We live in a world where grocers are selling insurance (Tesco), insurance companies are selling cars (Direct Line), lens manufacturers build laser printers (Ricoh) and software companies sell watches (Microsoft).

The nature of competition is changing. The US Department of Commerce recently stated that the total e-commerce sales for 2005 were $86.3 billion, representing an increase of 24% over 2004. The era of frictionless trading (as defined by Bill Gates, previously of Microsoft Corporation, in his book Business @ the Speed of Thought) is fast emerging when suppliers are literally one mouse click away.

No longer are competitors obvious and visible. They do not progressively eat away at your business over months and years. Competitors are more likely to be hiding in the shadows of a completely different market space and suddenly pounce to take away the business of unsuspecting, inward-looking suppliers; perhaps promoting new ways of shopping, easier ways to find and pay for products, shorter supply chains, pay-as-you-use service offerings, etc.

With all of this extra competitive activity, it's pretty obvious to onlookers that most western corporations have lost their way when it comes to creativity and ingenuity. The entrepreneurial characteristics that fashioned the 'American Dream' appear to somehow have been genetically removed from the day-to-day operating behaviour of most Western world corporations through successive rounds of good housekeeping polices and layer upon layer of risk mitigation under the brands of compliance, quality assurance and governance. How do you get creativity back into organizations that have factored out anything that creates risk?

Innovation means anticipating change, taking risks and spending good money on making mistakes (that's what learning is all about).

It means doing things differently, taking big steps, throwing ideas away that don't work and saying "Ah, well". The fact is that for most corporations, innovation is too much to stomach. It's too risky and unstructured. So much the better if you can just perpetually acquire little companies that invest in the navel-gazing work to come up with big ideas and place the weight of risk on their shoulders. But a global market means that these great ideas are free to seek out sponsors on a global stage.

Innovation is likely to find tiny pockets of the world where creativity is embraced.

As an Englishman I know all about the little guy that had a great idea and had to trek it around the world to find a sponsor. We English are the past masters of 'designed here, made elsewhere'. The mad inventors who make crazy inventions in garden sheds are at odds with our naturally reserved English *stiff upper lip* culture, and yet we produce many more of these wonderful but slightly crazy fools than any other country in the world.

There is a burning imperative facing corporations of the Old World to regenerate their competitiveness.

But how? Leaders can't just send an email to their workforce and say, "Hey guys, you know how I've spoken to you recently about corporate responsibility and the importance of control, compliance, conformity and quality assurance? Well I've been thinking about what I said and now what I really want for you to do is be CREATIVE! So get your thinking caps on and come up with some world-class innovations and let's make great things happen!" After checking to see what sort of wine the management team was served over lunch, workers would inevitably start by asking each other how they're MEANT to be creative without the right support and tools – and why should they bother anyway? What's the incentive?

Deep down every leader knows how to foster creativity. Never is it an IT silver-bullet technology, or a corporate think tank that originates innovation. It is about giving individuals a clear direction, head-room, resources – forming an environment where people are encouraged to be creative, where it's okay to make mistakes. Put simply, leaders have to set the right minds FREE.

Regenerating competitiveness is about creating *behaviours* that lead to these new processes, and the result is AGILIZATION. It is a pragmatic formula – a way to create a culture and behaviour that sources great ideas, evolves the right organizational structure and provides appropriate tools. Activities associated with creating innovation must exist within an operational framework that balances the value of innovation with reasonable risk-taking. Activities must be measurable, contributors accountable, and outcomes must ultimately deliver value directly to shareholders. Many factors influence whether great ideas translate into increased competitiveness.

I could summarize by saying that great ideas become good business when organizations translate them into customer value and turn that customer value into shareholder value. To do that requires the blend of processes and behaviours I describe in this book.

Why don't organizations just behave in an agile way anyway?

It's because, over time, a management culture develops that (often inadvertently) suppresses creativity. No doubt at some point in the growth of the enterprise, these embedded values and norms of behaviour delivered value to its customers. But its legacy is a 'kill creativity' instruction set that is retained in the latent memory of managers. This cascades through the layers of the organization, stifling creativity and inhibiting new thinking. The organization no longer supports curiosity. Managers continue to operate along the lines of this 'hidden rule-book' born of a different era. Without resetting this instruction set, the organization cannot set its creative minds free. And it's up to leaders to do it.

So what does it take to 'agilize' an organization?

Here is a simple list:

- **Leaders need to understand and embrace the new realities of markets.** They must know what customers want and engineer agility into enterprise behaviours and methods to embrace the next change.

- **People at all levels of management need to think differently.** It's no good believing that the way an organization makes its money today will always be attainable tomorrow. It's no good thinking creativity will just happen.

- **Organizations need to know *what* they are and focus their strategy.** It is not possible to find a good fit between what an enterprise is capable of delivering and what its customers want to pay for if the organization is not sure what it is. In a global market, everyone has to be world-class at something (unless of course customers have no choice – which does happen quite a lot in business!). It's a question of repeatedly finding a *fit* in the market.

- **Organizations need productive people.** Whatever happens to commercial markets over the next few years, it will be high-performing creative people (that drive forward corporate initiatives) that will have the greatest influence on competitiveness.

- **More than ever, organizations need to formalize how they work.** With loosely-coupled groupings of individuals working together to achieve corporate outcomes, good organization is essential to incentivize contributors, to measure productivity and outcomes, etc. It sounds bizarre, but to be more flexible, you need more formality. This is because the absence of formality to processes can make it impossible for managers to know how their enterprise actually works. This makes them powerless to make correctional changes.

- **Organizations need highly liquid information processes.** The idea of spending weeks debating how processes must work and then spending months hard-coding these requirements into new software systems does not work in a competitive environment where new markets and ways of doing business arrive and disappear within months, or potentially weeks.

- **Organizations must always keep tuned into market opportunities.** Customers with more choice can select products and services that are a perfect match to their needs – right place, right price, right time. Few organizations can do this without listening to customers. Customer insight has become a critical success factor.

- **Organizations must have excellent credentials and be able to show them.** It doesn't matter what business you're in, customers and investors will always need you to evidence that your organization can be trusted to deliver on its promises. Talk is cheap! The further you are from your customers, the more important it becomes to evidence values and capabilities – to build trust.

- **Organizations need to *externalize* and embrace new market *organisms*.** Market structures are evolving, combining with advances in communications and computing to form new 'market organisms' that perform new roles in the supply chain. These new entities will be new to most people's understanding of what an organization looks like. Not only do these new market organisms present new opportunities, for some organizations today they also represent the greatest threat.

- **Organizations need to avoid mistakes.** We all make mistakes but not all are visible. In the digital age, news gets around fast. Fail to deliver once and you could be saying goodbye to your business.

5

How Corporations Must 'Flex'

AGILIZATION turns an inward-looking organization into one that is constantly learning from its environment, seeks to understand how its markets are changing, and through the early identification of weak signals of change, learns what future customers think so it can 'flex' to deliver customer value.

Making sure a business always fits its most profitable markets is the big challenge facing business leaders. In the future, investors will demand that corporations leverage shareholder value by responding to new opportunities in an agile way. This does not mean corporations are going to start *kangaroo jumping* from one market to the next, but even within their chosen market space, leaders will be scrutinized to ensure they are protecting shareholder value by anticipating the impact of market forces.

There is always more than one way of achieving an outcome. The perfect match between the capabilities of an organization and the needs of customer groups might be achieved through the ingenuity of an entrepreneur, or through more scientific means. Whatever the source of innovation, it requires a higher level of dexterity and listening skills than is displayed by most corporations today. Engineers know that materials can absorb more impact if they flex. Having brittle business processes, even when cast in iron, is little comfort when market forces exert themselves. Whilst it may be a somewhat paradoxical statement, I believe that to mould an agile structure, leaders must invest time and energy in greater formalization of information flows that cut across their organizations. In doing so, they will liberate creative minds from mundane tasks and set them free to be curious, encourage learning and creativity, and exploit the talents and resources that lie beyond the enterprise.

Working to the theory that you can learn a lot about the future by examining the past, let's take a few steps back in history to understand why organizations aren't already agile and why the task of becoming 'agilized' is so challenging.

In the days of Josiah Wedgwood, if you wanted to invest money in an enterprise, you called into your local coffee house where you would find a selection of proposals tabled by many different *societies of gentlemen*, each willing to give you a share in their enterprise for the right stake. No stock exchange, no incorporated companies. Many of these 'coffee house' investments would be lost and, until the Companies Act of 1844, there would be nobody to sue if you wanted your money back. The names of these enterprises would surprise most of us today.

Walk into *Waghorn's Coffee House* in 1694, or the *Rainbow Coffee House* in 1709 with your money bag spilling over, you could have invested in societies such as 'The Contractors with the Czar of Muscovy for the importation of Tobacco into his dominion' or perhaps 'The Woollen Manufactory at New Mills in the Shire of Haddington'. If you wanted a safer bet you might consider investing in 'The Royal African Company of England'. For the brave-hearted investor there was the 'Company to develop an invention for making salt in all parts of England far more expeditiously and at less expense than by another method' or 'A stock for preventing and suppressing thieves and robbers'.

It was in these early days of capitalism that the founding principles of consumerism, capitalism and enterprise were formed.

Here are some of the foundation stones we now take for granted:

- Investors risk their private money in the success of an enterprise with the promise of future returns.

- An executive team is formed to invest this money wisely and shepherd scarce resources to achieve the maximum return by creating something that others are prepared to pay for.

- The executive team achieves economies by investing in processes and resources that reduce the cost of production, supply chains etc and yield maximum returns to shareholders.

- Offerings are introduced to buyers by taking products to a market and advertising their worth.

- A value is agreed and money is exchanged for products and services.

- Shareholders receive a dividend on their investment and agree a level of re-investment into resources that will improve the ability of the enterprise to make even more money next year.

The basic workings of business and markets have remained largely unchanged for over a century. Josiah Wedgwood, Henry Ford and Victor Kiam modelled their success on the fundamental rules of consumerism. Build good products. Make them affordable. Do it better than anyone else. Satisfy the customer. An aspect of the belief system formed from the teachings of these great entrepreneurs was that *mechanization* is good. It creates predictability, prevents variation and enables best practices to be translated into consistent processes that can be repeated time and again. **Mechanization is the core ethos that underpins 20th century organizations,** how people are conditioned to think about how organizations should work – the 'well oiled machines' of capitalism. This management ethos originated in the industrial revolution.

When capitalism was finding its feet, 'the wind blows trade' was how English sailors described the strong westerly and easterly winds that crossed the Atlantic, encouraging trade with the Americas. The profitability of many organizations of the day trading in coffee, tea, silk and cotton depended on the reliability of the wind and the skills of sailors to exploit its power. Clipper ships were designed for speed and built with passion. But they were powered by the wind and were dependent on its energy. For the industrialists and investors of the time, this meant 'no wind, no trade. No trade, no business.'

Then Isambard Kingdom Brunel brought together a steam-powered engine and Robert Wilson's underwater screw which meant that he could propel a vessel across the Atlantic waters within days rather than weeks by sail. The outcome of this small part of the industrial revolution was more control over the external conditions that impacted on trade, replacing *no wind, no trade* with point-to-point delivery schedules across the oceans of the world. Steam power was an iconic technology – the '.com' of the age. How steam must have resonated with industrialists as being the future, at a time when business seemed to have a symbiotic link with mechanization. It gave conformity, reliability and order to things that had previously been beyond the control of the industrialists – the power of the wind, the energy of employees – variables that could cost time and money. Industry had started its journey to regulate, to bring order to, the elements. In the following century, more and more mechanisms would be introduced to formalize the industrial age. Some would be organizational whilst others would be legislative (such as the Companies Act of England in 1844 that formalized the incorporation of joint-stock businesses).

With the advent of steam-powered ships and trains, the world became a smaller and more orderly place. Perishable crops grown in far-away lands could now reach new markets, displacing demand for less interesting domestic goods. UK businesses could compete on a world stage. People spoke of 'global markets' for the first time.

Some of the businesses forged by these changes in market conditions still live on under different names: companies like British Tobacco and Tetley's Tea. The underpinning values of the age were etched into a corporate ethos of productivity, logistics and supply chain: values that responded to a rapid growth in consumerism. Every English middle-class family wanted to invite their friends to take tea in the afternoon with the latest bone china, sitting on chairs made from American Spruce. With a social structure that rapidly began to measure social status by the consumer goods people owned, demand was high. Within the enterprising *societies of gentlemen*, the focus of management attention was on how to improve processes, build economies of scale – faster, bigger, sweeter, fresher, cheaper products that could service more and more consumers.

The assumption that demand would always outstrip supply has nearly always been proven to work. It was manufacturing productivity and product quality that mattered. These inward-looking management principles continue to underlie the culture and behaviour of most corporations even today.

The Industrial Revolution evidences the symbiotic relationship between industry and society. It was born from a sequence of interconnected and dramatic changes to society and the principles of supply and demand. England was enjoying a period of affluence and invention at a time when the middle classes wanted more of the products that helped them to climb the social ladder. People believed that humankind had barely started to discover its true potential. This spirit of invention encouraged investors to believe in the success of initiatives to invest in trade links with foreign lands, build salt-making machines and to fund the insurance of ships that could never sink. It wasn't until events like the sinking of the Titanic on April 14, 1912 and the Hindenburg disaster on May 6, 1937 that mankind started to realise that it had its limits, and resized its ambitions. At the turn of the 20th century, investors were prepared to look beyond what was known and discover new horizons. Industrialists saw the potential of mechanization to drive productivity and reduce costs through factory working, more workers were employed and earnings rose, leading higher disposable incomes. Women shopped for more upwardly mobile goods.

The result was a spiral of supply and demand that created our consumer society. This is how the social commentator Thomas Carlyle reported on the consequences of the industrial revolution. His comments on social change in the early 20th century exquisitely reveal the mood of the era:

"Were we required to characterize this age of ours by any single epithet, we should be tempted to call it, not an Heroic, Devotional, Philosophical, or Moral Age, but, above all others, the Mechanical Age. It is the Age of Machinery, in every outward and inward sense of that word; the age which, with its whole undivided might, forwards, teaches and practises the great art of adapting means to ends. There is no end to machinery. With individuals, in like manner, natural strength avails little. No individual now hopes to accomplish the poorest enterprise single-handed and without mechanical aids; he must make interest with some existing corporation, and till his field with their oxen. In these days, more emphatically than ever, to live, signifies to unite with a party, or to make one." (*Signs of the Times*, 1829)

A century of capitalism has forged a corporate culture that prioritizes risk management over innovation and inventiveness every time. In this book I comment on a changing world – globalization, instant intelligence, low response times, the power of the 'grouped individual' etc. – and the negative influence of the embedded risk-averse behaviour of corporations.

When Nick and I interview individual leaders they are well aware of the changes and the challenges they see today. So, when we talk to 'the organization', which is after all no more than a grouping of those individual leaders, why does that well-articulated view of the future disappear into the mire of risk paranoia and the obsession with the tangible things around them, like 'hierarchies', like 'systems', like 'all at the lowest possible risk of discomfort and surprise'?

It's because organizations are fixated by 'hard' manifestations of so-called good management practice. The din made by the running gear of the organization drowns out the murmurings and signals that markets are sending. Managers become deaf to these vital pointers to future success.

They – the organization's individuals – are not listening. Not listening to their customers, being attentive to their markets, their environment. Not listening to the warning signals. They often can't because they're not given the required mechanisms and resources. Sometimes they do not want to. They find it all too intangible, too indefinite, too uncertain, too challenging? And besides, their bonuses do not take into account any 'listening' or market sensing. They are acting in an understandable and justifiable way. It's just a pity that their organization will become increasingly less relevant and, like *the ship that could never sink*, it will one day meet its own iceberg.

Having focused their efforts on saving money in recent years, executives are now looking to find new business models that create value and tap into new sources of opportunity. Anticipating the impact of these changes, one in every two senior executives expects to see changes in their value proposition and the market sectors they serve. Business models have become more important than product innovations as a source of competitive advantage and understanding how the enterprise embraces new insight and turns it into new customer value for many organizations will be the key to their success. Processes that can support this listening, understanding and translation into action are devalued by senior management as being, at best, 'nice to haves', not 'have to haves'. The technologies that support business processes become all too important, their relationship to perceived reward (no understanding of incentivized contribution) is not understood and their output is not put into hard, 'bottom line' context. Technology is so seldom used as the strategic tool that it has the potential to be.

Yes, market-leading organizations must keep doing what they are good at and establish a defendable position in the supply chain, but they must also embrace values of greater empathy towards their customers' (and broader stakeholders') needs, and evidence a more visible and proactive social and environmental conscience. More than anything else, corporations must not stand still and become sitting ducks to more agile pursuers. As employers, organizations will be keen to acquire the best people by providing a work-life balance that is fashioned to meet the aspirations of a well-educated and skilled workforce. As players in highly competitive markets, these organizations will be characterized by their greater agility. They will demand the capacity to flex their business processes and resources to respond to changes in demand and capitalize on new market structures as they emerge.

The 'Wind-driven' enterprise of the 21st century

Today, the captains of industry face the discomfort of living within an environment that they are unable to control. No longer do they have the equivalent of steam power to drive their corporations forward and remove the variables of the external environment.

The captain of a steam ship had to make sure his engines were always running. This meant focusing more time on running the ship rather than spending every waking hour on deck waiting for the next puff of wind. What a great metaphor this is to parallel the role of senior management teams in today's corporations who spend much of their time looking inwardly at business processes and technology deployments to make the steam engine more efficient. How sad it will be for some of these captains to realise, only too late, that all they are doing is steaming faster onto the rocks – that if only they had spent more of their time on deck eyeballing the horizon, they would have seen and could have navigated a different course.

Commerce is reverting to a period when 'the wind blows trade'.

The opportunity for profitable, sustainable business depends upon the ability of executives to better understand what matters to their customers and be first to harness new untapped markets in a period when commerce will be less able than ever to control its environment. Instead of inward-looking management practices, corporations must reacquaint themselves with the skills needed to harness the prevailing external forces exerting control over their enterprise to achieve strategic goals.

The wind-driven enterprise is an adaptive, empathetic, socially and environmentally conscious venture that profits from being truly world-class at what it does best. This world-class capability is enshrined in its ability to always fit those markets that offer the highest return. Every time the market appears to nudge in a different direction and show a glimmer of an opportunity or threat, the agilized enterprise appears to know how to react, to capture these weak signals and harness its capability to exploit every opportunity to move forward. Its ambition is never to *mechanize* its structure – or culture – but to harness the power of external markets and to give the individuals that contribute to its success a compelling reason for participating in its journey.

Within an agilized organization of the 21st century expect to see:

- An organization that knows itself – how it listens, how it learns, what resources it has at its disposal, what assets are most critical to its success, what it does best.

- An organization that has *formalized* how it works – through greater formalization of roles, responsibilities, information flows, personal contributions, appreciation of outcomes, etc – with the goal of creating agility, creativity and structural (and process) liquidity rather than always focusing resources towards automation and seeking to strip away cost.

- An outward-looking organization that actively listens to its customers and markets.

- A loosely-coupled organization structure that embraces creativity within and beyond the 'firewalls' that protect its corporate boundary.

- A business that always fits its most profitable markets.

How to achieve this transformation is covered in section 2.

The message for organizational leaders is clear. Your organization needs to always fit the most profitable markets it has the capacity to serve. This means reacting faster to threats and opportunities than competitive peers if it is to enjoy sustainable growth in the perilous markets of the 21st century. It is not the ability to rapidly change that will define corporate success but the capacity to rapidly fit profitable markets.

Gone are the days of steam power and mechanization. Welcome to the new era where agilization rules.

Section 2

THE AGILIZED ORGANIZATION

It is not the strongest of the species who survive, nor the most intelligent; rather it is those most responsive to change.

Charles Darwin

Subjects of Agilization

After 6 years of research I've concluded there are 10 key subject areas that influence the ability of an enterprise to constantly change itself to fit its most profitable markets.

These are:

1. Vision and Essence
2. Leadership
3. Alignment
4. Operating Approach
5. Process Performance
6. Behaviour
7. Insight
8. Curiosity
9. People
10. Technology

It is how this diverse set of ingredients are forged and applied that differentiates the 21st century *agilized* enterprise from its 20th century *mechanized* predecessor. No single component could be described as more important than another. Indeed, it might also be the case that the performance of one component relies on or impacts on the performance of another. For example, what is *leadership* without *followers*? What are *actions* without a *vision*? The chapter progressively develops an understanding of each subject and the interlinkages between them – but it is the final section that we take these *elements of agilization* and apply them in a way that 'gets your house in order'.

I was nervous when writing this section that readers might find it hard work to get through the content. The way enterprises operate after all is complex and takes effort to understand. WHY BOTHER to invest time in learning about the intricacies of business operation? Isn't there an easier way to make money? Perhaps yes – but to create a sustainable enterprise that repeatedly competes and wins in the 21st century business world, thoughtful management and knowledge of these practical management issues is in my opinion essential.

It's not THAT DIFFICULT to learn these critical success factors but it does demand a little effort and concentration. But it's worth it! You will have the know-how to get the best out of the people you work with and work for. You will learn to get people and processes working that clearly aren't doing so. These skills you can develop just by reading. YOU CAN DO IT!

The fundamental management mechanisms I'm describing exist within every enterprise but unless you know what you're looking for, most of these things go unnoticed. For people familiar with business management, many of the terms are likely to be familiar but even for experienced managers it's probably worth having a refresher.

I wanted to start with an illustration that exposes the core elements of *enterprise logic* (i.e. how the enterprise thinks and acts) and how the enterprise is meant to work when it works well.

Illustration of the CORE ELEMENTS of Enterprise Logic

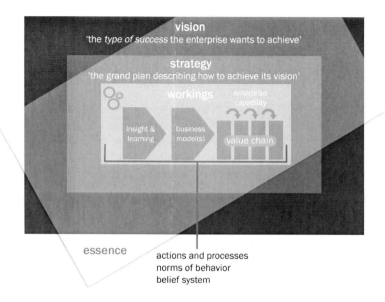

Here's a run-through of the mechanics of enterprise behaviour that I've illustrated in the diagram:

We assume that the enterprise exists for a purpose. That purpose is described by its '**vision**' (definition of success) and its '**strategy**' (how it plans to achieve success).

To achieve its success, the organization knows that it must understand what matters to consumers of its products, services or knowledge. Therefore to learn from its markets, the *agilized* enterprise has a finely tuned listening (**insight and learning**) system that takes weak indicators of market change and feeds this through to the decision making engine room whose role it is to translate these early warning signals into **business models** that turn *what the enterprise produces* into *earnings*.

The capability of the enterprise (see **enterprise capability**) to deliver this customer value is determined by its assets and capabilities. These are often described by '**value chains**' that normally start with 'raw materials' that flow through 'production' and result in the 'product' that its 'consumers' want to pay for. Of course, it's easier to see physical things than emotional attitudes and behaviours. These exist in an enterprise just as they do within people. So like the performance of people after a late night and early morning, we have to take into account the influence on performance of attitudes and behaviours. This is captured in the '**essence**' of the enterprise that is another layer that spans across every aspect of the way an enterprise works.

Useful Terms to Bookmark

I've just shot through a whole series of terms that might be new to you if you've never been heavily involved in business management, so I've provided a summary of them here. You will find me returning to these terms time and again in the following sections – so this is a good page to bookmark for later!

'Enterprise Logic' is an inclusive term that describes how an organization behaves. It's a relatively new expression in business management but it has got increasingly important for leaders to understand how enterprises think and act.

'Essence' describes the emotional values that shape the vision and activities of the enterprise. Organizational essence is a quality often missing within frameworks used for strategy planning. This can result in contradictions between the vision of an enterprise and its capability.

'Vision' articulates the ambition of the enterprise. In the modern enterprise, a *vision* is a statement of intent that advises shareholders of the *type of success* executives plan to achieve for their enterprise.

'Strategy' is a term used to describe the grand plan. A *strategy* should identify how the enterprise will husband its *learning, business model* and *capabilities* to deliver the desired outcomes that it views as essential to guide the enterprise towards its vision.

'Outcomes' is a term used to describe the *value* an enterprise produces for its shareholders (or in the case of public sector, the achievement of services tax payers are required to pay for).

The workings of the enterprise are characterized by:

'Learning and Insight' – how an enterprise captures and interprets contextualized information to gain a competitive advantage, such as understanding how to capture and apply customer preferences to create better products. The ability of an enterprise to capture knowledge and learn from it is also an aspect of enterprise capability but I've elected to separate it to aid the reader's appreciation of the relationship between insight capture and other aspects of information management (given that **insight capture** is critical to the success of the 'agilized' corporation but it is not a well understood topic).

'Business Model' – the mechanism by which the enterprise intends to generate revenue and profit or discharge its duties. In a private sector context it encompasses (1) how the enterprise brings value to its customers, (2) its cost structure (the relative proportion of fixed, variable and mixed costs found within the organization) and (3) how it generates its revenues – its **economic engine**.

An **'economic engine'** is the way an enterprise converts its customer value into earnings. Airline companies sell seat occupancy, private hospitals sell beds, banks sell transactions, and electricity suppliers sell numbers of units consumed. Wise investors focus their strategies on economic engines and how secure they are. Changing market structures can radically change how economic engines operate.

'Enterprise Capability' describes enterprise assets, skills and resources that are employed within the *strategy* to deliver outcomes that guide the enterprise towards its *vision*:

- The fixed and variable assets of an enterprise – people (and their skills), brand, plant, stock, premises, knowledge, etc.

- Partnerships with suppliers and channel partners – helping the enterprise in bringing value to its customers.

- Brand reach – the extent to which the enterprise is capable of delivering value to customers. If customers associate a brand with making cars, they probably wouldn't expect the same brand to offer them toothpaste!

- Management skills and capacity.

- Workforce skills and capacity.

Value chains are sequences of process steps that define the core activities of the enterprise. A 20th century manufacturing organization might have a value chain as illustrated below. See how one process step feeds the next (from left to right in the diagram).

An example of a typical value chain for a manufacturing company

At the foot of the *core elements* model on page 74 I highlight *behavioural* aspects of enterprise that influence how the organization works:

'Belief system' describes what the enterprise understands to be real – a collection of beliefs that management and workforce apply within every aspect of what they do and why they do it.

'Norms of behaviour' describe how the enterprise *behaves* or thinks that it should behave. Examples might include how executives define success and invest in their workforce; how workers use their time and discharge their role; how they treat customers; how rapidly they pick up the phone when it's ringing, how they are remunerated – even dress code.

'Actions and processes' describe the ability of the enterprise to efficiently discharge its functions through a formalized series of actions and processes that bring about a deliverable by the enterprise.

Section Introduction

In this section I've described each of the 10 subject areas that most influence agilization of the enterprise. Within each of these subjects I describe the net present state (i.e. how things are today in most organizations) and then I move on to what management teams can do to improve their enterprise capability.

For each of the subjects I have provided a summary table at the end of the chapter to provide practitioners with a check-list to measure the performance of an organization against these key performance factors.

The nature of business is that if you can't measure it, you probably can't manage it. So, should you wish to be more scientific in your analysis of agilization performance you can visit our website at http://www.agilization.com where you will be able to download (for free) a check-list and *agilization formula* for calculating your level of agilization.

Please feel free to access and use the resources made available on the website.

6

(V) Vision and Essence

The process of selecting a preferred future from a range of possible futures formed around a core set of values and beliefs that 'centre' possibilities and behaviours, everything the enterprise does or tries to achieve. The vision of an agilized enterprise is a *stated direction*, not and *end state*.

(1) A poorly scoped vision

Most organizations today have a poorly scoped vision. When businesses start, founders normally have a clear view of what they are starting a business for and what they expect to achieve – but this clarity can soon be lost. And the 21st century business can ill afford to stand still, otherwise the chasing herd will surely trample it underfoot!

Leaders have to look ahead and plan ahead. Setting a clear direction is the starting point of this journey and critical if a leader wants to encourage his or her workforce to be committed to their cause. Many organizations exist without a clear sense of ambition or direction. Most entrepreneurs start with a dream that turns into an ambition, and at some point evolves into a labour of love before finally (only sometimes) transforming into a reality. Without dreams and belief in themselves, most entrepreneurs would never achieve success.

Executives of larger corporations are often professional leaders that inherit a handful of cards and then have to work out what they've got to play with. Seldom in the past have the emotional aspects of organizational culture or 'fit' been a consideration when leaders set out to determine the future direction of the enterprise. Rarely is there the same emotional attachment to the enterprise unless the founder is still at the helm.

The foundation of a vision is to fundamentally understand what the enterprise 'is' – its values, its talent, its assets – to develop a clear picture of what it wants to achieve, and is capable of.

Thinking too small

Whilst focusing on what is core, leaders should not define markets too tightly. Some organizations fail to succeed because the bar is set too low. There are benefits of being a smaller fish in a bigger sea and leaders must seek to extend the aspirations of the organization beyond the confines of a core market – seeking to stretch ambitions from the top of the business downward.

Organizations that have achieved success in the past can frame themselves into a picture that they have historically dominated – their legacy market.

Whether it's Canon and cameras, McDonald's and hamburgers or Coca-Cola and fizzy drinks, many corporations achieve a point in their growth where they present to shareholders a level of dominance in their core market that would cause you to wonder why anyone would bother to compete. However, *confidence* can quickly drift into *arrogance* and a false sense of security. It can lead managers into becoming complacent about the power of market forces and forgetting the ingenuity of competitors and entrepreneurs.

It was Theodore Levitt, a Harvard Business School professor, who wrote a paper on "Marketing Myopia," in which he advanced the idea that organizations often fail because they define themselves too narrowly. One example he drew on was railroads that "let others take customers away from them because they assumed themselves to be in the railroad business instead of the transportation business".

Nick Lawrie reminded me of a story about Jack C Welch, the man who led the rapid expansion of General Electric Company. The story goes something like this:

Jack Welch walks into General Electric and all of the managers say, "Mr Welch, welcome on board. Yep, we're doing great. Dominant 80% market share in our primary market." Jack turns

around and says, "Okay. What I want you to do is to make your 80% market share 20%."

"What?" say the managers," So you're asking us to lose some of our market share!?"

"No," says Jack, "I want you to find a bigger market. In your world we've got 20% to play for. In my world I've got 80% to play for. I'd rather be in my world".

For organizations that have enjoyed strong, sustainable business from a specific market with the same business model for a number of consecutive years, it is easy to fall into the trap of not seeing beyond the next hill.

To example this:

Back in my history I led a consulting project with a global IT company that started out with a view that their present-day market extended to 2 or 6 major competitive peers.

As part of the 'discovery' project phase Nick and I met with a dozen middle managers from their European headquarter sales and marketing team. In a crowded room we explained that we had been working on the project for six weeks and were getting more and more confused about the market that we were meant to be dealing with. We asked the obvious question of the sales and marketing people, "Who is your major competitor?"

The marketing people gave us the name they had briefed us on. Bizarrely, the sales people not only quoted a different company, but a name from a completely different product technology segment!

The ripples of the meeting went through the organization for more than six months before the parent company sided with the salesmen and diverted their attention to the broader market that had been defined.

Belief that your organization dominates a market can disguise the bigger opportunity. Here's an example of leaders poorly scoping their market:

In the 1970s the most advanced technology for printing large volumes of data quickly was line printing. Kings of the line printer market were two well established German printer hardware companies. Then, in the late 1970s, a US company started to change the dynamics of the market by introducing products that had ruggedized plastic outer casings rather than the traditional metal cases of the Germanic products. Sure enough, the US Company started to make significant inroads into the line printer market. For two decades the three companies fought for global dominance of the line printer market. This led to a bitter rivalry between the players where one would regularly accuse the other of dumping products or somehow influencing channel decisions. Then suddenly, the nature of the computer printing market changed. Laser printers demonstrated more versatility in the business applications they could support and offered a higher quality of output. Data centres changed to become client server architectures with PCs on every desk.

Advances in networking and the Internet led to more on-screen reporting, which reduced the need for printed reports. Data storage also became more sophisticated and organizations felt less of a need to evidence transactions with paper-based records. The result? The size of the world market for line printers imploded. The new kid on the block, Hewlett Packard, had cleaned up in the laser printer market while these three Titans had been kicking each other under the table! In less than a decade, the market opportunity for line printers plummeted. In the early 2000s, two of these bitter rivals merged. Needless to say, neither of these suppliers ever became a serious player in the laser printer market.

This story presents a 20th century view of competition (where three known players fought for market share over a period of years) that ends with a very 21st century twist when a competitor with a disruptive technology appears from a different market space, and subsumes their market, not by doing things better but by innovating a better way of doing things.

(2) Defining a purpose and reason for being

In many ways, you either have a clear and well articulated vision that people are able to believe in – or you don't.

There is no hard and fast method of creating a vision. It's particularly difficult when placed in a crowded room with a blank white-board! Visions are not created in the boardroom. They generally happen in the shower, on the beach, in the car, on the train or when pushing a supermarket trolley. It is essential to form strategy around a stated direction that is qualitative, ambitious and believable. Building strategy without a vision is organizing to go nowhere! Without the energy of people who are energized to achieve a vision, organizations become empty vacuums that exist with no purpose. Posting a meaningless mission statement on your website is not a vision!

Organizational Essence

In a commercial enterprise, I personally see a vision to be a marriage between a financial outcome and the shared belief of a group of individuals to achieve it. To shape a vision that 'fits' the organization, the organization needs to understand its 'essence' – that core set of values that determines, from an emotional perspective, what the collective of individuals believes it should be capable of. It may perhaps be seen to be inappropriate to aspire to achieve a commercial outcome that has dire consequences on the lifestyle of employees, on society in general or on the environment as a helpless victim of corporate greed.

The changing cultural beliefs of individuals today and the greater importance placed on issues such as core values, lifestyle, community and environmental sustainability, mean that highly skilled workers are keen to understand the essence of the enterprise they serve. As individuals, they want to work for an organization that embraces and perhaps mirrors their own core values. Recent research on the decision-making behaviours of university graduates suggests 'enterprise essence' is a key influencer on how they short-list potential employers.

Canon is an example of an organization that clearly states and promotes its emotional values through a philosophy it calls Kyosei. Spearheaded by former President and Chairman, Ryuzaburo Kaku, Canon has made Kyosei a living principle by requiring employees to make a commitment to work and live in harmony with others. Kyosei encapsulates everything that is visionary about the company and lies at the heart of its brand values and behaviours. Kyosei means "living and working together for the common good" and is demonstrated in Canon's corporate mission statement, goals, culture and behaviours. Through this 'essence', Canon expresses the core of its collective being and extends this philosophy to the way people are encouraged to participate in the workplace.

Kyosei helps its workforce, suppliers and customers to understand Canon, to appreciate what centres its behaviours – how it thinks and acts. My personal experience working with Canon is that, on an emotional level, people – staff, customers, suppliers – get to know Canon, to understand how the organization thinks, and usually when they do this, they LIKE the organization. They trust in the organization. This deeper level of emotional attachment to the brand and its values makes a real difference to the commitment of staff to want to be a part of the organization. For customers it means that they do not see Canon as a heartless corporate machine. They are prepared to look deeper into the soul of the organization and see Canon employees to be the sort of people they aspire to be. The business impact of Kyosei is already visible in the way that Canon is trusted as a high quality product provider, in its ability as a corporation to attract the best people, in the feedback provided by customers on the quality (work ethic) of Canon people and in the deep business relationships Canon builds with its customers and partners – that create a deep trust.

This desire to externalize the emotional side of an organization is a very Japanese and European trait. It encourages a way of doing business that is not arrogant or aggressive but more laid-back, patient, thoughtful. This approach to business is finding favour with new generations of consumers – and for companies like Canon, *organizational essence* is becoming a differentiator that drives its economic advantage. I believe the greatest strength of Canon's philosophic approach lies in the fact that it has *always promoted* its organizational values and beliefs. As organizational essence starts to emerge as a key competitive differentiator, I suspect some organizations will attempt to 'retro-fit' values to their businesses. Introducing values into an organization 'down the line' is difficult. It can appear false and transparent to staff and customers alike, even though the emotional basis for doing so might be genuine.

The jewel

In England we used to have a style of retail outlet called a bric-a-brac shop (interestingly, a French term adopted by the Victorians to describe collections of curious, elaborately decorated items). Few of these stores exist today, but in their day you would look into the window of such a store and your eyes would enjoy a feast on colours from the rich tapestry of items that promised one day to be *clutter*.

As organizations grow, opportunities will often appear that offer the promise of quick revenue. Sometimes, these are too much of a tease for managers to turn down. Adopting new products and services in this way can easily result in business lines that do not encourage core strengths of the organization. This can result in an enterprise spreading its resources and focus far to thin. Eventually, the organization loses its reason for being, as none of its business lines represents a world-class offer.

On other occasions, product or service innovation can extend beyond the core customer community. Rather than growing business around a core of demand, new business threads form that require promotion to new customer communities. This is not always bad news, but a new product to a new market requiring new skills and new investment is a high risk game. Much of the time Nick Lawrie and I spend at NDMC is invested working with clients to establish what the 'jewel' is that should be at the centre of their 'shop window'. Another, sometimes painful, exercise is to de-clutter the shop window by focusing resources on THE JEWEL that promises business continuity and success.

How to determine the vision

Know your organization and what it is capable of

It is essential leaders have a firm grasp of the essence and capability – the 'what we are' – of an organization. It means that every strategic and tactical decision can be prefaced by 'Is this something that we believe in and that we can be great at?' Understanding what is core to any organization can be difficult to put your finger on. For example, local government is about making sure customers enjoy useful, quality public services. All too often, local authority executives place an emphasis on the delivery of service, and consequently invest in the systems and people needed to provide rather than manage the delivery, an overseeing role that demands fewer resources and can be a more effective route to meeting the needs of citizens.

Other examples:

- **Tesco** has become one of the world's most successful retailers by focusing on delivering quality products at affordable prices, recognising that the core to its competency is the need for exceptional logistics and knowledge of its customers' needs and expectations.

- **Direct Line** started as a phone-based insurance retailer but has recognised its own skills in administration and money assets to extend its offerings into Internet car sales and home contents insurance, all built around efficient administration processes and money assets.

- **The AA**, best known as a roadside maintenance organization, saw that its customers strongly identified its brand with reliable customer service. They leveraged this brand reach to provide a broad range of customer service-oriented offerings including insurance services and telecommunications.

One method used to distil an organization's core competency was created by Jim Collins, a student and teacher on the subject of how great companies grow and attain superior performance, who drew his inspiration from the defensive approach adopted by hedgehogs. So his logic goes, whilst the sly fox might think of a hundred ways to attack its prey, the hedgehog has only one way of defending itself. That does it do? It curls into a ball and shows its spikes! Whilst not terribly inventive, it is effective.

An organization's Hedgehog Concept flows from knowledge of:

1. **The organization's jewel – a customer offer that it can be best in the world at.**

2. **What drives the economic engine (i.e. how value is created).**

3. **What the organization is deeply passionate about.**

The Hedgehog Concept of an organization is derived from the intersection of the three factors above. Knowledge of an organization's core competency will give an indication of where it can go next. What it needs to get there is a strategy.

Checklist for **Vision**

If you would like to understand how agilized *your* organization is (either the one you lead or work for) use this checklist. If your ticks are in the unhappy zone the enterprise will be poor at adapting to new opportunities. Practitioners might prefer to visit http://www.agilization.com and download the more comprehensive agilization formula.

	Qualification	**Score**
☹️ **A poorly scoped vision**	**The enterprise has not stated its intentions and lacks a clear ambition or vision.**	☐
	The workforce is not driven to achieve its vision.	☐
	Vision is narrowly scoped and is not challenging.	☐
	Workforce is unclear as to what the vision is.	☐
🙂 **A defined purpose and reason for being**	**The enterprise vision:**	
	Describes its 'Jewel' – what it can be best in the world at.	☐
	Embraces its 'essence'.	☐
	Reflects what drives its economic engine.	☐
	Its people are passionate about.	☐

7

(L) Leadership

Do not bother just to be better than your contemporaries or predecessors. Try to be better than yourself.

William Faulkner

(1) Poor leadership

How do you know when leaders are not leading? A clear bottom line indicator is that the financial targets of the enterprise are not being met. There are other ways of measuring poor leadership performance.

Leadership is failing an organization when managers are directionless, workers are unable to explain how their day-to-day contributions are meant to deliver top level strategic goals, and attitudes between workers are inhibiting performance. Spend any time in an organization that has poor leadership and the signs are stamped everywhere. Poor resources, low self-esteem of workers, stale working environments.

(2) A coherent and shared strategy

It's easy for enterprise leaders to sit in their office and draw up a collection of objectives and then demand that managers get on and deliver them. This approach to strategy formation rarely works.

Formation of strategy should not be conducted in isolation by leaders alone. Instead, it should be recognised that building a strategy forms part of an inclusive engagement exercise with the stakeholder community, to develop a small number of objectives that are *mutually exclusive but collectively exhaustive* that will achieve the priority outcomes that matter most to the major stakeholder communities – shareholders, customers, workforce and partners/contributors. Ask a workforce to provide their opinions and ideas at an early stage and they are more likely to buy into your strategic plans.

Communicating strategy is a leadership priority

The best-laid plans are doomed to fail if not supported by well-orchestrated implementation. Ordinarily, organizations do not fail for lack of a well-defined strategy, rather, they fail to effectively execute it.

A common reason why strategy does not translate into action is because workers and partners do not 'buy in'. It is easy for a workforce to divorce themselves from strategy believing that it doesn't apply to them, that it's just one more boardroom initiative that will die after a few months. Convincing the people within an organization that strategy *is their* day job is a huge task. At this critical moment, I often see leaders locking themselves away from their organization, not spending enough time communicating their vision to gain the buy-in they need. The job of making a strategy successful is realistically less than a quarter done when the strategy is formed. It takes great energy to make sure that a strategy 'sticks'. Contributors must know how their own contribution is leading to the top level outcomes the organization is trying to achieve.

How to communicate strategy

To complete the task, leaders need to convince contributors that:

1. The strategy is good for them and is achievable.
2. This is one boardroom initiative that is not going to go away.
3. Achieving strategic priorities is part of every person's day-job.
4. As a leader – YOU believe in it.

Later in this chapter I introduce the subject of the *balanced scorecard,* which is a popular way of creating and articulating a strategy.

Sometimes boardroom methods are too academic and unfamiliar to broader audiences. At NDMC we favour the steering wheel model illustrated below that shows business strategy in a way that is visually more understandable to staff and stakeholders. The analogy with the steering wheel of a motor car (i.e. its role is to steer the organization) makes sense to most people. It helps to articulate what the leadership is trying to do and how. The steering wheel shows how a balanced set of objectives will achieve the vision.

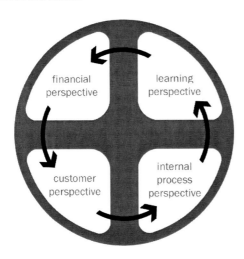

The steering wheel is a human approach to articulating strategy.

(3) Establishing and managing golden threads

Forming a small set of priorities is difficult. For large corporations, getting a management team to agree on less than 16 objectives is like pulling teeth! Big organizations have lots of people working towards many objectives, meeting thousands of personal targets to deliver thousands of actions. EVEN if you get these elements working in harmony, there's always a risk that the net result will not move the organization forward. Why? Because objectives are part of the here-and-now and can frequently change. What's needed is a counterbalance that always centres the enterprise. I use the term 'golden threads' to describe growth sustainability themes that cut across the activities of an enterprise.

Corporate management teams are coming to identify the need to integrate thoughts on social issues into all dimensions of the business, not just the making of strategy. 84% of the executives from around the world who participated in a McKinsey survey in 2006 agreed that their companies should pursue not only shareholder value but also broader contributions to the public good – whoever said business has a one track mind!

When faced with many competing demands on time and resources across the enterprise, *golden threads* are the very top level of strategic outcomes that encourage holistic thought towards sustainable growth. In the absence of a known business term, *golden threads* have been called many things in the past.

The purpose of *golden threads* is to:

- Improve the robustness of strategic framework for organizations that are today accustomed to silo-based budget planning regimes and management through 'top-down' strategic objectives.

- Create a small number of key priorities that ensure the enterprise is always heading in the right direction.

- Bring boardroom strategy into the day-to-day activities of departments and third party contributors, and harmonize and align strategic thinking.

- Work across the silos of operation. Golden threads are normally allocated to board room portfolio holder to ensure there is clarity on who has the responsibility of making sure day-to-day contributions are achieving these outcomes.

Golden threads are themes that cut across operational silos. They serve to bind the thinking of the organization together and focus its resources towards long-term corporate priority themes. Reporting systems constantly validate how silo actions are bringing value to the cross-cutting outcomes that ensure the sustainability of the enterprise. Every objective, action and task that occurs, at every level of the enterprise, is aligned to one or more of the golden threads that the senior executive team is responsible for. Senior managers use business activity monitoring software to understand how day-to-day actions will lead to the achievement of golden thread priorities. If a contribution does not readily satisfy ANY of the golden threads, managers have to ask the question 'Why are we doing this?'

Golden threads are the BIG GEAR wheel that put the entire resources of the organization behind a small number of long-term outcomes. This can be illustrated as follows:

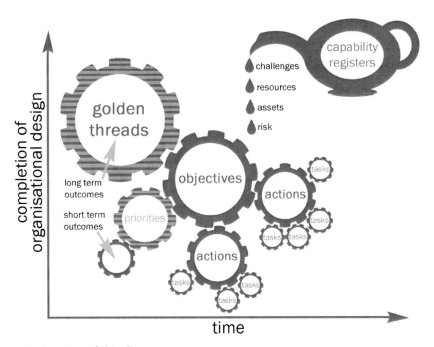

Explanation of this diagram:

The simplest definition of discipline of management is 'balancing scarce resources'. An organizational strategy sets out to balance scarce resources and to align them to desired outcomes. It maps out how operating silos manage the contributions of individuals, budgets, levels of risk, etc. to achieve the objectives and golden threads of the enterprise. This shapes its ability to learn and achieve strategic outcomes by managing day-to-day actions and scrutinizing itself (setting challenges) to ensure it is exploiting its assets and resources.

How to create a shortlist of golden threads

Golden threads should emerge as management themes when a balanced scorecard is produced (see Chapter 8). Sometimes it is necessary to encourage debate around strategic objective themes but generally what comes out if discussions are a series of long-term priorities that define the sustainability of the enterprise. You know the thinking works when golden threads clearly articulate priorities that underscore the sustainability themes of the enterprise and ALSO act as theme headings for the key objectives that have already been established. Executives might come and go but the golden threads your executive team establish should provide a sustaining view of the critical success factors that drive growth.

There are still remarkably few organizations that have identified their golden threads and yet this is changing because sustainability has become so much more important to organizations in the scarce resources of the 21st century. For clarity, I've described below a topical example of the application of golden threads in use:

The Olympics Delivery Agency (ODA) identified 12 'golden threads' that the management team agrees should be fulfilled by the 2012 Olympics. These priorities evolved through consultation during the planning application for the Olympic Park. They provide a useful means of identifying the key sustainability issues of the activities for which the ODA is responsible for, and aid continuity in its planning by aligning the day-to-day project contributions of contractors to the five London 2012 sustainability themes of Climate Change, Waste, Biodiversity, Inclusion and Healthy Living.

(4) *Followership* at all levels of the enterprise

Leaders must re-ignite *followership* in their workforce to create an enterprise that *thinks and acts* as one and fundamentally understands what the enterprise 'is' and what it is 'capable of'.

In order to be a leader a man must have followers.

Dwight D Eisenhower

Leadership is a huge subject area and many excellent books have been written about it by people who have done the job. I've therefore made no attempt to write another. The key question that I'm focusing on here is, "What will be different about *leadership* within an agilized enterprise?

You don't have to be a great orator or require the X-Factor to be a good leader but you do need *followers*. Leaders must encourage people to make an *emotional commitment* to a *project* that they want to be part of and contribute towards. Happiness is about doing something that is rewarding at some level. We all need *projects* to get ourselves motivated. Many people do not want to have careers as such, and are happy to do a 9-to-5 job, but even so, whilst they are doing the 9-to-5 job they do want it to be rewarding. *Followership* is about creating a *happy mental attitude* within a workforce. Whilst it's not possible to force people to be followers, you can recruit them more easily if you are able to paint a compelling vision.

We are moving into an era where decision making has to be more peer-based. This is because of the greater need for creativity within the enterprise at all levels. Organizations that discourage devolved decision making will not be able to harness change quickly enough. The greatest gift of leadership lies in the ability to encourage people to want to be *followers*. That requires **vision**, **energy** and **direction**. Time for a quick story – though I won't vouch for its accuracy as I can't track down the source! Anyway, it's a great story.

A successful Australian businessman was looking to retire to a beautiful vineyard located in the Australian outback, having made his fortune several times over. Relaxing in the sun and growing grapes, sipping his own wine as the sun went down was the main focus of his retirement plan – but when he arrived at the site he was inspired by the natural arena that presented itself to him. There were hills on three sides of a beautiful vine covered valley. He suddenly thought how wonderful it would be to organize an orchestral event where his guests could also sample the fruit of the land. During the period of his string of entrepreneurial successes, he had developed a high-performing executive team around him. They had a reputation for always getting the job done. He needed his A-Team.

A few days later, the A-Team was on-site. The businessman presented his idea – an orchestral concert and wine tasting party – and, this time, they thought he had gone completely mad. Organize a concert miles from anywhere with no facilities for catering? Everything would need to be flown in; food, toilet blocks, guests – the orchestra! The businessman presented a set of huge paintings to his A-Team so that he could illustrate what he had in mind. As his team studied the painted panorama showing an orchestra at the centre, marquees full of food framed by a landscape of undulating hills he overplayed the soundtrack of an orchestra playing, of people laughing, of champagne corks popping. The total effect was breathtaking. The businessman had literally painted a picture of his vision that his team could visualize. Once they could see what HE could see, they knew it would work. The event was a success and for a while became a regular feature on the events calendar.

In the world today, leaders continue to be promoted on their academic and technical expertise. How often do you see adverts saying "Do you have the ability to create *followership*, to engage staff to build high levels of motivation and morale in teams to achieve excellence?"

Jane Ling and Jenny Turner founded Ling Turner Ltd. in the late 1990s to support management teams in the complex task of installing positive norms of behaviour that help teams to achieve excellence. Jenny says, "Over the past ten years, we have asked more than 7,000 people from a range of private and public organizations to tell us what it is they look for or admire in their leaders. Without exception the same trends form every time. A clear message comes through on what staff are looking for from their leaders and when leaders listen and change in response to this, the shift in internal culture and external business results are truly amazing. What is really encouraging is that requests centre on behaviours and attitudes that cost nothing and people focus little on the tangibles that so many leaders believe is the key to creating motivation and morale. What are these crucial attributes? According to our research, people want to be respected, involved, valued, encouraged and supported, stretched and – most important of all – trusted."

Jenny adds, "The real differentiator for leaders is not in the traditional realms of IQ alone. What's required even more today in the agile organization are leaders who can truly inspire *followership* in their people. One such leader that we have had the pleasure to work with has a lovely analogy where he describes the emotional bank account. When you trust people and demonstrate values of respect, caring, involvement, openness and encouragement it earns you credits in the emotional bank account. When you have to make tough and unpopular decisions or, indeed, you make mistakes in how you deal with people these are debits from your account. The impact on *followership* however is negligible because you are constantly topping up the credits.

Here's a case story where one manager was totally overdrawn!

A colleague had given in her notice for personal reasons having worked with her employer for 20 years, the last 7 of which had been under the leadership of the same manager. During her exit interview she was taken aback by the complimentary feedback that she received from this manager, as she had never had this recognition from him in all the 7 years of working for him.

A week later when she requested a reference, she was confused, disappointed but more than that, she felt anger and frustration at his response to her simple request. She was told that the company policy and procedure only made provision for a brief note outlining the date of joining and date of termination. When she asked if he could include the positive comments from their earlier conversation he replied, "No, because this is not company policy".

This not only left a bad feeling with her, but moreover when she told her colleagues it incited a strong reaction of shared anger and resentment towards the manager. Logically he had fulfilled his organization's requirement, following policy and procedure, but emotionally he had destroyed all goodwill and *followership* across the team.

These destructive behavioural grenades are thrown frequently in organizations between leaders and their staff. Their impact can fester in peoples' minds over long periods and can, in some staff members, emerge as apathy, cynicism, aggression or even subversive attitudes. More than actions from leaders, a much more powerful requisite is that of emotional intelligence, whereby a leader will consciously take accountability for the ultimate way in which staff "feel" in every interaction that they have. It is this level of feelings, whether they be positive or negative, that determines whether staff will become true followers or passive spectators.

To get followers, workers need to know who you are – the real you. I'm always advising business managers and leaders to get out and talk to their workforce. It's so easy to get sucked into a work-day pattern that starts with email 'clutter' and overnight messages and ends with over-reaching meetings that extend into early evenings. I've worked for organizations whose leaders never mingle with their workforce. I have known executives walk into Reception only to find staff don't know who they are! If a workforce can't pick their chief executive out from a line-up, something is wrong.

There are so many ways of creating a bond with staff without having to trample on business etiquette and organization chart protocols but my personal favourite is the simple 5-minute 'good morning' or the 'water cooler moment' that creates a natural, non-choreographed opportunity to be approachable to staff. It's remarkable what leaders learn from their workforce when they make themselves available to listen. Just ten minutes a day between meetings isn't so much to ask is it? Most executives would agree but fall into the trap of opening their email inbox when they arrive at their office. Before they know it, another day has passed.

All the good leaders I know transfer a little of their enthusiasm and energy to their employees. No two leaders are the same. Some are larger-than-life with a voracious energy, whilst others are quietly-spoken and considered in their approach, truly gentle-men and women. Anything goes with leadership styles, provided that a little of that twinkle-dust rubs off on the workforce!

Leaders (at all levels of the business) must be decisive

Leaders at all levels must make decisions. Whether the decision is on how to achieve growth and shareholder value based on a deep-seated appreciation of what the enterprise does, or how it differentiates itself, knowing where it wants to go, how it's going to get there, what REALLY matters to customers – DECIDE! How often do you attend project meetings and find yourself debating the same issues agreed upon the week before? No matter what vision you decide upon, how you fashion your strategy and work out what you're good at and capable of, it is important to decide on what you're going to do and commit to it, because a bad decision is better than no decision at all.

The term decision comes from the Latin word 'cision' that literally means 'to cut off all other options'.

To encourage *followership*, leaders must set a vision that workers can buy into, they must emotionally commit to it, not set the bar too low, and they MUST make decisions.

The Spanish general Hernando Cortez (Hernán Cortés) was most famous for his conquest of the Aztec empire in the area today known as Mexico. To prevent any thoughts of retreat among his troops, Cortez burned his ships. Making decisions is critical but most of us struggle to cut off other options. Instead we elect to keep other options open just in case. Approaching decision making in this way is seen to be a lower risk option – to not burn any bridges. (It isn't of course.) If a leader does not have the self-belief to set a direction and commit to it, why should customers and workforce think any differently? Making a decision is truly a LOWER risk option. Risk is further reduced when the decision maker is constantly reappraising what matters to stakeholders. Franklin D. Roosevelt once said, "It is common sense to take a method and try it. If it fails, admit it frankly and try another."

Leaders are at all levels of the enterprise

When discussing the subject of leadership it is easy to forget that *followership* needs to happen at every level of the enterprise and not just around the boardroom table. Giving lower-level officers the 'headroom' to use their own initiative is a key influencer on the agilization of an enterprise. To make this happen, organizations need to produce the right environment and encourage the right attitudes. Even at departmental level, managers must possess emotional intelligence and encourage *followership*.

Historians now believe that the success of the German Blitzkrieg, the sweeping advance of German troops across Western Europe as far as the English Channel in 1940, was largely due to the ability and encouragement of lower-ranking officers to take the initiative and lead small teams of soldiers to overcome the challenges they faced in the field as they happened. By the later stages of the war, many of these innovative and talented section commanders had been lost, which meant that as soon as battlefield communications broke down the German Divisions quickly became dysfunctional.

Further reading and resources on this subject:

Jane Ling and Jenny Turner have produced some excellent materials outlining the development of programmes to embed *followership* into organizations. Visit their website at http://www.lingturner.co.uk.

Checklist for **Leadership**

Again, tick the check-boxes that most closely describe the current behaviours of the organization. If you are able to tick all of the way down the list of happy face areas then the leadership is exceptional!

	Qualification	Score
☹ **Poor leadership**	Targets are not being achieved.	☐
	Workers are unsure how their personal efforts contribute to strategic outcomes.	☐
	Workers feel unloved and poorly supported by management.	☐
	Environment is stale.	☐
☺ **A coherent and shared strategy**	Workforce understands what the management team is trying to do and how they aim to do it.	☐
	Workers understand how their personal efforts will contribute to strategic outcomes.	☐
☺ **Established and managed golden threads**	Leaders have identified core priorities that will sustain organizational growth.	☐
	Leaders understand how to meet the needs of stakeholder groups.	☐
☺ **Followership at all levels of the enterprise**	Leaders:	
	Encourage *followership*.	☐
	Make decisions.	☐
	Are at all levels.	☐
	Are people that workers want to help to succeed.	☐

8

(A) Alignment

The process of ensuring that all the people, processes and policies are headed in the same direction towards the same goal, thereby minimizing effort wasted in confusion and inefficiency.

(Mike Clargo, Managing by Design)

(1) The enterprise is misaligned

An organization that is misaligned probably has people working hard on activities that ultimately are not contributing to its strategic outcomes. Look around most organizations and you will see examples of poor misalignment with individuals seemingly getting nowhere because they are trying to open the wrong locks with the wrong keys. Alignment is never perfect for long. It is a moving target. Therefore, it is an aspect of enterprise logic that has to be continually assessed and modified according to circumstances.

Alignment has an enormous influence on organizational performance. It creates a dynamic that can either rapidly move organizations forward when done well, or severely hinder their progress when done badly.

An organization operating with poor alignment is like driving a racing car with the handbrake on.

There are several planes of alignment that must be properly managed in order for an organization to optimize the energy of its workforce (and broader community of suppliers and contractors that contribute to the achievement of enterprise goals).

These include the alignment of:

- Objectives to sustainability outcomes (golden threads)
- Organization structure to support and fit its most profitable markets
- Day-to-day activities to strategic objectives of the enterprise
- Resources to activities that contribute to strategic goals
- Insight to enterprise logic (i.e. how the enterprise thinks)
- Remuneration and incentives to reward workers for positive norms of behaviour that encourage curiosity and achievement of strategic goals

When an organization is poorly aligned, the energy of staff is seldom rewarded by the achievement of strategic priorities. This is normally as disappointing to contributors as it is to the management team!

I remember a personal experience that I suspect is representative of the pains of many poorly-focused people:

I was working for a small IT company in Northampton when the Technical Director asked me to prepare the launch of an exciting new product coming over from Japan. I wasn't too thrilled at the prospect of organizing a new product launch, given that my diary was already full-to-overflowing with pragmatic short-term marketing campaign activities and I was pretty starved of support as it was. Like a good *corporate citizen* though, I spent my evenings over the next few weeks preparing the product launch. I started with the product positioning, technical authoring and brochures before looking at the competitive landscape, pricing and go-to-market approach.

By week six I was on time and ready to go. I walked into the Technical Director's office (clasping my swatch of documents) to give him the good news. He look at me bemused and said, "What have you done that for? We decided not to go ahead with that launch weeks ago!"

When organizational structures are poorly aligned with the markets they serve, it becomes difficult for customers and suppliers to engage with one another. I have run consulting projects for companies that have segregated their product offerings to the point that customers can no longer speak to a single representative to share their product needs and requirements. This idea that five experts are better than one is particularly popular with manufacturing companies that have the perennial problem of making sure their production lines are busy. Their organizations mirror the product segregations determined by their production lines. Every product has its own specialist, but no broad expert exists on what matters to the customer and *their business* any more. This can result in the customer feeling that the supplier really doesn't understand *their* needs or *their* business. Supplier and customer lose synchronicity and understanding. They are unable to share a common perspective on how the world works.

(2) A Scorecard Performance Framework

A scorecard is the most popular approach used to clarify and translate vision and strategy, turning it into an actionable plan. Scorecarding today is widely used by Fortune 3000 organizations to shape and articulate their strategy. Known users include Barclays Bank, Tesco, HSBC and Ford Motor Company, to name just a few. Initially focused towards the private sector, it is the public sector that has now tended to standardize the balanced scorecard as a method of articulating strategy. Historically, organizational performance was based on financial measures. Leaders today know that measuring financial performance alone is not sufficient to ensure the sustainability of an enterprise. Attainment of financial 'bottom line' outcomes needs to be *balanced* with objectives for customer value, social and environmental responsibilities, and process improvements – hence the emergence of a *balanced scorecard.*

> **The greatest value derived from the scorecarding process is to bring together a loose collection of individual opinions on the priorities and challenges facing an organization and translating them into a shared view on a single page that everyone can commit to.**

The idiot's guide to scorecarding

The balanced scorecard methodology articulated by Robert S. Kaplan & David P. Norton in their book of the same name creates a consistent approach to clarifying and communicating a balanced scorecard. It also means that organizations are able to document their strategy in such a way that OTHERS can understand it. In some respects, scorecarding oversimplifies complex matters. With all its short-comings, it DOES assist many executives around the world in bringing clarity to their vision and communicating strategy to the people that really need to understand it – workforce, shareholders, partners and customers.

A *scorecard* should measure and predict the attainment of goals and set a descriptive but not prescriptive framework. Its broader application can involve cascading activities and measures to personal scorecards. By linking rewards and remuneration to measurable corporate outcomes, it focuses everyone's attention on their delivery. It empowers *individuals* by allowing them to understand how as individuals they can contribute to corporate goals. There are four *key perspectives* of the original Balanced Scorecard method matured by Kaplan and Norton that can align the actions of the organization to achieve *what matters most* for all key stakeholder groups.

There is no hard and fast rule that says there should always be FOUR perspectives, but it does seem to generally fit the balance of objectives that most organizations describe. These perspectives form a robust vehicle for balancing objectives.

They are:

1. Financial perspective

The financial perspective describes the economic outcomes expected by shareholders.

At one time the ONLY aspect of business performance that managers would measure was the bottom line. But chasing the bottom line can create a short-term view of the world and prevent leaders from encouraging investment in important projects aimed at securing long-term sustainability (for example research and development into the *next generation* product). In today's environmentally aware society, shareholders want to invest in organizations that demonstrate a commitment to sustaining the environment and demonstrating a social conscience through their actions.

The financial perspective is about measuring how implementation and execution of a strategy is resulting in improving bottom line results. When managers start thinking about financial objectives, focus turns quickly to measuring profitability such as operating income, return on capital employed (ROCE), or even economic value added (EVA). These are useful financial measures that remain core to assessing the comparative financial performance of businesses. Other financial measures to consider include cost reduction (perhaps through automation of manual tasks or other forms of productivity improvement), asset utilization and investment strategy.

2. Customer perspective

A scorecard recognises the need to achieve objectives that meet the needs of customers in order to achieve the economic outcomes of the organization. This has always made sense to me. How can you expect to sustain an organization and achieve economic outcomes if you fail to deliver what *matters to customers*?

Before attempting to develop customer-centric objectives, it is essential that sufficient thought is given to the definition of the markets and customers being targeted. Customer expectations might highlight product quality, fit, functionality, values relating to levels of customer service, responsiveness to requests, the quality of the customer interface and buying environment etc. Measures of the customer perspective might include customer profitability, levels of market or customer share (see also diagram on p101), customer retention, customer satisfaction, pace of customer acquisition, even the quality of customer relationship, brand perceptions and value.

3. Internal process perspective

These are the things the organization *must excel at* in order to deliver what matters to customers. Few people are accustomed to *thinking* about their day job in terms of *processes*. It is a word that people find difficult to grasp, unless they are used to its meaning through actively participating in business management. The dictionary definition is "a particular course of action intended to achieve a result." In the workings of organizations, internal processes are important because they describe how *specific tasks* result in *specific outcomes* that must be achieved. Measures of internal process performance are linked to the specific value chain of the enterprise in question. Therefore, if an organization is engaged in product development, manufacturing, distribution and retail, then its process performance measures will no doubt reflect the need to measure each of these core elements in its value chain.

4. Learning and growth perspective

These are the things an organization needs to act on to improve *internal processes* so that they deliver *what matters to customers*, resulting in the organization achieving its *economic outcomes*. The first time an organization develops a scorecard, many of the processes that are core to its success and *should* be day-to-day activities appear in the 'Learning and Growth' perspective of the scorecard. In the second year, these objectives can be expected to migrate into the 'Internal Process' perspective of the scorecard as the organization begins to align its resources more appropriately to achieve stakeholder outcomes. Learning and growth measures cover a broad range of subject areas from tangible issues like supply-chain performance and productivity, through to less tangible topics like customer value and education.

When objectives are placed within the four perspectives of a scorecard they reveal *cause-and-effect relationships* that help managers to understand how (1) learning and growth objectives contribute to improving (2) internal processes that deliver (3) *what matters* to customers and lead to achievement of shareholder (4) financial outcomes.

Articulating these cause-and-effect relationships in a strategy map (see overleaf) presents enterprise strategy on a single page that helps all contributors to understand how they bring value to the strategy. The *perspectives* of the scorecard are represented on the vertical (x) axis. The sum of all objectives should represent a mutually exclusive and collectively exhaustive view of what needs to be done to achieve the main stakeholder outcomes.

A strategy map shows strategic objectives aligned into the four scorecard perspectives revealing cause-and-effect relationships

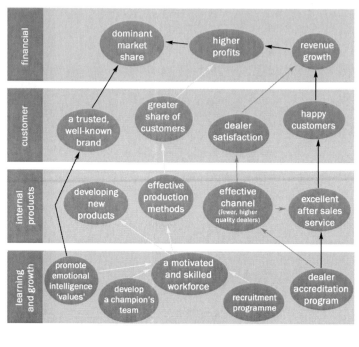

key: culture change
          effective sales channels
          customer experience

Each objective has an *objective code* (see L1, L2, etc.) that is used as an identifier when the objective is held as a record in a database. Arrows are used to represent the cause-and-effect links between objectives. Arrows will normally be colour-coded to identify management or stakeholder themes that might suggest portfolio responsibilities of the top executive management team.

To read a strategy map, begin with an objective found in the 'Learning and Growth' perspective (e.g. L1 – 'Promote emotional intelligence values') starting with the words, "If we...then", as exampled overleaf.

"If we install emotional intelligence values in our management behaviour, then we will create a motivated and skilled workforce which will enable our teams to innovate more effective production methods."

A balanced scorecard presents perspectives on the vertical axis and objectives (and their metrics) on the horizontal axis.

| | statement of what strategy must achieve and what is critical to its success | how success in achieving the strategy will be measured and tracked | the level of performance or rate of improvement needed | key action programs required to achieve objectives |
	objective	measure	actual/target	initiative
financial				
customer				
internal	*example:* cross sell our products	*example:* % revenue from new products	*example:* 1995 25% 1996 45%	*example:* train workforce on new product offerings
learning & growth				

Measuring performance

Having communicated your strategy, sustaining it is the next big hurdle – and for that you need measurement. Many of the measures will be new and will not be obtainable from existing information. Whilst you can manage performance using a paper and pen, scorecarding systems are made more sustainable by using a spreadsheet or – even better – a performance management software application that can be automatically fed data from existing information systems. The data that sits behind a scorecard can represent gigabytes of information that no one in their right mind would want to enter more than once. Collecting performance data can become a burden to workforce that, if not properly managed, can outweigh the benefits of measuring performance altogether.

Lead and lag performance measures

If you can't measure it, you can't manage it. Therefore each objective defined in a strategy should be measured. Unfortunately business people will adopt different terms to describe performance measures because there is no standard vocabulary for performance measurement. I prefer to use the term *lead indicator* to describe measures of progress, and *key performance indicator (KPI)* or *lag indicator* for measuring performance after the fact (also called lag measures). Performance measurement is vital to provide managers with the ability to monitor their level of success (updating progress of the steering wheel I describe in the Leadership chapter) without creating a major overhead on the organization to re-key information that should be captured only once through the day-to-day activities of knowledge workers.

How to align your enterprise

Much of the time invested in developing a scorecard is committed in workshops where the programme manager is educating the participants in the process. A balance has to be struck between making sure everyone knows *why* they are doing what they are doing and managing workshop time efficiently. In some cases I have heard of scorecard processes taking more than 6 months to complete. Hardly an efficient way of developing a strategy! For this reason, I created a 'rapid scorecarding' approach. Prior to workshops, participants receive primers that describe what they are going to be asked to do and why. With opportunity to prepare, participants can give thought to the subjects to be discussed before the work sessions. This way, no time is lost during the workshops to the process of educating participants. A scorecard strategy map should take no more than 6 weeks to complete by adopting a rapid scorecarding method.

The process of authoring a scorecard starts with financial objectives and walks through each of the four perspectives in order. Each perspective is represented by a single question. Questions are introduced one at a time to the working group charged with formulating the strategy. Delegates are invited to answer questions using a separate 'Post-it' note for each answer. Answers can be a single word or even a paragraph. Delegates are encouraged to offer up to 6 responses. The questions are:

Q1. (Financial perspective) – What do shareholders want?

This qualifies the financial outcomes that matter to shareholders (for public sector organizations the focus is on what voters will vote for.)

Q2. (Customer perspective) – What matters most to customers?

This question produces an 'outside-looking-in' perspective of what matters most to customers.

Q3. (Internal Process perspective) – What internal processes does the organization need to do well?

This question identifies the internal processes that the organization needs to do well to deliver its customer value. Delegates should be encouraged to think beyond the top-line banners of 'Communicate', 'Listen' and 'Share knowledge' to think about more the granular processes that exist within their departments with the aim of identifying process weaknesses and 'disconnects'.

Q4. (Learning and Growth perspective) – What does the organization need to do differently to achieve success?

This question exposes what the organization needs to do differently. This question is fortunately left until last to afford delegates two hours of thinking time before they need to summarize their views on what should be done differently.

Interpretation

Once delegates have been given sufficient time to answer each question, the workshop coordinator invites delegates to stick their 'Post-it' notes horizontally across a whiteboard. Comments are grouped vertically below an objective statement that describes the *antidote* – e.g. 'Better reception area' and 'Better toilets' might be themed under an objective of 'Improving facilities' that resolves these issues. This process continues until all of the issues are summarized into a consolidated series of objective statements for that perspective. The workshop coordinator proceeds through each question in this manner until all four questions have been completed and their answers catalogued and translated into objectives.

Outcomes

Feedback from staff and stakeholders is themed into what I call focus areas. These serve to group and concisely summarize a collection of comments. Focus areas *should* align to existing objectives if the management team is in sync with what matters most to customers and stakeholders. If there are new focus areas emerging then this would suggest a more radical change to strategic plans should be considered.

At the very least, inclusion programmes produce outputs that help to clarify what is meant by *the words* of objectives. The process of aggregating the opinions of staff and stakeholders and aligning this feedback to known objectives adds further accuracy and richness to objectives and actions. It means that when strategy is communicated, there will already be people out there who want it to succeed because they all can see their own ideas being put into practice!

General comments on creating measures

Just a few practical points about creating measures that Nick and I have learnt along the way:

- Take extreme care when choosing the wording of measures. It is important to make sure that the measure will be correctly understood if presented out of its strategic context.

- High numbers of measures are a sign of strategic focus being sacrificed for internal organizational reasons, i.e. legitimizing the existence of a particular unit, process or project by making the strategy fit the organization.

- Don't underestimate the power of inappropriate or poorly-defined measures to destroy your strategy.

- If THE SAME measure can be used for more than one objective, it is highly likely that objectives are lacking clarity (i.e. they are not mutually exclusive).

Checks and balances

Building *checks and balances* into a scorecarding process is critical to ensure that the correct conclusions are drawn from *inputs*. The scorecard process already has some *checks and balances* built in.

- Indicators determine whether defined objectives are valid.
- When aligning activities to objectives, if the SAME activity achieves more than one objective then the objectives are poorly defined. In the words of McKinsey, objectives should be mutually exclusive and collectively exhaustive. All criterion of a strategy should be addressed with the smallest number of *mutually exclusive* objectives.

Involving stakeholders in strategy formation is NOT optional

Having established the balance sheet view of what matters to the senior management team, assumptions of what stakeholders view to be important should be put to the test. Most scorecarding exercises to define strategy in large corporations are inherently flawed by a failure to test what really does matter to customers.

In the words of management guru Peter Drucker, "To satisfy the customer is the mission and purpose of every business".

Knowing *what matters* to customers is important to the usefulness of a scorecard. Assuming the strategy map works, an organization that delivers customer value will also achieve what shareholders want. It follows that internal processes should improve the organization's ability to deliver customer value.

Management teams can take for granted that their own understanding of what customers want is correct. Experience has shown this is rarely the case. Managers rarely have the time to listen to what customers expect or demand. Testing assumptions on what customers and other stakeholder groups (like staff) value most can deliver surprising results. Stakeholders who participate in formulating a strategy tend to adopt it as their own idea, so are therefore more inclined to support it!

Inclusion workshops are a good way of identifying 'well-poisoners' (i.e. people that have positive energy but negative attitude). Staff buy-in can be a huge hurdle and is best overcome at this strategy-formation stage.

Common failure points

My experience of implementing scorecards raises a few challenges:

- Sponsorship – There is always a need for leaders to lead. The management team has to be committed to the application of a strategy articulated by a balanced scorecard of objectives and this generally doesn't happen.

- A scorecard is a *point-in-time* balance sheet showing where the organization is now. It is not a definitive plan that never changes. The risk is that an organization builds a well-articulated strategic model that might look perfect on paper but does not reflect the 'coal-face' reality of the people charged with delivering it.

- Managers are not accustomed to developing lead indicators. These measures provide managers with early signals of progress towards their strategic goals as opposed to lag measures that can only report on what has happened when it is normally too late to do anything about it. A focus on the results of the past is no indicator of future events. Producing useful lead indicators is not easy and can be culturally challenging to managers.

- There is a risk that a prescriptive rather than descriptive management framework is created. This can produce an inward-looking management culture – where managers spend too much time looking inwards at the company's own micro management system rather than placing an emphasis on looking outwards to see changes in markets and customer behaviours.

- Management teams often fail to give attention to culture change issues, the influence of management style and the inclusion of staff in the strategy formation process. Failure to engage operational departments, line managers and workforce is the main reason why strategy does not get turned into actions. It takes time and money to ensure that stakeholders feel that they have been included in the thinking that sits behind the strategy but it is money well spent.

Scorecarding is more of an art than a science. Less than 1 in 4 scorecard projects get translated into *actionable* plans. That said, it represents the most effective means so far developed to communicate strategy on a single page – in a consistent way – that places *'what matters to stakeholders and how do we deliver it'* at the centre of the strategic planning universe.

Mixing priorities with objectives

Any organization, whatever the size, should have no more than 20 objectives. As managers attempt to distil those outcomes most important to their business success, getting to a list of 20 takes no time at all. Even though they might clearly be important, not all objectives are priorities.

Of the 12 to 20 objectives that result from a scorecarding process, something like 3 or 4 will reveal themselves to be the most influencing priorities.

Setting priorities places an emphasis on those activities where investment and management time are most needed. To me the term priority means 'do this first'. Not every objective can therefore possibly be a priority. Achievement of priorities should result in a step change in the success of the organization. How do you determine which objectives are priorities? It might be that an organization identifies 'happy customers' as an objective and sets a high customer satisfaction rating as a critical success factor. If customer satisfaction is deemed critical to the success of the organization, wouldn't you expect to see this objective on the scorecard every year?

Achieving customer satisfaction targets for one year is not going to change the world. However, if you're a retailer, getting produce on the shelves *fresh* can make a major impact on a year's performance. Priorities will normally align to the way an organization produces its customer value. A service-oriented business might focus priorities on processes that increase its share of any single customer's business, whilst a water utility might prioritize its ability to maintain and exploit its physical assets.

Bringing all of pieces together

Nick and I have developed to strategy deployment method that uses the same approach as that for baking an upside-down cake, i.e. starting with the layer that will end up on the top of the cake. After you've produced all the layers and cooked the cake, you turn the baking dish upside down to serve it. To achieve the vision that you want for your organization means leaders must think through strategic planning starting at the top layer of the organization and working down to the bottom.

The upside-down cake approach to turning strategy into action

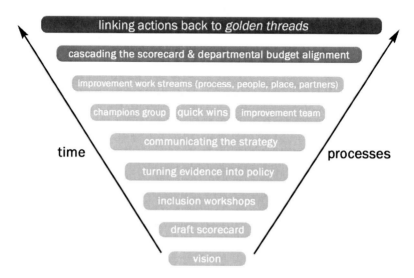

Whilst 'thinking through' the strategy starts at the top, delivery starts in the BOTTOM layers with individuals being set actions that will ultimately contribute to objectives being achieved. For this to work, departmental activities have to fall into alignment with strategic outcomes of the organization. Then unsurprisingly, the outcome of the strategy becomes the vision you intended.

Here's how it works:

'Vision' – The Management Team will establish the vision of the enterprise (i.e. what direction should the enterprise be heading in?).

'Draft Scorecard' – A programme of scorecard workshops is conducted to obtain a consensus view from the Executive Team or Management Board as to what the strategy should look like.

'Inclusion Workshops' – A programme of workshops is conducted to involve stakeholders in strategy formation.

'Turning Insight into Policy' – Outcomes of the inclusion programme are interpreted and strategic plans are shaped to balance the needs of the organization with *what matters most* to the different stakeholder groups. The result is a strategy that everyone can buy into including agreement on business model(s), defined objectives and priorities.

'Communicating the Strategy' – The Executive Team establishes an internal communications agenda.

'Champions Group' – A Champions Group is established by selecting individuals during the inclusion programme that show themselves to be *high energy* people, (some of these people may currently show negative attitudes towards the direction of the enterprise). These people must be 'turned around' to become the ambassadors of change.

'Quick Wins' – This inclusive approach to change is a sure-fire way of finding quick-win opportunities for improvement. A quick win is a highly visible improvement that can be implemented quickly – normally at low cost. At the start of an improvement journey, showing the workforce that you've been listening to them by acting on suggestions is not a bad idea!

'Improvement Team' – Establish a work team that will be responsible for improvement on an ongoing basis.

'Improvement Work Streams' – The Improvement Team will work with specialist third party practitioners to implement *people, process, place* and *partnership* work streams.

'Cascading the scorecard and aligning departmental budget plans' – In this phase, make sure all the action commitments outlined in departmental budget plans are aligned to the strategic plan.

'Linking actions back to golden threads' – The final step is to link departmental actions back to agreed golden thread sustainability themes. Performance reporting protocols are established so that senior portfolio managers can see, at any point in time, the progress of actions that will lead to the desired golden thread outcomes of the enterprise.

Do not try to miss layers out!

Executives often want to miss out some layers of the cake in order to jump to quick-fix initiatives that focus directly on the outcomes they want to achieve, perhaps seeking to reduce operating costs by automating or rationalizing operations, or magically turning ineffective managers into heroic leaders. The layer that executives most want to ignore is the inclusion exercise that tells them what matters most to their workforce and stakeholders. This is because the process costs money and – like all discovery processes – you can only measure the benefits once the exercise has been completed. Unfortunately, missing out steps in organizational improvement is like baking an upside-down cake without the sponge layer. The result of your efforts might produce the prettiest of cakes in the dish but it will not hold together when you turn it upside down!

(3) Management has developed 'digital DNA'

The success of many 21st century organizations will depend on their ability to (1) understand their role and capability and then (2) match this appreciation of self with new risks and opportunities that emerge from the external environment. A sound knowledge of 'self' comes from excellent management information that communicates the performance of well thought-out (efficient and effective) internal processes. Today, all the capabilities and behaviours of an enterprise can be captured in a database that distils *what it is, what it can do, what it does today and how it does it.* I call this the 'digital DNA' of the enterprise, i.e. a genetic data structure of the enterprise.

> **Management will go from art to science. Bigger, more complex companies demand new tools to run and manage them.**
>
> **Ian Davis/Elizabeth Stephenson, McKinsey & Co.**

The human brain has the capacity to memorize something on the order of 10 billion bits of information during the average human lifetime. My own brain appears reluctant to take up this challenge and is only able to cope with a little knowledge at any one time. I visualize my brain clearing out the *junk knowledge* that I haven't used for ages to free up shelves for the *new knowledge* that I'm desperately trying to squeeze in. And sometimes it hurts! If business leaders are anything like me, then they don't want to be expending valuable brain power on issues that can be made simple to understand and therefore act on. Isn't that what computers are for?

Ask most leaders what information matters most to them and they will probably tell you they need around 5 items of information and that the list changes all the time. This 'wish-list' normally mirrors the 5 events that are the key reasons why customers, shareholders or (in the case of government) ministers or council members will make a phone call at a silly time of the day demanding answers! The more leaders understand about what makes their enterprise tick, and the quicker they can absorb information from the 'cockpit' controls to make sure the engine is still working as it should, the better able they are to focus their time on those aspects of the leadership role that make a real difference such as supporting staff, developing useful partnerships, scanning the outside world of markets and customer value, and seeking new ways to fit profitable markets.

With more time to spend on creative thinking processes, leaders increase their chances of finding 'good fit' mergers and acquisitions, market opportunities and new ways of achieving success. So imagine that you could access on a single screen the complete make-up of your enterprise, its people, its purpose, its structure, its assets, its knowledge, its relationships, its brand reach, its capabilities and resources, etc. This is what I call the 'digital DNA' of an enterprise (i.e. the identity of the enterprise translated into a digital data set). This chapter dedicates some of its pages to explaining how relatively straightforward it is to turn this 'good idea' into a reality. In a market where the ability to fit the most profitable segments makes all the difference between outrageous profits and merely ordinary performance, knowledge of your digital DNA is essential.

Unless leaders fully understand the purpose, capabilities, customer value, golden threads (etc.) of their enterprise they are likely to:

- overreach their brand to a point that customers don't understand 'who they are anymore'.
- assume skills/ capabilities exist in the enterprise that aren't there.
- make poor acquisition and merger decisions.

Demands to improve activity monitoring are driven by:

1. The need to make effective policy and strategic decisions:
   a) (Public Sector) To evidence that policy-making decisions are addressing stakeholder needs with factual proof of the circumstances leading to a policy decision.
   b) (Private sector) To create more desirable products and services by adopting user-centred design programmes based on evidence derived from customer interviews.

2. (Public and Private sector) To align the actions of the organization to achieve the outcomes that matter most to stakeholders.

3. (Public and Private sector) The need for organizations to think and act corporately due to:
   a) The PACE of change in technology and market structures.
   b) The growth in the number of cross-organizational projects driven by compliance, governance, health and safety, diversity, ecology and the environment etc.

4. A change in the relationship with stakeholders and the importance of excellent Customer Service.

5. Pressures on organizations to develop a social conscience – to contribute towards society, support local communities, reduce their impact on the environment etc. – are leading to more cross-organizational projects and management activities.

Why don't organizations already have the capability to understand their 'DNA'?

Data that defines the digital DNA of an enterprise has largely existed within organizations for years. The problem for most managers has been trying to get hold of the information they need, when they need it, in a format they can use! Only now are affordable and useful software products beginning to emerge that have the ability to provide a common set of information flow capture, analysis and sharing features that non-programmers (non-IT) people can employ to service their own information needs. This change promises to consumerize IT like never before.

An organization that *thinks and acts* as one is better able to focus its resources towards achievement of its strategy

The information needed to manage strategy and performance has many demands placed on it. The volume and complexity of management information means that gathering and organizing it requires technology. Relational databases build associations between the different stakeholders and managers, presenting views of information that matter to them.

An Action Framework is the holistic, corporate 'thinking and acting' system that unites and supports an organization faced with constantly changing internal processes and behaviours. It is an essential tool for organizations living in a business climate where strategic plans might need to change at any moment. It is normally powered by a relational database to organise the data and the relationships between the different elements. Without technology it is almost impossible to support the information processing volumes required to do this.

An Action Framework creates an enterprise that is able to manage day-to-day actions and thereby its strategy.

There is a Japanese proverb that states, 'Vision without action is a daydream. Action without vision is a nightmare.'

Actions are *things that must be done* that occur in an organization every day. They are microscopic 'making-things-happen' units of activity. It is the successive completion of actions on a day-to-day basis that ultimately determines the achievement of outcomes and the success or failure of an enterprise. I am always disappointed by the number of organizations that are prepared to let the efforts of their hard-working workforce go to waste by failing to channel their energy and enthusiasm towards actions that would make a difference to the objectives of the organization.

Without measurement you can't manage, and without information you can't measure. Worse still, if you don't know why you're doing what you're meant to be measuring, people find themselves working hard but achieving little.

Actions are hierarchical. The *actions* of an executive are the *objectives* of his subordinates. The *actions* of an office clerk are the tasks of a senior manager. So an Action Framework honours the hierarchical structure of the organization so that all actions can be registered within the system whilst at the same time an appropriate level of *seniority* is given to the top line of activities. Honouring organizational design means that any manager or portfolio holder can quickly obtain information relevant to their role.

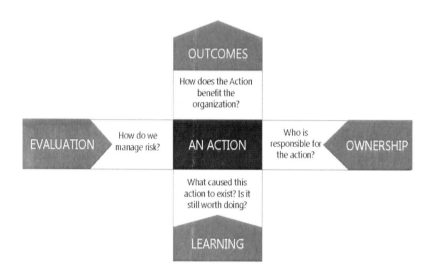

Illustration of the 'Action Framework' data model

An Action Framework places <u>actions</u> at the heart of the business planning framework by managing and measuring four key perspectives.

These are:

OUTCOME – Actions must achieve an outcome that benefits the organization. Any action that does not directly have a relationship to an organizational outcome is likely to be a waste of resources.

OWNERSHIP – Someone must be accountable for the achievement of outcomes to which actions contribute. This individual may not be the same person tasked with performing it. Several contributors may be required to fulfil the outcomes that an action is meant to deliver. Therefore, for any action, both ownership of the outcome and ownership of performing the action should be considered.

LEARNING – Organizations today can ill afford to stand still. Leaders at all levels must question why they are doing what they are doing. This requires a clear appreciation of what led to actions being formalized. Furthermore, new information that might influence how an action is performed (or whether it should be performed at all) should be easily navigated to the portfolio holder responsible for the achievement of the outcome that any action is meant to deliver.

EVALUATION – Performing any action expends resources. For any action there is an opportunity cost that should be evaluated so the organization can govern its behaviours appropriately.

Actions need to be effectively managed to ensure resources consumed within day to day operations are appropriately aligned to outcomes, are measured and also challenged according to good practices established within the behaviour of the enterprise. An Action Framework means this can be achieved without demanding a significant change in the way that people work, or how executive teams operate.

OUTCOME THEME METRICS

1. Purpose – No action should exist without a purpose. Actions should contribute to the sustainability of the organization – what I call sustainability *golden threads* – and towards measurable objectives that service the living demands of the organization.

2. Measure – Actions that are not measured can not be managed. All actions should at the very least have a lag indicator that informs the organization on how well it is performing. Ideally, actions should also have a lead indicator that suggests how well the action is being discharged before an 'outcome' becomes visible.

OWNERSHIP THEME METRICS

3. Owners responsible for discharging an action must be identified. Actions must be allocated to an action owner, the person responsible for performing the action. They must also fall under the portfolio responsibility of an executive. One individual might hold both responsibilities.

4. Organization – Organizations are not just one entity, they are made up of teams working within operational departments that might form into

companies as part of a group. To maintain a sustainable business activity and performance management system it is vital that leaders understand WHERE actions are occurring within their organization. This becomes even more critical as work teams operate across organizations and become ever more *virtual*. An Action Framework maintains a record of the associations between actions and the organizational tiers where they occur.

LEARNING THEME METRICS

5. Focus Areas – There should always some basis of evidence as to why an action has been arrived at. The basis of evidence is normally held within the prompts, suggestions or recommendations that instigated it. Normally there are events that led up to the formation of an action and this data can be presented in focus area themes to aid learning. Grouping actions, and any insight that leads to the formation of actions, into *focus areas* enables pertinent market information to reach those people responsible for discharging related actions in the enterprise. This approach to action analysis means that a post-mortem can be performed on actions 'after the event' to understand how well the organization is working (i.e. to ask the question, "Why did we instigate that action in the first place?").

6. Insight – Insight data in the form of suggestions and prompts should be themed under focus areas and associated to related action occurring within the organization to support learning processes.

EVALUATION THEME METRICS

7. Opportunity – When actions are instigated, their potential value should be viewed within a context of how much cost and resources are required to fulfil them. This activity is normally manifested in some form of budgeting process. All actions should be associated to their opportunity and cost profile.

8. Challenge – All Actions must be resourced (people, finance, etc.) and so there is an opportunity cost associated with performing actions that should be evaluate prior to an action be instigated. Once instigated, Actions should continue to be assessed and challenged. All actions should be associated with challenges that might be simple assessments or sophisticated risk register style assessments.

How to get aligned and stay aligned

Organizational alignment is a subject that sounds academic and not terribly important if you want to be a 'seat-of-the-pants' type of leader that has a passion for business and thrives on winning deals. That's probably why it is one of the most misunderstood and misrepresented topics in business management. You would be wrong to think that it doesn't matter very much. I suspect businesses lose a great deal of their best talent this way, through inappropriate incentive schemes or creating circumstances where good workers are expending all of their energy doing the wrong things. From my experience of business, a good way – probably the only way – to set and maintain the correct alignment of an enterprise is to validate its structure and actions through an Action Framework. An Action Framework highlights – at any point in time – where day-to-day effort has fallen out of alignment with strategic outcomes. It means that managers can quickly take action to prevent people from working 'hard, but not smart'.

Checklist for **Alignment**

	Qualification	Score
☹️ **The misaligned enterprise**	Actions are not measured. Workers do not know how their activities contribute to strategic goals.	☐ ☐
☺️ **A 'scorecard' performance framework**	The management team has agreed: A small number of objectives (less than 20 if possible). A smaller number of priorities. A scorecard that measures the performance of the enterprise against a balanced set of priority outcomes. Key performance indicators and lead indicators to help the organization to plot its progress against its plan. In addition: Individuals understand how their activities contribute to the outcomes of the enterprise.	 ☐ ☐ ☐ ☐ ☐
☺️ **Digital enterprise DNA / Action Framework**	The enterprise has the capability to rapidly understand its 'DNA'. The enterprise has the ability to align day-to-day actions with outcomes, budgets, resources, corporate challenges, etc.	☐ ☐

9

(O) Operating Approach

The basics of the business must be as efficient as human beings can make them: they always deteriorate over time unless somebody deliberately tightens them up. But nothing is sacred. Organizations must be prepared to kill any aspect of their structure or operating approach that gets in the way of its ultimate ambition.

Sir John Harvey-Jones

(1) Organizations adopt inflexible structures and poorly-defined management processes

During my own career I have experienced more organizations with inflexible, debilitating structures than any other form. As departments grow, they create cultures and attitudes that prevent innovation, creativity, knowledge-sharing, and ultimately agilization.

Many strategies fail because of departments that work well, but not together. Chinese walls build between the silos and hinder cooperation, information sharing and corporate thinking. Sometimes organizations dilute management responsibility to the point that decisions can not be made at all. Having too many managers can mean that no single manager has authority to make decisions and any decision that needs to be made demands a whole team of managers to get involved. I'm sure this all sounds petty and bizarre but it's just the sort of decision making quagmire that organizations get entangled with.

Operating silos are easy to form but very difficult to kill off.

The way an organization builds silos goes like this:

- An organization produces something someone is prepared to pay for.
- As the result of success, it grows.
- More people and more internal processes demand more structure and formality in management practices.
- Operational silos evolve around core disciplines – sales, marketing, finance etc.
- To reward managers for keeping *the machine* well oiled, remuneration is based on the performance of the operational silo they are responsible for. Consequently, attention moves away from the performance of the *organization* (which unless it fails completely is unlikely to affect them) towards the performance of the *silo*.
- As corporate management teams wrestle with a growing number of business challenges – diversity, environmental policy, IT deployments, customer service strategies – they adopt an ever-broadening assembly of cross-departmental work teams. Key workers inherit two or three bosses, complicating job prioritization and accountability.

Over time, organizations inadvertently *encourage* departments to be self-sufficient by installing incentives that promote achievement of department outcomes over organizational goals. They let departments form their own management structures, information technology systems and operating procedures.

Dr Eli Goldratt's Theory of Constraints is well known to organizational consultants. It states that the core constraint of virtually every organization is that organizations are structured, measured and managed in parts, rather than as a whole. This results in lower-than-expected performance with constraints constantly shifting from one place to another and chronic conflicts between people representing different parts of the organization.

An inward-looking management focus, blended with an ever more complicated organizational structure, creates an inherent inability in an enterprise to respond to market forces with the potential of seriously denting the profitability of the organization. This is the structural legacy of the mechanization latent instruction set.

Nick and I have met with so many excruciating examples of where these self-made 'Chinese walls' prevent a business from being as productive as it knows it can be, or delivering customer value in the way it thinks it should.

Siloism is today so well acknowledged and understood that it doesn't really need evidencing. Almost every business person can describe a great example of an organization with silos not working well together. Most managers greet the subject with a sigh. That frustrates me even more because this is a serious subject that managers have to DEAL with and not just adopt a stance of, 'Well there's nothing you can do about it, is there?'

Getting an efficient and effective organizational structure – one that has people working in teams, sharing ideas and retaining an intimacy with customers whilst sharing resources, skills and costs to minimize operational overheads – just isn't easy. Consider the well-documented case example of ABB, a truly massive organization formed as the result of a merger in 1988 between the Swedish-based engineering group Asea AB and Brown Boveri Limited, headquartered in Switzerland. Both companies were players in the European electrical equipment market. Their innovative CEO Percy Barnevik saw an opportunity to develop an organizational structure.

He constructed small work teams that could take into account local conditions in the countries in which the company had its operations to maintain a close intimacy with customers and expedite localized decision-making processes, supported by thin layers of support service teams for shared disciplines such as IT, finance, marketing and HR that each decentralized unit could exploit to minimize operating costs and leverage the global footprint of the organization. This matrix model concentrated on maintaining small teams that could work closely together. But eventually the high costs and complexities of this organizational structure became too onerous. A major problem was the frequent iterative changes needed to sustain growth whilst keeping work teams small. Doesn't this sound like an agilized organization?

Was it a bad decision to attempt to keep the organization close to its local markets and customers? I believe time will show that Percy Barnevik and ABB were absolutely on the right track, but as is common with innovation, it was good thinking that emerged at the wrong time in the wrong climate, and ABB lacked the technology, tools and systems that are now available to corporations today.

(2) The organization thinks and acts as one

To have everyone working together to achieve a common goal in the most efficient and effective way is no longer a nice idea, it is a business necessity.

Picture a management training course. Three or more people are asked to balance a 6-foot wooden pole parallel with the floor, each using just the tip of one finger, starting 5-foot above the ground. The challenge is to work together to help the pole to descend whilst remaining parallel to the floor. The only rules are that the pole should remain parallel and that no one is allowed to stop touching the pole with their finger. What happens? Everyone might be working hard to contribute to the endeavour but as soon as participants feel the pressure of the pole lightening on the tip of their finger, their natural reaction is to raise their finger to make sure they don't lose contact. Instead of going down the pole goes up.

This exercise provides an excellent example of the leadership challenge faced by many executive teams the world over. Leaders require their people to work together to achieve the outcomes of their enterprise but instead they find departments are working *interdependently* but not *together*. It is a subtle but significant difference. In order to thrive within a constantly changing social and economic environment, the enterprise must always know who and what it is. It must be able to apply learning, sense new opportunities and threats and have the ability to rapidly realign resources towards new opportunities and challenges as they emerge. The way to achieve this is by doing the following:

1. Qualify the intentions of the enterprise – what it is trying to achieve – and let everyone know!

2. Encourage joined-up, organization-wide, management behaviour and a performance management framework to manage sustainable growth on a day-to-day basis.

3. Create a forensic understanding of how the enterprise thinks and acts that encourages the creativity and participation of individuals.

4. Make sure individuals know how they contribute and give them space to work together and the time to make mistakes and learn.

5. Measure performance and link the contributions of individuals to strategic outcomes.

(3) Management looks ahead, thinks ahead, plans ahead

It's not easy driving a car spending all your time looking in the rear-view mirror, but management teams can fall into the trap of running their businesses in this way. Management must see beyond the current crop of objectives and seek to envision what the organization needs to look like and how it needs to operate in order to meet the next market opportunity. Organizations must install new mechanisms to anticipate emerging customer value areas. Early signposting is therefore business-critical for agile organizations – an issue that I spend more time on in Chapter 12.

(4) A loosely-coupled structure

Leaders must adopt supple organizational structures in order to compete. Some managers I have worked for have wanted to see every role with a detailed job description and every department a hierarchical structure. Others adopt a more flexible approach where broad disciplines are recognized and team working is encouraged to *fill holes* in the formal contracts and documented job descriptions. As an enthusiastic musician myself (but not a particularly good one) I naturally liken organizational structures to the way musicians are organized within the different genres of music. Perhaps the two greatest extremes are orchestras and jazz bands.

When at school, I played first trumpet in our regional orchestra. When you perform as part of an orchestra, everyone has a fully scoped and specific role. There is a hierarchy. If you are second trumpeter your role is not as influential as the first trumpeter! You take your steer from the conductor and always watch the baton irrespective of the challenges of following the sheet music and playing your instrument. The result can be a very organised and pleasant sound. But orchestras operate in a way that makes no provision for variation to the structure of the music or of contributions made by individuals. Apart from soloists the other contributors are required to play the notes in front of them and nothing more. No variation is allowed. None whatsoever. When I was a child, the conductor of the Orchestra I played in would even stop occasionally just to check you were paying attention!

In a jazz band nobody is in any doubt about who plays what instrument or the tune being played at any point in time. However each performance is different. The musical contributions embrace the influence of other players, and the performance varies according to the feedback that comes from the audience. It is a more intimate performance that can be more challenging but more fulfilling for the performers. If you were to describe each model, you could easily describe a group of individual musicians working together to produce a collective sound. From the outside in perhaps, there is not a great difference, but the way that the musicians produce the outcome, how they work together, where they get their direction from, the level of change in the performance that results are all very different.

Like a jazz band, the agilized enterprise:

- has a less prescriptive and more reactive organizational structure where responsibilities are not defined through function alone, but also through a shared appreciation of individual skills, contributions and knowledge.

- devolves decision making to peers

- exploits the skills and innovation of individuals, finding the best knowledge, innovation and skill wherever it might be. This adaptable structure brings sustainability through the professionalism and ingenuity of the individual contributors who are encouraged *to be* individuals, and to excel at what they do best by leaders that can encourage *followership*.

- rewards individuals by ensuring a high quality of life – and lots of freedom to assert their individualism.

- has a state of mind that believes in the benefits of change, learning and improvement, where the enterprise embraces *the power of new* as a constant. Improvement is incorporated into operations at an *atomic level*.

The Alter-Preneurs

Alter-preneurs is the name given to a new community of people who go into business for lifestyle reasons, as an alternative to the regular corporate job. They achieve economic independence by leveraging their knowledge and skills. A survey by *More Than Business*, a UK-based business insurance firm, found that 70 per cent of these new business owners were not financially or career-motivated. Fifty-nine per cent of those surveyed said they started a business to 'gain more control over their lives' and 54 per cent said they did it in order to 'be happier'. Growth in numbers of Alter-preneurs has been significant over the past few years as utility, financial services and IT companies have shed jobs and these people, having experienced a life-change, have elected to become independent contractors with the aim of achieving greater flexibility of work-life balance rather than returning to the corporate machine.

This community is significant because it provides the raw material for a change in organizational structures as businesses seek to harness talent beyond their firewalls. To exploit the potential of this *knowledge and skills rich* community of workers a more adaptive workforce model is required. Ironically, *even more* formality of processes and behaviours is needed to manage contributions from individuals that are not full-time employees and not working from the same building. Whatever the employment contract structure, individuals should adhere to corporate standards of behaviour, embrace business values and be measured in terms of their knowledge, creativity, contributions to processes and customer value.

To create a supple organizational structure requires this greater level of formality, keeping everyone pushing forward together with building blocks that I covered earlier – a great vision, a committed, engaging and enthusiastic leader, a strategy that everybody believes in.

There are three areas to master, the formalization of:

1. How positive norms of behaviour are maintained in a way that delivers customer value and to ensure that workforce induction and appraisal measure behaviour.

2. How the 3R's of human resources – roles, responsibilities and remuneration – are managed to ensure that the efforts of the workforce are rewarded and aligned to strategic outcomes whilst under-performance can also be suitably addressed.

3. How information flows through the social networks of the organization in such as way that it becomes possible to understand the contributions made by individuals.

Sitting around the boardroom table in 2018

You can almost track the years by the rise of boardroom power roles:

1950/60s   Advertising and Marketing Director

1970s   Production and Finance Director

1980s   Data Processing Director

1990s   MIS and Human Resources Director

2000s   Customer Service and Finance Director

Boardroom roles today closely resemble the departmental structures they govern, where the highest officer for each silo achieves boardroom status. The traditional way of aligning senior officers to operating silos does little to focus minds towards strategic outcomes. It creates too many chiefs who adopt an inward-looking focus towards the performance of their own silo. This results in only a small number of executives (commonly human resources, financial, IT and chief executive roles) focusing their energy on cross-cutting and outward-looking initiatives.

Organizations that align management responsibilities with strategic outcomes are likely to have fewer executives with broader portfolio responsibilities. Role titles more accurately reflect the outcomes that the organization identifies as being key to its success, moving away from alignment with departmental structures. Roles that exist in leading organizations today will blend with new definitions of role responsibilities to form a very different boardroom. Senior executives will have less direct involvement in (inward-looking) day-to-day matters and will focus more towards the management of the golden thread sustainable growth themes.

Which senior executive roles will stay?

(Leadership) Chief Executive Officer – This role is unlikely to disappear! The Chief Executive will retain the responsibility for steering the organization and scoping what he or she believes the organization is 'good at'. The Chief Executive shares with the Chief Operating Officer the role of determining the most appropriate growth strategy – which could be through organic growth, merger or acquisition. Finding ways to empower the workforce to achieve the outcomes of the organization remains the principle role of the Chief Executive.

(Delivery) The Chief Operations/Financial Officer will continue to oversee the financial health and performance of the organization with increased attention given to benchmarking core processes against competitive rivals and leaders in other industries. The attention given to corporate governance and stakeholder accountability will be sustained into the mid-2000s but (for public sector organizations) will include a renewed attention to evidence-based policy-making as the paternalistic 'government knows best' attitudes of the 20th century lose their grip. Risk management will become a common component in financial management housekeeping procedures.

What are the new senior executive roles?

(Customer) The Customer Advocacy Director is a new role that emphasizes the strategic importance attached to understanding what matters to customers and stakeholders. The Customer Advocacy Director is responsible for insight and dialogue management processes and is measured on the usefulness of these operational areas. A key aspect of the role is to analyze and interpret signals to 'scan the horizon' to identify business opportunities in advance of competitive peers. The Customer Advocacy Director plays a key role in encouraging a culture of curiosity and ensuring the organization is always listening.

(People) The Performance Director combines a series of traditional role disciplines such as strategic and operational human resources with new responsibilities such as the management of the service profit value chain, embedding diversity policy and programmes to ensure the organization is meeting its social responsibilities.

(Place) The Facilities Director is responsible for providing a workplace that fully supports and enables the productivity of employees. The workplace includes information systems, physical workspace and will its scope will often be extended to encompass asset performance.

(Improvement) The emergence of formalized organization departments that have a full-time responsibility to improve the way the organization thinks and acts will result in senior board level roles accountable for measurable success in this area.

(Partnerships) Organizations are collaborating with many more suppliers and channel resellers. These relationships will require the executive team to make investment decisions that extend beyond the traditional scope of role for sales and marketing professionals. It is likely that the level of risk and management capacity overheads attached to partnerships will result in executive roles being formed to manage commercial relationships.

Which senior executive roles are likely to *disappear*?

The IT Director role is being subsumed into the business transformation role as information systems become ubiquitous in the world of business. In this new environment, the traditional employees of the IT Director – business analysts and programmers – are all going their separate ways. Adoption of 'no code' software is removing the need for full-time in-house programming skills. Those business analysts who can demonstrate a willingness to embrace other discipline areas and skills are likely to find themselves in a more senior but broader role as Process Value and Improvement Managers ('Process Managers' for short). The Human Resources Director is merging into a more strategic Business Transformation Director role that places a greater priority on the holistic service-profit chain. This role is also absorbing the Change Management role that organizations have adopted as a short term 'fix the organization' approach. There is likely to be far more governance over the sales and marketing functions. This will result in Sales and Marketing becoming roles that report to the CEO, CFO or COO.

The rise in non-executive advisory roles

Boardroom expertise is likely to be supplemented by advisors and experts in sustainability, employment law, governance and compliance, legal, quality assurance and specialist business matter areas relating to vertical market or core competency.

(5) Formalized for flexibility

According to a survey conducted by the Economic Information Unit (EIU), when asked, 1 in 4 senior executives in 2005 identified the automation of manual processes as a key strategy in improving operational efficiency. Productive professionals make big enterprises competitive, yet these employees now increasingly find their work obstructed. Creating and exchanging knowledge and intangibles through interaction with their professional peers is the heart of what they do. Yet most of them squander endless hours searching for the knowledge they need—even if it resides in their own companies—and coordinating their work with others.

McKinsey & Co. Quarterly, June 2006

Most organizations have already automated many of their core business processes. What remains are those information flows that are by necessity more *fluid* and require a greater degree of versatility and constant enhancement. We've coined the term *liquid information processes* (LIPs) to describe these more fluid *human-centric* information processes.

There is much to be said about formalizing the way information flows within the enterprise. The success of 20th century industrialists was often the result of the rationalization and automation of production processes. This attention to the design of processes to eliminate waste, variability and inflexibility has been slow to filter through to informal networks and the fluid social networks of the office environment that represent the poorest performing productivity area of enterprise operation.

Departments that tend to have the highest population of liquid information flows are the highly administrative disciplines such as sales administration, marketing, design, human resources, finance and customer insight capture and analysis. It's bad news that these poorly-performing productivity areas are where knowledge workers exist who are now seen to be the major competitive differentiator because they are originating new ideas, finding the next big product, translating insight into market advantage and 'wordsmithing' the perfect marketing slogan.

One of the structural changes facilitating this formalization of information movement is the recognition that information flows have to be owned by an individual. These *information flow owners* (people responsible for managing information flows) must be made accountable and responsible for the movement of specific types of information within specific processes. It's not rocket science to recognise that these people probably already exist. Many of them are unsung heroes who push the limits of their job specification to *grease the cogs* that make the enterprise work (Oops, that was a mechanical, steam-powered metaphor – sorry!).

All too often informal support networks emerge to cover over the cracks in poorly-formalized information processes. If you've ever received a 'Please help me, I've no-one to turn to' email from a colleague with two or more people on the circulation list, you know the originator has no idea who owns the information flow and you can be sure that you have a problem!

The consequence of relying on informal support networks to manage information flow is that, at some point, the *do-gooders* get tired of being unrecognized for the long hours and 'above and beyond' work and simply leave, without managers truly understanding why they feel aggrieved. Without formalizing accountability and ownership, information flows *don't flow* as well as they should.

Exercise your LIPs

There are a few reasons why the software industry has been so dreadful at finding workable solutions for information worker productivity – seeking 'silver-bullet' technology fixes for people issues, trying to stretch the usefulness of office desktop software to perform a role it was never intended for, getting immersed into husbanding unstructured content rather than thinking about its value and contribution to business processes, etc. – but the main challenge has been to define what the *underlying problem* is. Technologists have known for some time that most corporate knowledge is held within informal information networks – i.e. on email servers and people's laptop hard-drives, etc. – but the challenge was thought to be 'How do we encourage information workers to invest the time to share their knowledge?' As it turns out, that wasn't the real problem. The IT sector is only now waking up to the fact that it's all about how you exercise your *LIPs*.

Liquid Information Processes (LIPs) appear to be ad-hoc because they demand variation in content and contributions from participants but they *are* in fact repetitive exercises and can therefore be automated and formalized.

LIPs are the biggest reason why office productivity has not improved over the past 20 years, because the IT sector:

1. Failed to qualify the problem and instead directed its focus towards the management of desktop documents.

2. Did not have interoperability and operating platform standardization that could enable the development of software needed to formalize information flows found within liquid information processes.

Spend half a day in any busy workplace and experience the consequences of poorly formalized information flows. You are likely to see information workers authoring spreadsheets, word processor documents and PowerPoint presentations to gather and share information often trapped within hard-to-reach back-office systems. You can also expect to see others replying to email requests for information the organization already knows but finds hard to share. You might overhear staff complaining about a lack of response from colleagues and the degradation of trust through poor collaboration. Every enterprise has its own peculiar list of informal processes that are hidden within the informal social networks of workers. In today's office environment, most tasks are performed using office desktop software. The fact that most are repetitive goes unnoticed. This is the information found on laptops, memory sticks and network servers. In formalizing these tasks, more creative time is made available to information workers. Formalizing the flow of information across human-centric processes means that communications can be captured in a secure data environment.

Examples of information flows found in organizations today

Discipline	Information flows that are not commonly database-driven
Corporate	Strategy formation Applying market research Gathering customer feedback Processing complaints Responding to corporate challenges
Marketing	Understanding what matters most to customers Product release processes Price list distribution Competition analysis Monitoring of product quality and performance
Finance	Budgeting Regional budget plans Risk register Governance and best practice Benchmarking statistics
Sales	Client correspondence Tender responses Sales opportunity analysis Customer complaints
Human Resources	Directory of people Succession strategy Training needs analysis

Ongoing multi-year tasks such as launching new products, building new businesses, or fundamentally redesigning a company's technology platform usually call for small groups of full-time, focused professionals with the freedom "to wander in the woods," discovering new, winning value propositions by trial and error and deductive tinkering. Few down-the-line managers, who must live day-to-day in an intensely competitive marketplace, have the time or resources for such a discovery process. McKinsey & Co. Quarterly, June 2006

Relational database-driven information flow software helps to formalize the movement of information across enterprise networks by:

- Creating a virtual workspace that delivers improved workforce productivity by using databases to manage data movements.
- Bridging between front- and back-office systems energises the enthusiasm of staff and stimulates their creativity.
- Empowering workers to capture and structure their data to make it accessible to – and re-usable by – a broader community of users, collaborators and stakeholders. No time is lost in re-keying data.

The common forms of information flow are illustrated here:

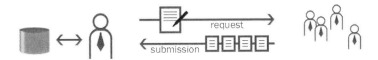

1. To gather information

To compose and present a structured information capture method to a community or team that will enable contributors to submit information in a consistent and regulated way. An information flow owner develops a formalized database-driven template form to request information from a group of contributors whilst ensuring that information is gathered in a consistent way and can be stored in a single relational database where information can be analyzed using themes that cut across all the report submission processes. This type of information flow is commonplace in reporting environments such as human resources, accounting and head office compliance roles.

Example: A Finance Director authors a departmental budget document that is distributed for each departmental head to complete. Departmental plans are submitted electronically to the Finance Director. At the point of submission, information is immediately added to a relational database which means the

Finance Director obtains a near-instant view of the corporate resource requirements and financial challenges and risks for the coming year without having to personally concatenate a variety of departmental budgets into a holistic document.

2. To share information

To publish information to a community or team in a form that is simple to navigate and digest. In the second example, an information flow owner develops formalized operating guidelines or procedures taking good practice or evidence of previous behaviour from a relational database system that has been capturing this data. The information flow in this case is educating contributors as part of the communication process, yet still provides an opportunity for structured feedback.

Example: A Quality Assurance Manager might choose to publish a monthly report mentioning areas of poor performance or non-conformity to recommended good practice behaviours based on evidence captured through automated information feeds from back-office systems.

3. To inform, share and gather information

To inform, invite participation in an information flow, and then provide the mechanism to gather information.

In the final example, an information flow owner informs a community of contributors of the requirements of a process and in the same communication requests their contribution for submission.

Example: A Marketing Director might create an information process to announce the release of a new product or service and provide go-to-market information whilst at the same time requesting that Regional Sales Directors complete an estimate of potential first year shipments for their region.

Software that can rapidly formalize information flows is important but it only plays a supporting role. For projects to succeed it still takes vision, leadership and management commitment. Transport for London is one such organization meeting its strategic objectives by formalizing information-sharing processes with industry partners.

Every day London's roads carry 11 million cars and motorbikes and 400,000 cyclists. Upwards of 7,000 buses carry 6.3 million passengers and London Underground ferries 3.5 million people around the capital. Transport for London (TfL) is the main government agency responsible for managing and delivering transport services across the capital and making sure the traffic keeps moving. There are a multitude of reasons why works undertakers need to dig up roads. Many major works are planned well in advance, while others operate on a tighter timescale and provide benefits to consumers such as the installation of new utilities and communications services. Emergency failures are estimated to be around one tenth of the total. Coordination of these road works plans has traditionally been a major challenge for traffic management and works professionals.

Until recently, the exercise of sharing road works plans between highways agencies and undertakers of road works has been a little like playing the game 'battleships.' Highway engineers from each agency would meet once every few months around a table and, from information extracted from their computer systems on spreadsheets, they would present their road works plans whilst colleagues from other agencies would listen, at the same time reviewing their own spreadsheets to see if the planning data conflicted with their own. This was a costly, people-intensive exercise and a poor use of highly skilled people. What was needed was a multi-agency approach to managing and sharing road works information.

In 2006, a pilot system was developed to formalize the capture of data from all the agencies involved and present information in a way that it could be entered and viewed via a website. Engineers from undertakers and highways authorities worked with the TfL project team to formalize and translate the complex information flow into a software system using Encanvas, a software application designed to formalize information flows. A technology deployment was designed, prototyped, user-tested and deployed within weeks.

Screen showing TfL's Information Flow Application for Streetworks

During the first six-month pilot, the longer range road works coordination system proved its worth, res significant savings to the agencies concerned that were estimated at many millions of pounds. Disruption to the road network was avoided by harmonizing planned activities. Use of geospatial maps meant that all stakeholders had a clearer view of data that traditionally had been exchanged on spreadsheets. In some cases, economies were gained through trench-sharing or pragmatic coordination of surface reinstatement activities. But clearly the biggest beneficiary has been the general public who – in the run up to the 2012 Olympic Games – can expect less congestion from planned works.

Through this system, TfL has improved its ability to work with partners and enjoys a deeper, more collaborative, trusting relationship with stakeholders because of the increased visibility of plans. TfL is able to work with its industry partners to respond quickly to emerging requirements such as the introduction of an event – e.g. Chelsea Football Club winning the Premier League or the Tour de France coming to London. Through the formalization of information flows, Transport for London is becoming ever more efficient in supporting good management of road use in London.

(6) Lower-cost business models

Agilized organizations seek to embrace business models that are inherently low-cost such as a manufacturer who traditionally sells products via a reseller channel moving to online web-based sales. Cutting out a stage in the sales channel can achieve significant economies whilst potentially improving reach. Exploring other aspects of the enterprise value chain to determine which areas are core to the business whilst others might be only supportive can result in the outsourcing of logistics, research or even manufacturing where these functions are delivering minimum customer value and competitive differentiation.

More challenging decisions arise when the economic engine itself is considered for an overhaul. It is a high-risk strategy to fundamentally change the mechanism that makes money for an enterprise. Whether it is sales of seats (airlines), the number of transactions (utilities) or the number of machines-in-field (photocopier sales companies), the introduction of a new model is a huge decision.

Factors to consider include:

- Whether the new economic engine will generate enough revenue to support the melt-down of the 'legacy engine'
- Whether the brand reach will stretch → whether customers will identify the business as a supplier for the product or service
- Whether the company's skills and resources will equip it to service the new economic engine
- Whether processes will support the new economic engine

(7) A virtualized enterprise

An agilized enterprise supports a new 'virtualized' value chain and organizational structure that extends through into the boardroom.

> **"A new organizational model for today's big corporations will not emerge spontaneously from the obsolete legacy structures of the industrial age. Rather, companies must design a new model holistically, using new principles that take into account the way professionals create value."**

Lowell L. Bryan, Claudia Joyce – McKinsey & Co., 2006

One definition of management is the husbanding of scarce resources. This almost implies that you own the resources you 'husband' but in today's business world that doesn't have to be the case. Outsourcing is growing at a raging speed, fuelled by specialization of process disciplines. There is hardly an area left of business operation that does not have the opportunity to call upon third party specialist support. This introduces a very different view of the way organizations utilize 'people' resources. There are significant changes to the resourcing of innovation. Insight and new processes are now shaping the operating structure of organizations.

> **An agilized enterprise is an enterprise without walls that considers it inappropriate to define the boundaries of its resourcing and innovation by the perimeter of its firewall.**

An agilized enterprise forms a network of loosely coupled organizations and individuals formed around an interest, brand or common deliverable. It is able to harness the collective skills of third party suppliers, channel partners, government agencies, industry clusters and knowledge communities and individuals because it thinks differently and because it operates formalized information flows that shape behaviours and measure contributions.

My one concern about describing this new model as a virtualized enterprise is that it infers an enterprise lacking emotional cohesion and strong values, but the agilized enterprise is more energized and 'together' than its 20th century counterpart. Knowledge workers are increasingly able to achieve more return for their skills by contributing to projects sponsored by many different virtualized organizations. Internet and the emerging portfolio of participative technologies are making it easier for knowledge 'solvers' to use their skills and extract the greatest value from knowledge 'seekers'. In this new environment, and with old world corporations needing to re-generate their competitiveness, there will be huge drivers to tap into the creativity of open networks of high performance individuals. Those corporations that retain a focus on insourcing their innovation will quite simply be unable to compete.

Creative people are inhibited by the straightjacket of corporate policies and procedures. But creativity is not always productive. It can be a wasteful process as many ideas can come to nothing. Many failures might occur before that next great idea appears. Creatives need a sustainable funding source that can only be achieved through loosely-coupled retainer contracts. It makes sense for businesses to share the risks for creative processes.

The unbeatable ideas factory – Fishing in 'PONDs'

Industry is coming to terms with what can be achieved through exploiting knowledge experts who exist beyond the walls of the enterprise. These *Creative Networks* – which I call Primary Open Network Devices (PONDs for short) – are places where individuals have the opportunity to participate as part of communities with a common interest in investing their knowledge, fuelled by an incentive provided by the host. I expect that most large organizations in the future will need to identify the primary open network devices (PONDs) they will adopt in order to remain competitive in markets of the future that embrace external creative networks as a matter of course. These highly organized, open knowledge marketplaces exist today.

One of the earliest and most successful examples of an open network was developed by innovative American company InnoCentive Inc. An e-business venture by Eli Lilly and Co., InnoCentive connects scientists and science-based companies online to collaborate on complex scientific challenges. This virtual research and development network involves 125,000 registered scientists worldwide who work for companies including Eli Lilly, Dow Chemical, Solvay, Janssen and many non-profit entities.

InnoCentive has created an efficient marketplace that allows research "seekers" to access the best ideas and research "solvers" to solve them – thereby removing the barriers of distance, specialization and organization from the sciences, facilitating global collaboration and driving scientific discovery.

Dr Alpheus Bingham, Founder and Board Member of InnoCentive, is clear on the challenges facing organizations wishing to develop open networks of their own, "In the first instance, organizations must recognise that their biggest competitor is the status quo, with companies by default continuing to operate the way they do now. To move forward you have to achieve a critical mass. In launching InnoCentive, our strategy was to go inside the research and development organization and find 20 challenges that offered a range of problem types and complexities for 'solvers' to address.

This was necessary to give solvers enough to work on and also evidence that solving any specific problem wasn't just a fluke. In spite of early success, maintaining the momentum of the market also requires active planning and participation. At present, as an example, we are actively pursuing new domains. The original 20 challenges were actually pretty scientifically narrow in their orientation. We are constantly planning and have clear domain concepts that we're working on. Development of this form of community still needs to be managed, fashioned and to some extent engineered."

Dr Bingham sees a bright future for open networks formed on the business model that InnoCentive has innovated. He says, "My ideal scenario is that businesses will evolve to embrace a new approach to leveraging distributed intelligence by building it into the foundation of how they work and not attempt to tack this useful resource pool onto their existing organizations.

Today, most organizations use their internal resource pool to find solutions to problems when they should be focused on problem definition and pushing problem-solving tasks to an external collective."

More PONDS

The opportunity to create primary open networks exists not just for scientific research.

There are many other 'primary devices' that an enterprise can install to bring together and leverage the skills and resources of a broader open network of individuals through relevant incentives, shared risk and appropriate use of Internet workspaces.

Research   (Like the InnoCentive case example I describe).

Design   OpenAd is a POND adopting a 'seeker/solver' model that brings together client organizations (seekers) looking for advertising innovation and creatives (solvers). *Solvers* are either self-employed people or individuals who work for smaller companies that lack the brand reach to serve large advertisers. In OpenAd.net is the world's first online marketplace for buying and selling advertising, marketing and design ideas. The organization accesses over 11,000 creatives in 125 countries. Clients who have already used the service include MTV, LastMinute.com, Emap and the Make Poverty History Campaign. I my opinion this is a great idea that is sure to do well. Advertising agencies struggle to maintain the energy and originality of house designers. In future I expect advertising and creative agencies will take responsibility for the scoping and delivery of client projects rather than expecting to be the sole source of creative thought.

HR   Whilst there are several successful recruitment sites like www.gumtree.com that use the Internet as another form of promotion, we have yet to see core competency-based 'super-temping agencies' adopting the primary open network model. I can imagine a time where 'seekers' will advertise their staffing requirement and 'solvers' will provide the right-price, right-fit people creating a marketplace for any given competency.

Insight   Information providers like Factiva, Butler Group, Gartner Inc. and Platts are developing information portals tailored around the specific needs of clients. Use of these portals is already becoming an embedded part of operational behaviour within corporations. No doubt in the near future these same corporations will adopt incentive schemes to capture new and unique market knowledge using loosely-coupled open networks to encourage the capture of insight that has a known value to the enterprise.

Legal   Bringing seekers and solvers together in the legal market around specific case work is another obvious POND, particularly as the industry gets ever more specialist in its case handling.

These new forms of third party specialized knowledge pools and markets, systems and resources will demand new investment and operational models to support them. The compelling commercial value of PONDs is funding the development of new technologies to create virtual workspace environments (exampled by the InnoCentive website) to support collaboration and the creation of knowledge markets. In future, we can expect PONDs to become the prime mechanism used to capture knowledge from both *outside* and *inside* an enterprise.

The value of knowledge has to be recognized as being incremental to a worker's contribution to the enterprise they work for – and this has to be paid for. It is often assumed by executive teams that if one of their employees comes up with a useful and original idea, then they instantly own it. Strictly speaking this might be the case in law, but in the future, the proliferation of open networks means that employees are more likely to log into an open network and sell their ideas to competitors for the highest price unless employers start to recognise that knowledge has a value.

How can a corporation aim to compete with only its internal resources available to it when there are fleet-of-foot competitors out there able to harness the knowledge and innovation of potentially thousands of independent contractors? A company employing a handful of full-time workers has the opportunity to enjoy an instant 'virtual' research team of thousands of expert scientists overnight. An enterprise *without walls* is characterized by:

- A small nucleus of employees on full-time contracts.
- Use of sub-contractors and outsourced service providers.
- Use of Primary Open Network Devices (PONDs).

Supply chains and sales channels become so intertwined with the organization that the 'walls' of the enterprise become almost indistinguishable.

How to develop an excellent operating approach

Operating approach is one of the most complex topic areas. Each of the seven operators is worthy of a small exercise book, so I won't attempt to explain in a chapter end summary how to develop improvement programmes for each of them. Instead I recommend two excellent resources below for further reading.

Further reading and resources on this subject:

Organizational Structure – Lowell L Bryan and Claudia Joyce have recently written a book on the subject of organizational structure. *Mobilizing Minds* explains how companies need to put the same energy and focus into designing their organizations as they have devoted to the design of new products, processes or entry into new markets.

Primary Open Networks – Visit http://www.InnoCentive.com to see an example of an open primary network and take any opportunity you can of hearing Dr Alpheus Bingham explain his vision of the future!

Checklist for **Operating Approach**

	Qualification	Score
🙁 **An inflexible structure**	Targets are not being achieved. Organizational silos exist.	☐ ☐
🙂 **Enterprise 'thinks and acts as one'**	A holistic business-wide management perspective. Performance measurements and contributions of individuals linked to strategic outcomes.	☐ ☐
🙂 **Management looks, thinks and plans ahead**	Leadership sees beyond current objectives and is always thinking and planning for the future.	☐
🙂 **A loosely-coupled structure**	A responsive structure. Knowledge and skills sourced from wherever they might be found. Management believes in the benefits of change and constant learning.	☐ ☐ ☐
🙂 **Formalized for flexibility**	Management thinks about and formalizes 'liquid' information flows.	☐
🙂 **Adopts lower-cost business models**	An enterprise adept at finding / adapting to new models.	☐
🙂 **A virtualized enterprise**	A small nucleus of workers on full-time contracts. Use of Primary Open Network Devices (PONDs).	☐ ☐

10

(R) Process Performance

The real question to ask is not 'Is the practice good?' but 'Is the practice appropriate for us' – does it fit with our ideology and ambitions?

Built to Last, Jim Collins

I spend little time in this book commenting on the subject of process performance but this is not because it isn't important. The fact is it is a well known and deeply understood topic. In the context of this book, the big question is "How does process performance influence business agilization?"

My experience of process performance is that agile organizations tend not to have a problem with known processes that are core to the operation of the enterprise. It may be that they don't spend enough time questioning them and asking themselves whether they are still appropriate or not as the organization re-models itself towards new customer demands or market conditions. The bigger issues of process performance are normally down to weak areas of formalization that usually happens for three reasons:

1. Changes to business models and structures have caused processes to become misaligned to new demands of the enterprise.

2. Processes are so *liquid* in their nature that technology and structures have failed to keep up with demands.

3. The pace of change has overextended the internal resources of the enterprise to build new processes, probably because the organization lacks suitable IT tools and resources or because dedicated improvement skills and resources do not exist.

Look around most large corporations and you will find examples of poor information flows being covered up, hidden by the exceptional efforts of information workers using email messaging or spreadsheets to glue together critical exchanges of information where processes have not been properly formalized. In consequence, organizations function at a sub-optimal level but probably don't realize it. Well understood processes are important to business success AND to the process of agilization because formality brings flexibility. Formalized processes help individuals to realize how they contribute to activities and who is responsible for outcomes.

(1) Poorly-formalized processes

An organization that fails to understand its own processes will inevitably find it difficult to maintain quality in what it delivers, It has no hope at all of optimizing day-to-day activities. But measuring the performance of processes in isolation can be a dangerous game. Managers can be tempted to benchmark the performance of processes they operate and assume that the sum of these high performing processes will be a higher performing enterprise. This is a BIG assumption and risks too little focus being placed on questioning the appropriateness of processes.

In 2000 I attended a supplier meeting of a local authority that wanted to ensure that it was achieving *best value* in the operation of its business processes. It was apparent, from the presentation made to the gathered audience of private sector product and service providers, that the authority felt it could benchmark its process performance by asking private sector companies if they could run the same processes any better. To aid this exercise, the lead director responsible for coordinating the event offered suppliers a detailed list of the processes they currently operated within each department of the council. What was missing was any detail that described how the processes delivered value – to customers, to the organization, to staff or any other stakeholder! Without any clear appreciation of how a process delivers value, it is impossible to say what 'good' looks like, to identify the contribution that any given process makes to the success of the enterprise or to assess the appropriateness of the process to current and future needs.

Process improvement managers have to temper the desire to achieve excellence by putting each sliver of a process under the microscope. Instead they must think about a holistic view of operational excellence with the constant mantra of achieving and measuring customer value.

When processes are not documented

The absence of any documentation is a pretty sure sign that an organization is failing to run quality managed processes. How can you *share* good practice if nobody has documented how a process works? This is why any good quality management system looks first at whether an organization has documented and is following its own processes. The pace of change means that maintaining and improving quality processes becomes an ongoing but unavoidable task.

Workers are not familiar with the workings of the processes they contribute to.

If workers are unable to describe the processes that they are meant to be contributing to – YOU HAVE A PROBLEM.

(2) High-performing reinforced processes

The organization has installed process quality management

If the organization is able to produce a document that explains how it does what it does and why, in such a way that every contributor knows how the processes that they contribute towards work – then it is on the way to having a good process quality management system. A quality management system becomes excellent when an organization also operates behaviours and processes that map 'what it does' according to the customer value that it seeks to deliver. Managers must be able to influence the shape and structure of processes to constantly remain aligned with the needs of the enterprise to support new business approaches as and when they are needed. In most successful companies I have encountered, processes and behaviours are supportive of one another. They are 'clustered' together so that an inappropriate behaviour or process stands out like a sore thumb.

One organization I class as being truly world class when it comes to customer service is Pret A Manger, a high-street chain in the UK providing coffee and light refreshments. In a very aggressive marketplace and facing much larger rivals, Pret consistently achieves higher customer satisfaction ratings than its competitive peers. Each of the processes it operates, from managing and replenishing stock to cleaning toilets, is faithfully wrapped into a customer value-driven ethos that always asks the question "How will the customer benefit?"

This dogged commitment to a qualitative standard of operational behaviour means that any process falling outside this profile becomes exposed and in obvious need of correction. In this way, replenishing shelves is supported by staff training, which is supported by a 'freshness first' focus on the supply-chain and manufacturing process.

This package of operating approach and behaviours serves to create a virtuous circle that assures that Pret always maintains its customer value focus.

The fit of processes is regularly reviewed

Monitoring the appropriateness of processes should be an embedded part of operational business planning and project review. It's easy to fall into an operating behaviour that fails to question the role and suitability of processes, particularly when performance incentives and measures become institutionalized.

The deep questioning management behaviour outlined later in Chapter 11 (point 3) is the surest method I am aware of for achieving this ambition.

Corporate challenges

I believe that corporate challenges are grossly under-represented in the business performance management methods of most organizations. They are a necessary tool to encourage deep thinking about the effectiveness of day-to-day activities.

A *corporate challenge* could be nothing more than a list of questions that question the value and performance of an organizations internal processes and operational behaviours.

Corporate challenges might be internally sourced – encouraged by the curiosity and inquisitiveness of managers – or externally sourced from good practice 'ambassador' organizations such as trade and industry associations. There are many corporate challenges that organizations must administer. Some examples are listed in the table below.

Challenge Description	*Example*
Performance challenges	**QFD**
Quality challenges	**ISO**
Governance challenges	**Risk assessment** **Customer experience**
Best practice challenges	**Policy and process guidance**
People and diversity	**IiP, DDA**

Corporate challenges ensure that a sufficient number of checks and balances exist in the assessment of quality, corporate behaviour and performance, ensuring effective governance. The ability of corporations to manage and administer corporate challenges can be limited by management capacity. It's easy to imagine an organization that only has time to 'do the day job' with no time to ask questions about how or why it operates the processes it does. Use of relational database technology makes it possible for organizations to author software applications that minimize the amount of time staff and managers need to invest in operating a system of effective corporate challenges whilst producing more complete, better-structured, better-evidenced responses to questions.

The main benefits of corporate challenges are:

- To determine the 'fit' and usefulness of internal process to meet current and future business requirements
- To benchmark the performance of internal processes and identify areas of improvement (efficiency and effectiveness)

- To learn from good practice ambassadors about better ways of running internal processes
- To measure levels of risk associated with internal processes
- To encourage 'doing better things' not just 'doing things better'

(3) A dedicated resource to monitor, improve and introduce new processes

A dedicated 'organization' department

On a research field trip to Germany, I found it common for companies to have an *Organization Department*. This team supports change and improvement processes with a blend of skills including IT, strategic human resources, business process analysis and training. Clearly German organizations know that if you want to *always* improve, the role of *improvement* needs to become a full-time job for someone!

Installed business process managers

Process value and improvement managers* ('process managers' for short) are allocated to each internal process and take a holistic view of all aspects of process improvement to make sure the fit and performance of processes are in tune with the needs of the business. PVI managers are measured on their ability to streamline and improve processes both in terms of their benchmark performance against industry peers, alternative models of delivery, and in terms of their contribution towards objectives.

Process managers are central to the operational excellence of an agilized enterprise. They become the recipients of all insight and innovation to do with the internal process they are responsible for and help the organization to rapidly learn from insight that is captured.

(*Volkswagen is one major corporation that has already introduced the role of process managers. The introduction of this new role has helped Volkswagen to govern the continual improvement in processes by devolving IT responsibilities deeper into the business and to harness IT skills in a way that instils a sustained improvement agenda.)

Further reading and resources

This is a well-documented subject but I don't think I've read anything that improves on the book *In Search of Excellence* by Thomas J. Peters and Robert H. Waterman Jr. – one of the most influential books written on the topic of operational excellence. Built around case examples, this book manages to offer up some excellent examples of good practice and innovative thoughts that have relevance to organizations today.

Checklist for **Process Performance**

	Qualification	Score
☹ **Poorly-formalized processes**	Processes are not documented.	☐
	Workers are not familiar with how the process they contribute towards operates.	☐
☺ **High-performing reinforced processes**	Process quality management in place.	☐
	The fit of processes is regularly reviewed.	☐
	Corporate challenges are used to analyze the performance and suitability of processes.	☐
☺ **A dedicated resource to monitor, improve and introduce new processes**	A dedicated organization department.	☐
	Process analysis expertise installed in the form of process managers.	☐

11

(B) Behaviour

The gorilla story. The story starts with a cage containing five gorillas, and a rope leading to a large bunch of bananas hanging above some stairs in the centre of the cage. Whenever a gorilla attempts to climb the rope the entire group is hosed down by water. After a few attempts the gorillas pounce on any one of the group that attempts to climb the rope. Later another gorilla is introduced to the cage. As soon as the new gorilla attempts to climb the rope, the other gorillas pounce, even when the hose has long been removed.

(1) Latent instruction set

Organizations over time develop a deeply-embedded set of instructions that fashion how the people within them think and act. This is encouraged by the lack of good approaches for delivering ambitious management goals and the consequences of making mistakes, and increases the inclination of managers to err on the side of caution. These conservative, 'no-risk-taking' behaviours become entrenched in the *enterprise logic* of the organization. How can leaders attempt to change this latent instruction set that rests within the heads of their workforce? Imprints of behaviour remain, sometimes for decades. People who have worked in the top tiers of management all of their lives know that *norms of behaviour* must be challenged and changed from the top down.

Bob Kiley knows a thing or two about leadership. He has developed an international reputation for being able to save transit systems experiencing serious problems. (He is currently advising the London Transport Authority *Transport for London* on *Crossrail,* a new railway proposed for London and the South-East that is setting out to deliver a rail service from Maidenhead and Heathrow in the west right across the capital into Essex and Kent in the east by 2015). Kiley says, "The *belief systems* that continue to operate within some organizations today date back to the late 19th century. Institutions encourage newcomers to follow patterns of behaviour that have existed within the enterprise for years and embrace the status quo. Starting in *the middle* doesn't work. Driving a change in behaviours requires constant and continual focus that only comes from the top. You need to examine the key people and how they discharge their duties. If you're going to attempt to do it, modifying 'norms of behaviour' has to be a topic in its own right".

You can imagine how a latent instruction set inhibits new ideas from being drafted into the way an enterprise thinks. Today's corporations are largely methods-based. The individuals they employ are conditioned to always think in terms of methods to bring automation, structure, control and conformity to business processes. Even creative industries such as advertising and marketing have developed a methods-based approach that conditions how its creative people think, bringing confidence and a security blanket to corporate decision makers who like to know – deep down – that even people who wear ponytails and body-piercing are following a methods-based approach. Business is still truly in love with mechanization. Senior managers will default to this mindset seeking a formula, and most of the time that's the right thing to do! Methods are *scientific*. At school I remember my science teachers drumming in the message that any experiment should have a documented method. But methods are not always essential, and for creative exercises they can be restrictive and counter-productive.

I grew up with my mother's deep crust steak and kidney pie. My mother was a self-taught cook. When I reached puberty I asked Mum to show me how she baked such great pies with the anticipation of developing the skills to guarantee a future supply when I left home. To my everlasting disappointment, whenever we went through the exercise of measuring the ingredients and writing down the timings for each of the steps we were never able to recreate that mouth-watering deep crust!

Creativity is rarely encouraged by methods-based formulaic processes. Whilst there need to be some ground rules, maintaining the spontaneity and passion that exist in creative thinking demands an environment without walls. To create an agilized organization capable of responding to market changes demands new thinking characterized by the Wind Driven Enterprise I describe in Chapter 2. Moving to this new enterprise logic does not just happen. Thinking needs to change – and be encouraged to change – within management teams. This starts with leaders introducing positive new behaviours.

Leaders must change the latent instruction set of their organizations if they that want to become 21st century 'agilized' powerhouses.

Belief Systems

A belief system is a series of ideas organized in the mind to project an image of what we believe is 'Real'. These ideas are manifested through interaction with others such as parents, peers, mentors or *work colleagues*. Beliefs have a profound impact on the way people live their lives and perform their work role. Every enterprise carries within its 'DNA' a belief system that is the sum of what everyone thinks to be true. This influences the way an enterprise works and makes decisions. Consider also what is taught by academia about the way marketing works. Over time, academia has developed a latent instruction set formed around mechanization that sits in the memory of college lecturers and professors while the practice of management has moved on.

Agilization is partly about changing the latent instruction set from the inward-looking 'risk averse' *mechanization*-centric belief system of the 20th century enterprise to the outward-looking 'creative' agilized belief system demanded of the 21st century enterprise. Whilst some of the internal processes, assets and resources might be shared, to me the mindset and behaviours of the mechanized and agilized enterprise are poles apart! The diagram overleaf illustrates these differences. The mechanization enterprise logic of the 20th century corporation has its management capacity predominantly committed to inward-looking activities to analyze internal processes with a view to understanding methods and seeking to automate them to deliver efficiencies and improve effectiveness.

Illustrating the transition of enterprise logic to the agilization model

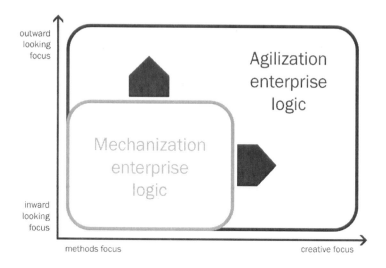

The agilization enterprise logic of the 21st century enterprise embraces its operational effectiveness and builds on it. Leaders need know that when they formalize information flows they will be better positioned to encourage flexibility without creating a rigid framework that inhibits processes that thrive on creative thinking. Leaders invest more management time being outward looking so they are better placed to identify and harness new market threats and opportunities.

Encouraging the right workforce behaviours is about setting the right minds free, scoping the purpose of the enterprise so that every worker can contribute and introducing *new thinking* in the areas of learning and innovation, procurement, the role of technology, the use and flexibility of workforce, exploiting external resources and the nature of customer relationships.

Tapping into the existing values held by executives, stakeholders and the workforce can serve as a valuable indicator on the general health of an enterprise. Beliefs also exist in the minds of **shareholders** on what they should expect from an enterprise in terms of profits and behaviours, in **executives** on how they should manage and in the **workforce** on how they think they should behave and be rewarded. Ask a chief executive to describe the belief system for their enterprise and you might get a funny look – but most would agree that it is important. What we believe influences how we behave. For example, it could be my employer has a policy of answering phones within three rings. Unless I feel it's the right thing to do or that I will be found out if I don't do it, then that policy might as well not exist. The way that belief systems reveal themselves is through **norms of behaviour**.

Whilst it's a knuckle-cracking frustration for executives, you can't directly act to replace one belief system with another. You can change what people think over time by evidencing that the foundation of *their current belief* is not actually correct (i.e. gravity – apple – ouch). At the core of belief systems lie preconceptions, self-interest and self-identity – i.e. what *I* believe, how it affects *me*.

Agilization is about getting the hearts and minds of organizations to buy into a new set of values that establish new 'positive' norms of behaviour, that are a perpetual good fit with market opportunities – knowing that this transition will positively influence the performance of people, processes and outcomes.

In no particular order of priority, here are a few examples of beliefs commonly held within the 20th century mechanized enterprise. The 20th century enterprise believed:

Shareholders	Sustainable growth and shareholder value comes from asset worth and market share.
Leaders	We should have a mission statement.
	We achieve sustainable growth by attaining a position of market strength where market share is greater than our competitive peers.
	It's natural for men to dominate the boardroom!
	We must review our business model once every few years.

Leaders (Continued)	We learn by paying for market research and watching what our competitors do.	
	Customer satisfaction is nice when it happens.	
Workforce	I want a job for life because it is more secure.	
	My company will look after me.	
	I have no choice other than to commute to work.	
All	The environment can take care of itself.	
	Brand is the responsibility of our marketing people.	

In contrast, the 21st century agilized enterprise believes:

Shareholders	Sustainable growth and shareholder value is about achieving market fit better than competitors.	
	Organizations must recognize their responsibilities towards society and the environment as part of what they do and how they do it (values and behaviours).	
Leaders	The enterprise knows the direction it is heading in, described through its brand values.	
	The enterprise achieves sustainable growth by always fitting the markets it serves.	
	The enterprise knows what it is capable of.	
	The enterprise has a happy mental attitude.	
	Leaders must encourage *followership*.	
Workforce	Job security is not dependent on a single employer.	
	Change is constant but isn't threatening.	
	It is the quality of the journey that counts.	
All	Brand is democratized. We share in the values.	

This *new thinking* has to be driven through by leaders. Leaders must appreciate the attitudinal differences between an *agilized enterprise* and its 20th century predecessor inwardly focusing on mechanization. Leaders must consider how to:

- How to steer the enterprise through change whilst sustaining the current business model and economic engine.
- Heighten the awareness of the enterprise and individuals to the consequences of doing nothing.
- Redefine the purpose of the enterprise, how it thinks about its customer value, planning, workforce productivity etc.
- Invest in new ways of capturing insight and innovation to engage with staff, channel partners, suppliers and other groups.
- Create an enterprise that is capable of actively listening and reacting to new external threats and opportunities.
- Monitor and continuously review business models and the best way of operating them profitably.

Breaking through the Chinese walls

Breaking through *silo mentality* that exists in most large organizations and encouraging managers to be prepared to look outside the organization for the best knowledge, innovation and resources is not easy. To create an enterprise without walls requires management teams to actively involve their workforce and broader stakeholder community in every aspect of business activity from the outset. Ultimately, if more people are aware of the 'game plan', more people can contribute ideas that will make the enterprise more efficient and dynamic. Getting people to work together as one organization is easier when everyone is working in the same place (preferably an open office or well connected virtual environment). The idea of working in silos has to be rejected in favour of openness.

Rackspace Managed Hosting is an excellent example of an enterprise without walls. Since its formation in 1998, Rackspace has become one of San Antonio's largest and fastest-growing high-technology companies, with revenue topping $200 million in 2006, up from $139 million in 2005. It has expanded from a

handful of employees to 1,120 today, including 839 locally. David Bryce joined Rackspace in October of 1999 as Director of Operations. Together with his group of fanatics, David developed and implemented Rackspace's passionate approach to customer service, known as "Fanatical Support." Rackspace has encouraged David to pursue his desire for building one of the world's greatest service companies.

Keeping staff happy with unique perks is identified by managers as a critical success factor in delivering the company's "Fanatical Support" commitment. Graham Weston, Executive Chairman of Rackspace, gives employees the keys to his midnight-blue BMW 3-series two-door convertible sports car to drive for a week, or the keys to his guesthouse on the Comal River in New Braunfels to encourage positive norms of customer service behaviour. That generosity earned the company recognition in Fortune Small Business Magazine, which recently named Weston one of USA's best bosses.

To reward employees for their hard work, Rackspace's teams plan quarterly events ranging from bowling to scavenger hunts. Top employees are rewarded by tying them up in a straitjacket at a party and taking their picture. Their photo then hangs on a wall of fame at San Antonio headquarters along with other so-called "Rackers." All of them deliver what the company calls "fanatical customer support" and embody such core values as embracing change and treating fellow "Rackers" as friends and family. This forms part of an approach to management that encourages a 'really small big company' culture.

Rackspace is a business without walls where:

- The values of the business are presented at every opportunity: on walls, coffee mugs, official papers, marketing materials, even tee-shirts! These values are seen as foundation stones providing the right 'fit' for a workforce that is encouraged to opt into a culture and norms of behaviour laid down by the management team.

- This culture is motivated and reinforced through both casual and formal activities such as social events, social interaction activities, formal briefings, open briefings, open-door days, etc.

- A value chain of the key business processes is displayed on office walls to enable individuals to contribute ideas towards doing better things. Ideas are generously rewarded as an incentive to others to become innovation activists!

- Individuals who put great energy into providing customer value through exceptional 'above and beyond' customer service are heralded. Storyboard examples that evidence and support enterprise values are shared and encouraged.

- Every opportunity is made to share the essence of enterprise values across the virtual team of participants.

All this effort to foster an 'opt-in' commitment to behaviours is made not for philanthropic reasons. Managers know that workforce buy-in and commitment to the cause are critical in achieving customer value and sustainability.

(2) Positively modifying norms of behaviour

For objectives to demand the full attention of the organization and direct its energy in a consistent and shared direction, they have to become embedded into the operational psyche. Lofty management precepts can quickly be drowned out by the actions people see around them. As soon as people see business going on as usual without individuals being criticized for poor performance or demonstrating inappropriate behaviours or attitudes that discourage cooperation and teamwork, any hope of transformation and change is lost.

Leaders must find a way to change the latent instruction set that their managers continue to discharge, and introduce a new reality formed around what it takes to operate in today's commercial environment. Stakeholder groups, particularly senior officers, must come to realise that an inward-looking 'nothing can harm us' belief system doesn't fit any more.

Ask any Chief Executive how important it is to monitor markets for threats and opportunities, or to listen to *what matters most* to customers, workforce and other stakeholders (yes, even shareholders!) and they will say, "It's extremely important." However, management capacity trained on 'actively listening' to stakeholders is normally low. No surprise perhaps. This behaviour reflects the latent instruction set held by managers.

Tough love

Getting great performance from workers means investing in mechanisms that encourage the right *norms of behaviour* and discourage the wrong ones. It's also about being prepared to face up to and *fix* the problems.

Jane Ling and Jenny Turner appropriately describe this HR management style as tough love. It's a question of getting the best out of people but tackling attitudes head-on that don't fit. It's about attempting to get the best out of everyone, but being realistic and accepting that some people just won't want to play ball. That's their choice. Respect it, but deal with it. The diagram below shows the balance of the attitudes that exist in most organizations.

Illustration of a popular workforce appraisal model

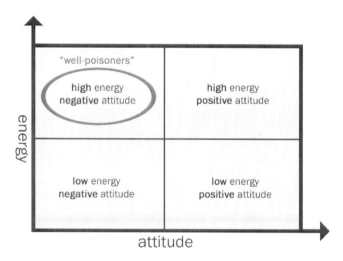

Leaders and managers always want people with a positive attitude. We all know that a positive attitude rubs off on everyone – try smiling at people! On the flip-side, negative attitudes also rub off, and can kill enthusiasm and ideas. When taking stock of workforce capabilities, it is the 'well-poisoners' – those people with negative attitudes and high energy – that need to be identified and brought on-side fast. The well-poisoners of yesterday make your greatest advocates tomorrow if their negativity can be turned into positive attitudes.

Attitudinal areas to address should include:

Purpose	Define or redefine what the enterprise does.
Learning and innovation ideology	Encourage the enterprise to look beyond its firewall for learning and innovation.
Procurement ideology	Encourage processes and attitudes that seek competitive advantage and innovation rather than simply 'following procedure'.
Workforce ideology	Encourage processes and attitudes that seek competitive advantage and innovation rather than playing 'follow-the-leader'.
Technology ideology	Pay for software as a service and focus on the flexibility of systems, recognizing that nothing in an agile world stays constant forever – and if it does then perhaps it should be outsourced!
Customer relationship ideology	If appropriate, invest in the development of tribal brands, develop a two-way dialogue, and actively listen to customers.

How do leaders start the process of changing attitudes?

1. Establish and communicate a new and clear expectation of what *good looks like*, that individuals can buy into.

2. Install actions and formalized processes that encourage the enterprise to think and act as one.
3. Ensure the early contributions to success made by individuals and teams are clearly visible.
4. Install standards of behaviour and install a behavioural *management guardian* (more about this later).

Walking through this list makes change sound painful. Sometimes it is. What makes matters even more complex is that the process of improvement has to balance investing time to precipitate change with the need to manage the deliverables of the organization today. Unfortunately, you can't switch off the organization for a couple of months to make changes to the way it works and thinks. Business must continue, and this presents significant capacity issues – particularly within management teams. This is one reason why many organizations will bring in external consultants to assist with change. But another good reason to seek external advice and support is the benefit of expertise that manages change as a 'day job' and has the opportunity to see old problems and challenges with fresh eyes.

I'm a big fan of *The Service Profit Chain* workforce appraisal model. It originates from a book written by James Heskett, W. Earl Sasser and Leonard Schlesinger that explores these issues. Their argument is that by efficiently engineering the linkage between employees, customers and profits, better business performance can be achieved.

The service profit chain (J. Heskett, W. E. Sasser, L. Schlesinger) links profit and growth to loyalty, satisfaction and value

Organizations such as **Ling Turner Ltd.** in the UK help organizations to equip themselves with the skills needed to adopt a *tough love* HR approach and formalize high-performing *norms of behaviour* that transform the ability of an enterprise to satisfy its stakeholder expectations.

(3) Deep thinking (QFD)

Managers need to think more deeply about how they manage projects across the enterprise; particularly when multiple departments are engaged and project contributors are geographically dispersed, which is increasingly common. As Mike Clargo, CEO of Tesseracts Ltd. (and thought-leader in this subject area) is quick to stress, "Unlearning poor practice is as important to effective management as learning good practice."

This process of discovery only really begins to work when managers – and the organization as a whole – start to challenge conventional wisdom and start to be 'curious'. Some managers appear determined to have no curiosity. This is where the Quality Function Deployment (QFD) process comes in that Mike Clargo has shaped into a practical programme for 21st century business activity management.

QFD is not a new tool. It was first applied in Japan in 1972 at the Mitsubishi Kobe shipyards, where engineers were struggling to make sense of how to turn customer value into the complex assemblies and systems that go to make up a ship. Engineers Shigeru Mizuno and Yoki Akao hit on the simple idea of using a visual matrix to show relationships between the main areas of the ship specification and the key systems and assemblies required to deliver them.

QFD enables an organization to develop a highly intuitive, deeply questioning, business activity planning method that means managers at all levels are constantly reassessing their performance and the rationale for why they do what they do. At its simplest, QFD is a matrix, a series of rows and columns (see overleaf). Each row reflects a clear business objective, and each column reflects a separate delivery mechanism (i.e. function, unit, department or process of that business). Each cell represents the potential for that business mechanism to influence the attainment of the objective.

Notice that the right-hand side of the matrix provides each business objective with a description of the measurement, target and actual performance of the organization and its ability to meet the objective. The matrix produces a holistic view of how parts of the enterprise (which might also include external agencies) are contributing to the achievement of objectives.

Developing a framework for the matrix provides an opportunity for the management team to reconsider the organization's mission, logic and operating structure. Discussing each cell of the matrix brings together the collective actions of contributors and encourages debate on how to achieve outcomes in the best way possible by working together and sharing resources and expertise. The cleverest aspect of the QFD model is the roof at the very top of the matrix. This is where the delivery units understand common areas of delivery and have the potential to explore how they can work better together to achieve the common ambition of the organization.

Illustration of a QFD Matrix (©Tesseracts Ltd 2007)

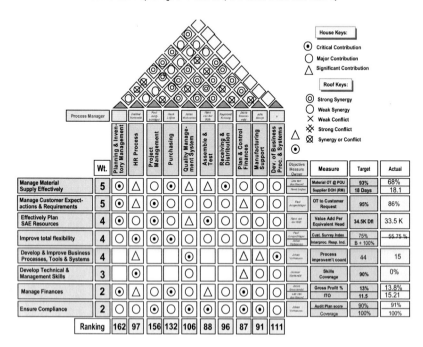

It is in this discussion that the true value of QFD shows itself. Surfacing challenges, sharing solutions, bringing context and analysis to problems – all of these elements are essential when developing the sense of teamwork needed to encourage positive norms of behaviour that place organizational outcomes above attainment of departmental targets.

The rigor and structure that QFD provides gives freedom for the management team to consider goals and strategies that they might otherwise consider unthinkable or irresponsible, even to the extent of redefining themselves, their role, and their operation. It is discussion that is the real value that comes from QFD. It is a framework for deep thinking across the enterprise.

For me, a key element of Quality Function Design (QFD) is another system that Mike Clargo promotes for managing the day to day running of projects that he calls **Quad-Charting**.

Illustration of a Quad-Chart

A **Quad-Chart** presents project status on a single page.

1. The top left quadrant shows the current progress of the project against forecasted targets. Use of visual tools (like smiling or frowning faces) makes comprehension simpler.
2. The top right quadrant charts the progress of the project.
3. The bottom left quadrant analyzes performance
4. The bottom right quadrant enables the Process Manager to articulate the challenges the project faces and how these challenges are to be overcome.

Use of Quad-Charts means that people can share problems and ideas in an intuitive and easy to understand format. It means that everyone in the organization shares their project update information in a consistent way. The Quad-Chart approach offers a drill-down to more detailed analysis of each task associated with the activity.

(4) An externally aware enterprise – Happo Baraki!

The Japanese martial arts term 'happo baraki' means "a total awareness of one's surroundings". It is a phrase that echoes the essence of traditional Japanese philosophy: a deep awareness and appreciation of our surroundings.

In the fast changing market conditions of the 21st century it is easy to see why this concept of being self-aware and in constant communication with the environment resonates with the desirable behaviour of leaders and enterprises. All too often, being alert to external signals of market change and listening to customers is identified in the incumbent enterprise logic as an aspect of transactional data analysis – i.e. who bought this product? What do they have in common with other purchasers? Is there a common purchasing behaviour?

One of the new battlegrounds of agilized organizations is their ability to anticipate change. Organizations can today use horizon-scanning intelligence-gathering search systems and sophisticated self-organizing map analysis tools to identify, make sense of (and therefore anticipate) opportunities in markets and plan to exploit them faster than their competitors.

It's a process I call *anticipationomics*.

Creating an enterprise that is always 'listening' and in tune with its external environment in this way demands not just one but a series of significant changes in the way that organizations think and act.

In summary they are:

- Develop and ability to scan for weak signals of market changes.
- Forming a culture of curiosity.
- Releasing time for workers to invest in being curious.
- Establishing methods, roles and skills to listen to customers.
- Embedding insight-capture into operational procedures.

How to build the right behaviours

Getting behaviours right starts at the top, with the management team. It is so easy for leaders to assemble people around them who think the way they do. I've never known 'good behaviours' to arrive in organizations unless there is a healthy blend of *different strokes* in the executive team. This is the kick-start that most organizations need.

On one occasion, at the break-up of an inclusion workshop that I had facilitated in a local authority, one of the delegates took me to one side and asked me for my advice. She was a member of the customer service team but she was finding that any suggestions she put forward were being ignored by her boss. It was clear from my workshop that the organization's management team had become stale. The entire management team was a reflection of its leader. After explaining how unhappy she was and describing her circumstances through a forensic monologue, she asked me what her next move should be. It's one of those situations where inevitably too little knowledge is a dangerous thing, so I fluffed an answer. But inside I was saying, "LEAVE! LEAVE!"

Further reading and resources

For more information on how to positively modify norms of behaviour, visit the Ling Turner website, which can be found at http://www.lingturner.co.uk.

Checklist for **Behaviour**

	Qualification	Score
☹ **Latent instruction set**	Managers do not question the latent instruction set that exists within the enterprise.	☐
☺ **Positively modifying behaviour**	Management establishes and communicates a new and clear expectation of what good looks like.	☐
	Management installs actions and formalized processes that encourage the enterprise to think/act as one.	☐
	Leaders ensure early contributions to success made by individuals and teams are clearly visible.	☐
	Management establishes behavioural standards by nominating a *behavioural guardian.*	☐
☺ **Deep thinking – QFD**	Deep-thinking business planning that enables managers to repeatedly question what they're doing and why.	☐
☺ **An externally aware enterprise**	A culture of curiosity.	☐
	Time released for workers to be curious (unproductive tasks reduced or removed).	☐
	Insight capture embedded into operational processes.	☐
	The organization employs *anticipationomics.*	☐

12

(I) Insight

An organization's ability to learn, and to transform that learning into action rapidly, is the ultimate competitive business advantage.

Jack C Welch, former CEO, General Electric Company

Speed is a key competitive differentiator. It is about identifying new opportunities first and being able to turn insight into actions that transform knowledge into value for the enterprise. Technology exists to make this easier to do. It has been around for some time.

(1) A cocooned enterprise

A *cocooned organization* is one that builds cultural and structural barriers over time (creating an impenetrable wall) that prevent managers from learning from customers and markets.

The vital 'weak signals' that signpost a change in customer demand or market behaviour that emerge from the external environment are prevented from influencing the formation of strategy and day-to-day management decisions.

A cocooned organization is characterized by top-table executives shielded from the irritation of customers by lines of middle managers who spend most of their time behind a corporate firewall. In some organizations, talking to customers is seen as something that you do when you sell something or you receive a complaint. Only some departments are 'allowed' to talk to customers. It isn't a common day-to-day occurrence across the organization.

Listening to customers strengthens relationships and develops a stronger bond of trust. Deep down, managers know this. But few organizations encourage *open dialogue* with customers or have structured the roles, responsibilities and information processes needed to work in this way. Much of the feedback received from web crawls and day-to-day customer dialogue is *unstructured* content, i.e. text extracts of opinions that are not easily captured in a database and do not feature in the structured transactional analysis process. New sources of insight such as social behavioural analysis, user-centred design field surveys, tender analysis, complaints-processing, focus group feedback, etc. – unstructured as they may be – need to be captured, interpreted, contextualized and hopefully acted on.

Neither is the technology there to make it happen. But it *could* be there if managers thought it important. It isn't a question of technology not being able to deliver. It is a question of management priorities, of mindset. The inward-looking, mechanized enterprise does not *think customer*, does not *think agilization*.

(2) Employs dedicated insight management skills

Distilling *useful insight* from data requires a deep appreciation of context – i.e. what is important to *this* organization, how does *this* organization think and work?

Managers must fundamentally appreciate what the organization is capable of and the directions it might wish to take in the future. After all, how can you ask technology to interpret signals that might have nothing to do with today but might have everything to do with what you might want to do tomorrow? Insight capture and management processes place new demands on technology and the introduction of new skills to the organization.

Very few organizations today have a Customer Advocacy Director (one notable exception is Sun Microsystems). Even fewer have a Head of Corporate Insights, Head of Asset Performance or Vice President of Enterprise Alignment.

These are potentially future roles in the agilized enterprise.

(3) Customer insight capture is seen as 'strategic'

The agilized enterprise focuses on achieving greater customer value through a deeper appreciation of what customers want, knowledge gained by formalizing the process of capturing customer insight.

Insight management describes the process of capturing, analyzing and channelling insight from customers and markets to the right places in the organization so that it can be rationalized and put to a practical purpose that delivers value to the enterprise, and ultimately to customers. Insight management guides priorities, steers decision-making and directly influences day-to-day activities.

It differentiates the agilized enterprise of the 21st century from the mechanized enterprise of the late 20th century.

Capturing insight from customers and markets

The reality is that most organizations pay lip-service to their customers. As a result, they do not know what matters to them. Nobody is responsible for listening to customers and no formalized process exists, and few leaders recognise the *value* of what customers might tell them. Some organizations don't even know WHO their customers are.

Since 2002, through NDMC, Nick Lawrie and I have enabled organizations to sell more products and services, and to improve their quality of services, by delivering insight that helps organizations to understand their customer priorities, demands and behaviours. We provide these services across Europe to organizations that are committed at senior level to knowing their customers better.

Within NDMC, our experience has shown that many corporations that claim to listen to customers actually don't. Organizations in the public sector, in financial services, consumer goods manufacturing and retail will use their customer satisfaction surveys and their investment in Customer Relationship Management systems as evidence of their willingness to listen. But they don't listen.

What really matters to your customers?

You wouldn't believe it from the way some organizations treat them, but customers are people too and (as a general rule) they are articulate and intelligent. When asked their opinion, they will often give it if you ask nicely. Customers can help organizations to understand where their processes are weak, where products and services are failing to deliver customer value, where the organization is not learning from its mistakes, what they will buy next. Good enough reason to invest time in listening to them?

The value organizations place on understanding *what matters most* to customers IS changing. As major organizations come to terms with over-subscribed global consumer markets they know that if they don't get closer to customers and understand their world, they will lose the edge of being first to market with the next product or service. Those organizations that listen more actively to customers and have installed formalized means to act on this insight by translating it into better-fit products, messaging and go-to-market strategies will inevitably rise above those organizations that do not. This is a hard lesson to learn for corporations that have been successful for many years, dominating their markets to such a degree that they could ignore the impotent rumblings of markets transforming about them.

Today, many corporations appear to see customers as so many transactions. Several of the large European retail banks continue their inward management focus, eating away at the cost-per-transaction by outsourcing contact centre services to Asia while their customers drift to alternative providers that offer the personal service and advocacy that customers with choice can demand. It matters little how much a transaction costs should customers move their account business elsewhere! Design and usability product differentiators are set to become even more important as products become functionally comparable. Parity of product and service offers between different vendors in oversubscribed markets places a premium value on customer service differentiation. As leaders see revenues fall and business ebb away, the value they place on customer insight will surely grow. Knowing what matters to customers matters.

Managing customer insight is a new process that is not well understood. One of the MOST misunderstood aspects of listening to customers is the recognition that an enterprise must appreciate its *reason for listening*. This reasoning is built into the way the enterprise thinks – its *enterprise logic*.

Without understanding and formalizing the incumbent enterprise logic, information will 'hit' the outer walls of the enterprise, or pass through them untouched without the right people ever seeing it or having had the ability to apply it. This is because recipients don't realize that the information is valuable to someone somewhere in the organization.

The world beyond satisfaction surveys

Have you ever had someone stop you in the street and ask you to complete a supplier survey where they ask you 20 or so questions but none of them is the question you really want to answer such as, 'When it comes to *[blah]*, what matters most to you?' or 'How can we improve our product?'

Organizations spend too much time talking and not enough listening. Customers are rarely given the opportunity to have their say.

So much of today's business culture and approach fuels one-way push communications traffic from corporations to their customers – 'We sell, you buy' or 'We ask the research questions, you answer them'.

Stakeholder relationships deliver MUCH more when both the supplier and consumer move from one-way traffic to two-way dialogue. The only time most organizations actively invest in listening to customers is when they want to capture customer satisfaction statistics to enrich their performance management information. Rarely is this a qualitative survey, and generally the results are used to populate a small number of performance indicators. Customer insight is not seen as performing any further role in educating managers as to how they should align their activities.

Formalizing the process of capturing customer insight

Capturing customer insight is not easy. For one thing, customers are not always willing to tell you what they think. Unless suppliers reward them, why should they invest the time? It is normally only when customers reach an extreme level of happiness or unhappiness that they become sufficiently energized to take action and find justification to volunteer their opinion. Nick and I call this the 'apathy curve'.

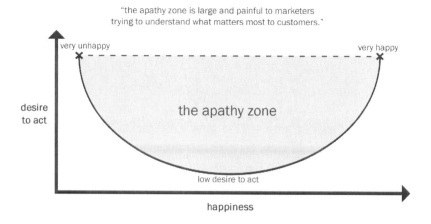

"the apathy zone is large and painful to marketers trying to understand what matters most to customers."

very unhappy · very happy

desire to act

the apathy zone

low desire to act

happiness

Market research from the direct mail industry suggests that people who have had a particularly poor product or service experience will tell *seven other people* about their bad experience while people who are very happy with a product or service will probably tell one or two people. Those who are somewhat happy or somewhat unhappy with the product or service they have received are normally not energized enough to take any action whatsoever. This is a challenge for customer advocacy professionals who need customer feedback in order to know how to improve the ability of the organization to deliver customer value.

Sources of insight

Customer information (which becomes insight when it is contextualized by the organization) takes many forms. The knowledge a sales representative captures when they meet a client becomes useful insight when it reveals opportunities to improve products and services. A conversation between a customer and a customer service agent in a contact centre becomes useful insight when it helps to determine what most interests the customer and how the customer qualifies value. Gathering insight from all customer touch-points is a characteristic of the listening culture that agile organizations adopt.

There are **four types** of insight capture processes distinguished by their source and currency of data:

1. **Direct in-line** insight capture occurs when organizations gather information in real time from customer conversations. In my opinion, this is the best way to capture insight given that the customer is already willingly communicating. The challenge facing insight specialists is that the direction of the conversation cannot easily be directed towards *things the provider wants to know* without risking what I describe as a 'betrayal of trust' – an event that causes the customer to feel that the provider is abusing use of *their time* by directing dialogue towards topics that have no bearing on the individual customer's interests or requirements. If you've ever phoned a company for customer service only to find that they want to try to sell you something different whilst you're on the phone, you'll know exactly what I mean!

2. **Direct off-line** insight capture occurs when a customer is directly approached for the specific purpose of acquiring information that will assist the organization in better understanding customer needs, levels of satisfaction and perceptions of value. Examples include customer questionnaires, satisfaction surveys, exit polls, focus groups, front-line staff surveys and the process of Issue Signature Analysis that we touch on later in this chapter.

3. **Indirect in-line**, where customer information is captured through customer contact / interactions with third parties such as third party websites. This information is either volunteered by the customer or is captured by tracking mouse-click selections on websites.

4. **Indirect off-line**, where customer information is gathered through indirect means such as third-party market research.

It's good to listen, but beware of talk-back

It is human nature that when someone talks to us, we interpret their words in either a positive or neutral context depending on our perceptions and state of mind. This might come down to who the person is that we're talking to and our personal relationship with them (i.e. 'I know they don't really like me and they think I'm mad, so whatever they say must be sarcasm or some devious plot to catch me out'). Over time, organizations interpret whatever customers say in a way that echoes their latent instruction set. This is a condition I call *talk-back*. In cases like this, it makes sense to put an independent set of ears and brains between the feedback and the organization. This way, the information fed back to the organization is more likely to be untouched by preconceptions.

When listening provides a competitive advantage

I once flew to Germany to meet a client and a few of his customers. After the first meeting my client said, "That was the most valuable and rewarding thing I've done in years. I should have done that a lot sooner."

What did I do that was so miraculous? I sat with my client and his customers and occasionally prompted a simple question that

I was not expected to know the answer to (even if my client was). And what was the result? His customers told him about his company, its products and the quality of his support services, the performance of his workforce, what his competitors were doing, what he could do next and why it mattered.

Yes, customers provide income to your business, but they can also tell you what matters to them so that you can always know what to offer and how to offer it. Customers will only invest the time to talk to you *if* they think their comments will be taken seriously and they will be rewarded by receiving better products and services in the future.

The risks of listening

There are risks associated with listening to customers. It is dangerous to adopt a slavish policy of believing everything that customers say and using this as the sole basis for policy formulation. For organizations that have continued over a period of years to broaden the scope of their offering to many different markets, it can be more useful to know what customers *don't want* and reduce the size of their product portfolios. Trying to satisfy all your customers all the time can be a recipe for disaster.

Social research scientists who study evidence-based policy formulation for the government have over recent years become more skeptical about the efficacy of outside *intervention* and the capacity of well-meaning *outsiders* to grasp the highly specific institutional and cultural contexts of complex organizations. Listening to customers can confuse the issue as to who owns an idea. Corporations run the risk of taking a great idea and investing in it, only to find some day that the telephone rings and someone says "That's my idea. I'm going to sue!" In my opinion, the level of risk attached to this is low if appropriate risk measures are adopted. I would say when you consider the sustained value that comes from customer feedback, it has got to be worth it.

Some organizations like McDonald's have adopted formal policies not to accept any suggestions from customers. Their website reads, "Thank you for your interest to share an idea for a product or service that you believe would be beneficial to McDonald's. Please know, however, that it is McDonald's company's policy not to consider unsolicited ideas from anyone other than our corporate employees, franchise owners and dedicated suppliers. It's not that great ideas cannot come from our valued customers. Each year, however, McDonald's receives thousands of unsolicited ideas and proposals for products and services. Due to the mass volume of these unsolicited ideas and the business challenge of determining what is truly a "new" idea versus a concept that is already in development, being tested, or previously considered, we must adhere to a strict policy not to accept or review any unsolicited ideas that come from outside the McDonald's system of our corporate employees, franchise owners and suppliers. As a result, we must decline your invitation to review your idea, and hope you can understand and appreciate our business reasons for making this company decision. We do, however, greatly appreciate your interest in McDonald's." (As published June 2006).

Contrast this with the UK's Pret a Manger sandwich and coffee chain, which prides itself on customer service and does it better than any other organization that I have encountered. Visit their website and you will find an 'I have an idea for you' page that provides a response form to complete.

(4) Installs formalized analysis of customer issues

Understanding emotional and functional issues of customers is critical to an agilized enterprise. Some suppliers appear to think that their product is the only thing their prospect is thinking about, but they'd be wrong. In between making decisions on work related issues, buyers – like everyone else – will be balancing their timetable to pick up the kids and arrange the next holiday.

Issue signature analysis (ISA) charts the customer decision-maker's world from the inside out – i.e. taking a view of business priorities and perceptions from *their* vantage point. Decision-influencers are interviewed and asked a series of questions formed around what matters to them. The purpose of the exercise is to understand where the buying priority sits in the complex and congested world of the decision-influencer. Emotional and functional issues described by a decision-influencer are charted, and a 'signature' is created that represents a unique inside-looking-out view from the buyer's perspective. Resulting signatures can be aggregated to reveal a composite view of what a buying community thinks.

Issue signature analysis chart example

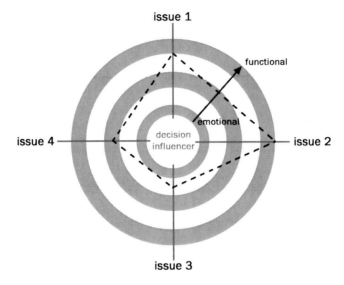

Each of the identified issues is measured for its *functional* or *emotional* impact on the buyer. The level of importance for each issue is weighted. The results are presented on a target chart for ease of interpretation as shown on the previous page. ISA is the only way I know of doing this. Decision-makers are more likely to be influenced by issues that are personal.

Emotional issues are illustrated on the target chart by their close proximity to the centre. It is not necessarily the case that customers will change their buying behaviour and prioritize *emotional* issues over *functional issues*. For instance, let's say you need to buy a new suit for work. I'm sure there are many better things you could think of spending your money on but that doesn't mean that you won't buy a suit if you need one!

So why is it important to develop a deeper understanding of customer issues? I believe it's important because, by recognising and addressing emotional issues suppliers can significantly differentiate their offers, particularly when deals come down to a short-list. For example, let's say that you need to buy a new car and the two cars you have on your short-list are pretty-much the same price and specification. For you, the fact that one supplier is offering free servicing for three years makes a difference because you've just had a bad experience with excessive service costs on your previous vehicle. If the salesperson knew of these bad experiences, it is likely that he could have clinched the deal by simply placing an emphasis in his offer on peace-of-mind on servicing. The outcome is to all intents and purposes the same – the customer buys a car – but the supplier that knows more about the emotional needs of the customer, and how to satisfy them, is more likely to win.

The influence of ISA on offer communications strategy

The influence of emotional and functional issues on product and service sales will vary from industry to industry. For example, functional sectors such as utilities or telecommunications providers might not care too much about emotional influences on the sales process if theirs is the only option available. But the nature of 21st century markets means that most organizations have to care more about emotional buying considerations and reflect their deeper appreciation of customer needs in the way they communicate their offers.

Nick and I employed ISA for an assignment that looked into the usefulness of software tools for professional digital printing companies. Our client wanted to introduce some new products that would add value to their hardware.

They wanted to know which products would appeal most to buying decision-makers. Using ISA, we were able to quickly understand that workforce skills and a shortage of trained people was the most significant emotional issue. It meant that any software demonstration disks supplied to customers would most likely remain on the desk unopened because the production managers responsible for making buying decisions had no time to look at them.

One hot topic of the moment was variable data printing, which production managers said they were enthusiastic about. However the software industry had been authoring solutions for use on personal computers whereas it was more common for designers to use Apple Macs.

This meant that if production managers were to adopt a variable data printing software product for PCs, they would probably be using the software themselves and have to work even longer hours.

In response to this feedback our client partnered with a software company that provided an Apple Mac solution for variable data printing. This meant that *designers* could include this task as part of their day jo, and the production managers were no longer required to shoulder the responsibility. Nick and I recognised at the time that without the thoroughness of ISA and its ability to visualize the emotional needs of the customer, we could easily have fed the message back to our client that the production managers we had spoken were really interested in variable data printing.

In our experience, ISA provides a competitive advantage to organizations by helping marketers understand how to shape their offer messages in a way that tugs at the emotions of the target reader. I remember interviewing a customer for one of our clients at an event and he said to me, "I like these events because they help me to understand the questions I need to have answered." When buyers are choosing between similar offers from reputable market players, the factor that will often tip the balance is the commitment of one supplier to invest money in educating the customer. This type of insight results from use of ISA as a day-to-day operational process.

In 2005, Nick and I were asked to research IT network security needs of companies based in Europe. Network security was emerging as a key issue facing the industry that supplied multi-function printer-copier-scanner-fax products. All the players were suffering. Nobody in the market had managed to piece together the information that network managers needed to satisfy their bosses that the technology on offer was 'safe'. A year later, the technology available in the market really hadn't changed much but the subject was no longer a concern to the network managers. Why not? Because network managers by now understood the questions and the answers they needed to

build contingencies and appropriate risk management precautions into their procurement and operational strategies. Had one of the players in this market understood the concerns of network managers and fashioned collateral to outline the issues, they would have been able to steal a march on their competitors.

Insight-driven marketing methods have consistently helped q to keep its clients six months ahead of the market. What could *your* business do with six months' head start against your competitors?

The positive influence of issue signature analysis

Once ISA charts have been authored for the many different customer segments that an organization serves, it becomes far easier to distil the opportunities that exist for delivering customer value. When appropriately applied, deeper insight into *clients' issues* results in *better fit* offers and relevant user-centred design built into products, but its influence can go much deeper and change the way an organization structures itself to align its resources, and satisfy the evidenced needs of the client groups it serves.

Illustration of the issue signature analysis (ISA) alignment model

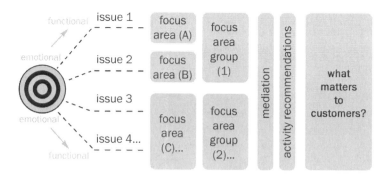

This happens by examining the relationship between the client group *issue signatures* and the digital DNA of the enterprise. Supporting software captures and examines customer *signals* derived from the ISA process and assigns these to known *focus area themes* that formalize how an organization *thinks*. The mediator assigned to the focus area topic will be responsible for *making sense* of the signals. Activity recommendations that result from the mediation process might suggest that a change to actions already adopted is necessary or lead to an even more dramatic influence on strategic direction and the structural alignment of the organization.

In 2004, Nick and I conducted an ISA project examining the buying priorities of production managers working for professional printing companies. This was an important client group for our customer.

Whilst the feedback from customers was overwhelmingly positive towards our client, the project uncovered a series of customer issues. These issues had little to do with the scope of the work the marketing team had asked us to focus on, but we felt it had strategic significance for the way the organization structured its operations. Our project sponsor agreed that it would be worthwhile to have a separate meeting with a broader audience of managers to discuss the alignment issues.

In readiness for this meeting, Nick and I authored a *report* that presented the ISA findings and the important emotional and functional issues that had been uncovered by the ISA process. Some of the focus areas covered by ISA issues included such things as training, materials and supplies policy, helping the customer to win more business.

The report helped to provide the management team with a window to align their business activities and act on some of these issues in advance of their closest competitive rivals who were seen to be equally lacking in the way they conducted their business.

It came as a great endorsement to the effectiveness of the ISA process to find, six months later, that the issues the ISA process had identified were being represented by competitors in their messaging at the Dusseldorf Messe trade show.

(5) Embeds USE of insight in decision-making

I call the integrated information system that gathers customer insight from all these sources and forms a holistic view of what the enterprise knows about its customers an insight management system. Insight management brings the external world of customer value into alignment with the digital DNA and strategy of the enterprise.

Illustration of an insight management system

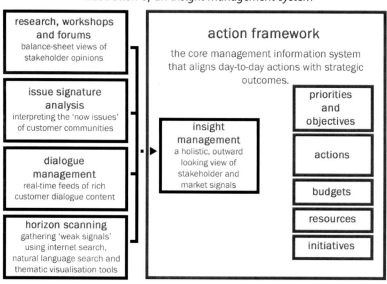

How insight management works

Each item of insight is called a *signal*. As signals are submitted to the insight management system, further attributes are added that qualify the relevance of the signal to the organization, a weighting to qualify its perceived importance, the date it was entered, who entered it, where it has come from etc. They are also catalogued into *focus areas* that start to describe the way the organization needs to think. Focus areas are essential to align signals to the appropriate people in the enterprise *(the mediators)*, who know how best to act on the signal, and to the strategy and actions of the organization.

Signals are aligned to the way the organization thinks by assigning focus areas that provide an alignment to the organization's strategy

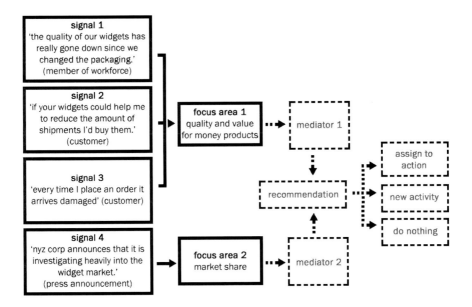

It has been our experience that there are three common outcomes that might occur when processing signals:

1. The signal relates to known customer value and actions that are already taking place. On these occasions signals can be associated with the relevant action and their contribution considered complete.

2. The signal introduces 'new information' that the mediator believes demands a new activity to be considered.

3. The signal requires no action to be taken, perhaps because it is old news or its value is already known.

Described over the next few pages are a selection of insight capture systems that operate today. They are:

Internal insight   Tools and methods to gather and share insight that already exists somewhere within the organization.

Staff inclusion   Programmes to involve staff in the formation of strategy that creates an opportunity to gather workforce insight whilst encouraging 'buy-in'.

CRM 2.0   Tools and methods to gather and share insight that already exists somewhere within the organization.

Horizon scanning   Capturing weak signals that indicate changes in market conditions.

The usefulness of insight is closely interlinked with how knowledge is generally managed and used within the enterprise. There are two main knowledge perspectives that organizations must come to grips with if they want to extract value from knowledge:

Inner space   Knowing and leveraging what is already known to the organization but is poorly shared.

Outer space   Scanning the horizon to learn what's going on in the market to identify threats and opportunities.

Internal insight

Extracting value from information sources within an enterprise requires both *curious people* and effective processes to rapidly build relationships between pockets of information to create 'new knowledge' – a process that I call **information bridging**.

Bridging is about tapping into pockets of knowledge that exist within and beyond the enterprise to forge new value. Common bridging forms include people-to-process, people-to-data, across systems and across organizations. Harnessing pools of information (normally held within silos) means the usefulness and value of knowledge can be transformed. Nowhere is this more relevant than in the process of client engagement.

In one case, NDMC was invited to support a knowledge-bridging project for a global professional services organization that wanted to leverage its broad portfolio of skills to win new business.

To harness this knowledge and translate it into value, customer relationship staff needed to know what solutions and resources they had at their disposal. This information was held in Human Resource (HR) management systems and customer databases. A solution was needed to build a coherent, holistic view of information from a variety of sources – and in doing so created new knowledge. To achieve this, a series of **information bridges** was required:

1. Bridging between MARKETS and CLIENTS – To identify events, current affairs etc. within a market and then define relationships between these events and the specific circumstances and interests of a client (i.e. how could emerging events impact the client?)

2. Bridging between CLIENT NEEDS and CAPABILITY – To identify a problem or new challenge facing a client and then define relationships between this new requirement and the ability of the provider organization to deliver a product or service.

3. Bridging between CAPABILITY and CREDENTIALS – To evidence, through credentials of previous work, the capabilities of the organization such as projects performed for other, similar, clients.

4. Bridging between CAPABILITY and RESOURCES – To define relationships between the identified capability requirement and the resources available to the organization to deliver a product or service (such as technical competencies and staff skills).

The implementation of this solution meant that the client could fully exploit its 'pockets' of information by looking across a range of data sources.

There are many circumstances where new information bridges bring value to corporations. I highlight two examples here:

Bridging between old and new systems, for new business models

When business models change, so too do the demands for information. Often, new strategies fail to be implemented successfully because new information requirements cannot be met within reasonable timeframes. As organizations seek to find new ways of engaging with existing and new customer communities, working with channel and affinity partners becomes a strategic priority for some. Bridging technologies provide a new useful top layer to back-office information systems. They are an essential for the effective gathering and sharing of information across social networks.

Bridging between back-office systems

Corporations frequently identify new requirements for exploiting information held within multiple back-office systems – perhaps to support process rationalization, cross-organizational customer-focusing strategies, migration of operations to a regional shared service centre, or harmonization projects resulting from mergers or acquisitions. In such cases, bridging technologies provide interim or permanent integrated information solutions, creating new, better-fit operational systems. The reason why this is so difficult is because process specific systems are normally all different in the way they manage their information and were never really designed to 'share'.

Information bridging across multiple systems (housing example)

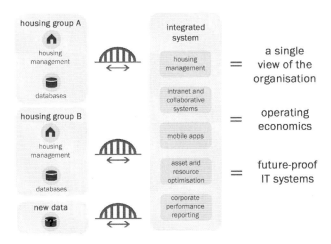

The preceding illustration examples two housing associations merging and identifying a need for a common information platform that bridges across existing systems. In this example, whilst some of the information needed to support a new web-based information management platform originates from existing database systems, new demands for data management (i.e. databases) are created, encouraged by new ways of working and operational demands that result from harmonization.

This is a common situation that can easily be resolved by information-bridging software that has the ability not only gather information from existing resources, but to build new ones, either creating new tables and fields in existing databases or new databases to satisfy new information processes.

Staff inclusion

Since the 1970s companies such as Ford Motor Company, Marriott and 3M have used *future search* conferences to involve hundreds, even thousands of people simultaneously in strategic change processes. Entire factories would come together to contribute their ideas for strategic action plans. Taking your organization 'off-line' for a day in the 2000s is not an option.

NDMC developed an *inclusion workshop programme* to support the strategy formation process. It consists of a balanced set of interviews with a sample set of stakeholder groups, a practical means of gathering a balanced view of the robustness and suitability of a strategy. Stakeholder insight, when captured in a consistent way and fashioned into a formalized information flow by relational database technology, evidences the basis-of-decision at that point in time. Managers are able to remind themselves why they chose the path they did after time has passed and outcomes of the policy decisions have become clear. Inclusion programmes immediately start the 'energizing' process to knit an organization together and help management teams to identify 'pressure points' that inhibit change and harmonize all existing plans together to form a joined-up view of strategy.

This content is added to other sources of insight to create a holistic view of *what matters* to stakeholders that might include:

- Workshops specific to the strategy formation process.
- Surveys: mystery shopper surveys, Internet surveys and internal surveys (e.g. departmental customer surveys, Investors in People, Institute of Customer Service, etc.)
- Focus groups.
- Customer reception and one-stop-shop exit polls.
- Customer service and satisfaction surveys.

The Inclusion Process

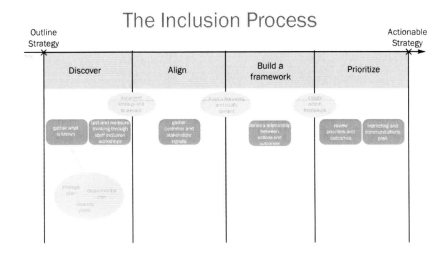

How the process works

Outline   Workshops are conducted with the Chief Executive and management team to distil the vision of the organization. Some thought should be given to the approach adopted here. Is it better to meet with the Chief Executive, the Board and the Executive Team individually or in groups? There are advantages and disadvantages to each approach but the greatest risk lies in engaging executives who might lose their jobs as the result of a strategy being implemented – when the boardroom is aligned to a smaller number of portfolio areas.

Workshops   These are conducted with all levels of the stakeholder community – managers, workforce, Board members, customers, partners, etc. It is helpful that there is no cross-over of seniority levels, as few people will be prepared to speak openly with their boss in the room (should their comments be critical about management support or facilities). The workshop format closely follows that of the process for building a balanced scorecard strategy map. The same four *scorecard perspective* questions are incorporated to provide a comparative analysis. Responses are catalogued into *focus areas*. Once each question has been answered by the workshop participants, delegates are invited to vote on the recommendation they feel should be put forward to the CEO. This bonds the group together by giving them the confidence that they are directly contributing to policy formation. It also gives planners a *weighting* towards priority stakeholder issues.

Report   This early stage report incorporates a 'straw-man' strategy map and scorecard. It is likely this will be the first time that the organization has seen a view of itself according to its stakeholder community priorities and perceptions. One can expect to find a few surprises that require careful handling with Board members and executives. Normally a closed-door session with the CEO is required to provide advance warning of the good and bad news carried in this report.

Alignment   The next process stage is to draw together all the captured insight resulting from the *inclusion programme* so far and align it with existing departmental and strategic plans to build a complete picture of what managers think needs to be done. This will typically uncover a whole range of activities occurring at departmental level that have been hidden away in departmental budgets and that appear not to contribute to the end goals of the enterprise. What is needed is a pragmatic assessment of what should be done about these actions in the light of the big picture view that has now been established.

Framework   Develop an Action Framework (see Chapter 8) that focuses the available resources of the enterprise and its partner contributors on actions that deliver the most important strategic outcomes.

Signals and focus areas

The comments of stakeholders are like grains of sand in your hand. The value of a single grain might be worth more than the Sahara but the trick is not to let the grains of sand pass through your fingers until the value of each grain can be assessed. This is why a database-driven insight management system is needed to manage the volume of content effectively and not lose value due to the sheer volume of data.

At one point, Nick and I were engaged in a project with an IT hardware company. We had been asked to meet with their customers to understand and feed back on a particular aspect of their strategy. We were flying around five countries in Europe to provide a balanced view of what customers were saying. Nick had the opportunity to meet with a senior IT officer of one of the largest Dutch banks, which was in the early stages of moving forward with a major deployment with our client. They had a number of their hardware products already onsite and had plans to buy many more units. Nick sat through a four-hour interview with this IT officer as he presented the weak points of our client's offer and client engagement approach.

Nick knew at once that, even though in this project we had spoken with close to 250 organizations, this single interview meant more to the success of our client's strategy than the other 249 put together. This account represented our client's best-fit customer profile. The interviewee, the most senior technical decision-influencer within the client account, was evidencing a succession of dysfunctional processes and behaviours that were inevitably going to cause real issues with other – similar – customers and ultimately determine the ability of our client to compete for business.

Once signals have been captured they must be contextualized and presented in a way that the organization can make sense of and act on.

- Use of focus areas makes it much easier to translate stakeholder issues into themes an organization can understand.

- Focus areas align insight to existing objectives and management themes. New subject matter tests assumptions that are the basis of strategy formation.

- Authoring of focus areas is achieved by examining the incoming signals and aggregating subject matter in a way that mirrors the strategic thinking of the organization.

- Signals captured during an inclusion programme provide a useful indicator of what needs to happen next and bring clarity to the next steps needed to achieve stakeholder outcomes.

A chart reporting on the outcomes of an inclusion programme

management			staff		delivery		concentrating on the customer	
leadership	empowerment	culture of communic- ating	skills	attitude and behaviour	process	resources	value for the customer	access
22%			21%		34%		23%	
19%	14%	67%	19%	81%	76%	24%	43%	57%

What the chart shows:

Signals are grouped and measured by their **focus area group** – in this example we have *Management (22%), Workforce (21%), Delivery (34%)* and *Concentrating on the customer (23%)* – which are themselves aggregations of focus areas that in the Management focus area group are Leadership (19%), Empowerment (14%) and Culture of communicating (67%).

This top line view makes it easy for executives to understand how to prioritize and align their activities to respond to stakeholder feedback. At the same time, all of the source data – the original signals – are held within the insight management system to provide an evidence trail.

Establishing a common set of questions with which to gather stakeholder opinions encourages a consistent formula for analysis that means feedback can be aligned to known activity areas.

The benefits of stakeholder inclusion are many:

- Stakeholder feedback is the most important 'checks-and-balances' mechanism to sanity-check strategic plans.
- It qualifies the scope and fit of objectives and their ability to fulfil stakeholder expectations.
- It shapes actions and suggests new activities.
- People rarely argue with their own suggestions.
- It identifies *future champions* and *well-poisoners*.
- It identifies weak processes and quick wins.
- It provides a barometer of the enterprise's state of health and ability to think and act as one.

I have conducted a number of inclusion programmes. Without exception they have proven to be valuable to our clients. There is a genuine excitement that comes from new ideas and quick wins that spring from the minds of fellow workers, people who have been shuffling past the door of the CEO for years and who have never had the opportunity to share their wonderful ideas. Whilst I could never do them all justice, here are just a few of the many learning experiences that have resulted from inclusion programmes:

The refuse collector who believed in contingency planning

During one of our workshops with a mixed contingent of front-line workforce for a local authority, as we were walking around the table to share ideas on the 'learning and growth perspective', one of the refuse collectors said, "I'm not sure how important it is, but I think the management team should think about contingency plans". Surprised, I asked him what he meant, and he informed me that the Council had recently changed the refuse collection timings and this had led to many customers being missed because they weren't informed of the change (apparently letters were due to be sent out but failed to get out to all the customers). He explained that as a consequence of the error, customers had called in to the Council in their hundreds. The call centre could not cope with the dramatic increase in the volume of inbound calls. The manager of the section decided to go out with one of the refuse collection teams to 'be with his men' but this left the receptionists in tears as they were trying to respond to aggressive and sometimes abusive customers without any management support.

The delegate made the point that the Council had no procedures to deal with this situation even though at some point it was likely to happen – and could happen again in the future.

When we shared these comments with senior executives they confessed that they had no formalized contingency plans. It should come as no surprise that some refuse collectors are intelligent and alert workers, who can contribute good ideas.

The IT Department's green form

Seemingly ridiculous levels of bureaucracy can form over time, crippling the activities of an organization and remaining invisible to the executive team. I was leading a workshop with the administrative team of another local authority when one of the delegates raised an issue about the level of IT support. She explained that IT insisted on all its customers completing a green form. The purpose of the green form was to qualify what IT was being asked to do and obtain three levels of management sign-off before IT even started to look at the request. This process could take days and sometimes weeks, and sometimes the request would be received by IT only for one of the IT team to tell them they were asking for the wrong thing. In the example quoted to me, a part-time member of the workforce had been working with her for six months without a working PC, which made her appointment far less useful to the rest of the team. In accordance with the protocols of the IT department, a green form was completed on the day the temp arrived. The process of administration and qualification took its course – six months to be precise. On the day the temp was leaving her PC arrived. Perfect timing!

Keeping a copy of every message

Trust can decay to such a low point that new interrupter processes emerge to cover over the cracks. On one occasion we were asking the workshop group what their colleagues could do to help them to be more effective and one of the delegates answered, "It would be great if I didn't have to keep a duplicate record of every message I take."

When we investigated this comment it transpired that the administration team were copying and filing a record of every message that they passed to 'certain colleagues' who could be relied upon to say that they had never received messages that were taken by administration. This had led over time to a blanket procedure to keep a written record of all messages taken. Trust at a low ebb.

A brief word about rationale-based policy making

In the private sector, the fluid nature of markets and the need to qualify customers not in terms of segments but as individuals has fuelled interest in evidence-based policy making. Likewise, as UK politicians face a more critical and challenging public, the public sector has also started to recognise the need to evidence the relevance and usefulness of policy decisions. Evidence-based policy-making is a term that is in vogue in the UK public sector and is no doubt circulating in the corridors of Whitehall and the Treasury. So what is it?

The terminology sounds self-explanatory but there are two interpretations:

1. The way policy is formulated is based on evidence.
2. Decision makers seek evidence that justifies policy decisions they have in mind.

I believe a more appropriate description of a balanced approach to policy formulation is *rationale-based policy-making* – i.e. executives should be able to explain at a future point in time the rationale behind the decisions they have made. Leaders should not adopt a slavish approach to making decisions purely based on what their customers and other stakeholders may say. Customers or citizens with the best of intentions may not understand the complex nature of organizations and the political and operational nuances within which they are forced to work. At the same time, would Sony have ever produced a Walkman if they had waited for a customer to evidence the need?

Even in the future, leaders will stick out their necks and follow their instinct and intuition when making policy. They are likely to do this however with the benefit of more stakeholder feedback. At NDMC, we encourage policy-making based on a clearer understanding of what stakeholders want and the opportunities and threats that become visible through research. That doesn't detract from the occasional need for inspirational thought and entrepreneurial instinct.

Horizon scanning (Tools to support *anticipationomics*)

The successful organizations of the 21st century will possess a capacity to scan their horizon for weak *signals* that indicate early signs of changes to market conditions, including early warnings of competitive activities – noting that competitors might emerge from different markets. Horizon scanning is a method used by organizations to capture weak signals of market change.

It is a 'threats and opportunities' radar, a technology and process layer that captures and helps analysts to filter weak signals of change – the slightest breath of wind – so that the enterprise can position itself to exploit it.

Visualization technologies funded by the patents, gambling and military sectors have emerged over the last decade to capture and interpret vast amounts of content and distil potentially newsworthy reports. This technology is able to crawl through large amounts of structured and unstructured content in search of conceptual themes formed around natural language search tools.

Unfortunately, inward-looking management teams have encouraged organizational structures that have been slower to evolve. They have not geared their processes to look outwardly at markets and stakeholder needs. Limited capacity to make use of emerging threats and opportunities being captured has diluted opportunities to benefit from this technology-driven capability. This has led to a ponderous take-up of *horizon-scanning* technologies.

Horizon-scanning technologies can profile market changes and the activities of competitive peers and major clients

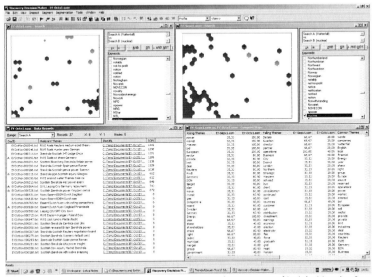

Screenshot courtesy of Insight Mapping Inc.

Organizations that fail to take *horizon scanning* seriously are likely to be those that are culturally slow to change and embrace innovation. These organizations are the first to fall when new market structures emerge. There is a further risk that some organizations will place too much reliance on technology when developing processes that are intended to listen and interpret the needs of stakeholders and markets. Horizon-scanning technologies have been around for many years and they work. It is governments that have taking the lead in horizon scanning. Driven by the major 21st century threats of disease and terrorism, governments are actively seeking mechanisms that will give them advanced warning of what might happen in the future. The UK Government's *Modernizing Government White Paper* encouraged civil servants and policy makers to *become more forward-* and outward-looking, to exchange ideas with other countries on policy making, on delivering services and on using information technology in new and innovative ways. By 2002 the UK Central Government's *Department for Environment Food and Rural Affairs* (DEFRA) already had an active horizon-scanning programme with its own definition for the term.

It reads, "The systematic examination of potential threats, opportunities and likely future developments which are at the margins of current thinking and planning. Horizon scanning may explore novel and unexpected issues, as well as persistent problems or trends." It has to be said that this policy has commonly been interpreted by the UK public sector in systems that scan only pre-vetted information sources. Not a great way of capturing new insight! But initiatives such as this have created a demand for technology solutions that have prepared the ground for commercial tools and good practice methods for horizon scanning.

The challenge has been convincing corporations not used to looking outwards at markets that they really should. What's the argument? You need this new capability because if you don't SCARY THINGS WILL HAPPEN? (Take it from me, the "big-hairy-monsters-in-the-closet" appeal for common sense doesn't really work in business).

True there are plenty of examples where inward-looking management teams have been caught out by markets in transition and this is only likely to increase, but there are no guarantees that just because you look out to sea you're going to spot the icebergs. However, when your ship ventures across 60°latitude, it would be unwise not to put out an iceberg watch!

It is difficult for managers to come to terms with the fact that in the next few years they will have to master the processes needed to scan their horizon for changes in market conditions. Unlike some information processes however, the technology for horizon scanning has been around for some years and works well. So why isn't everyone doing horizon scanning? Well, it's what I call an umbrella technology – you only need one when it rains. And it's still only starting to drizzle. With horizon scanning installed as a business process, an agilized enterprise will be at the door when opportunity knocks.

Building a *corporate radar* that identifies weak signals requires that:

1. The enterprise must firstly instigate a **content value assessment** to determine what knowledge matters most to its success.

2. The enterprise must develop an **accountability model** that qualifies WHO has the potential to extract value from this knowledge.

3. An **insight management system** is installed that manages the process of carrying the 'grains of sand' through the enterprise to the appropriate people and then manages the mediation process to determine whether this information is valuable to the enterprise, and if it is, how to act on it to achieve the greatest benefit.

4. **Advanced search technologies** are installed that have the capability to spider across all internal and external sources of information including funded news feed sources like Factiva® and Bloomberg®.

This is how it works:

1. Search 'radar' scans the horizon (web, news-feeds, internal sources) for weak signals relating to the areas of knowledge value identified in the 'content value assessment'

2. Content is combined and visualized using intelligent self-organizing mapping software that reveals thematic relationships between different elements of content.

3. An analyst monitors these visualizations and reports on themes that are identified as representing potential opportunities or threats.

4. On a regular frequency – perhaps monthly – a meeting is held to discuss these new threats and opportunities and to assess the usefulness of this knowledge and how it can be turned into value by the organization.

Rabbit holes

It takes time, skill and therefore investment to find new opportunities for innovation and market advantage. The idea that management teams should be aggressively hunting for opportunities emerging through changes in market conditions is for most organizations a distant ambition. Most management capacity today is absorbed by inefficient information systems and an inappropriate inward-looking management focus. The process of learning from customers and markets is inevitably time-consuming and requires a blend of creative thinking and analytical skills. It is often the case that you need to look down a great many *rabbit holes* before you find a *rabbit*. Supporting the insight process is arguably a task best left to people and organizations that search and analyze knowledge as a 'day job'.

Making sense of knowledge

Taking information from the outside world and placing it in information processes that take place within the enterprise is critical in extracting value from the horizon-scanning process. As a child, did you ever play with one of those picture mazes that show a series of scribbled lines mixed together in a picture and you have to work out where each thread begins and ends? Then think of the way that organizations 'listen' to the outside world as being a giant version of this and you'd be close. Each thread of information must be carefully woven into how the enterprise thinks and works. It must be routed through to the right person, with the correct balance of knowledge, awareness of issues, aptitude, etc. – otherwise the value of this information is lost.

The analysis of data will not by itself produce new ideas.

Edward de Bono

In most organizations, the only time information gets contextualized and passes through the outer shell of the organization is when (a) somebody happens across information by luck, or (b) somebody can contextualize the information into a vocabulary that the organization can understand and then can place the information in an information flow that directs it through to the right people.

How to listen and learn from customers

Listening to customers is a competitive differentiator, but as a subject area it is poorly understood. Remarkably, it is finding its feet as a profession. As soon as the word 'customer' is mentioned in personnel departments, thoughts turn to Customer Service, which has for a long time and in many organizations been about attempting to sell – rather than listen – more to customers.

The secret of listening to customers in the 21st century is no different to the skills that Alfred Tack promoted to field sales people in the 1970s. It's about taking an interest in what the customer has to say and genuinely believing that, if you listen hard enough, they will tell you more about your business, your products and your future than you could ever have imagined.

Further reading and resources

For resources on issue signature analysis, visit the NDMC website at http://www.ndmc.uk.com or email info@ndmc.uk.com.

Checklist for **Insight**

	Qualification	Score
☹ **A cocooned enterprise**	The management team has cocooned itself from customers.	☐
	Managers rarely speak directly to customers.	☐
	Customer feedback comes via customer satisfaction surveys.	☐
☺ **Dedicated skills**	Specialist skills are employed to understand customer value.	☐
☺ **Insight capture is seen as 'strategic'**	Made a strategic priority.	☐
	Insight capture embedded in core processes including:	☐
☺ **Formalized analysis of customer issues**	Formalized processes such as ISA are used to analyze customer issues and requirements.	☐
☺ **Insight is used in decision-making**	Insight is used in decision-making processes to influence tactical and strategic decision making.	☐
☺ **Internal insight**	The organization employs information bridging techniques.	☐
☺ **Staff inclusion**	Inclusion workshops.	☐
☺ **Horizon scanning**	Horizon scanning.	☐

13

(C) Curiosity

God gives every bird a worm, but he does not throw it into the nest. Swedish proverb

(1) A work environment that discourages curiosity

An agilized enterprise has to anticipate what might happen next. This requires an unrelenting culture of curiosity.

Curiosity is the life energy of a 21st century agilized enterprise. For organizations that depend upon innovation for their competitive edge, it is *THE* competitive differentiator. Without curiosity, knowledge has no value because the way the organization listens and acts on knowledge does not change. Knowledge is not translated into anything of value. It takes a delicate blend of *curiosity and useful information* to result in a competitive advantage. To kick-start this magical chemical reaction, the enterprise workforce needs TIME to invest in being curious.

Building a culture of curiosity

I first came across the phrase 'creating a culture of curiosity' when the then Chief Executive of Norwich Union expressed his desire for his management team to encourage it within their workforce. I was left wondering why the leader of an insurance company that offers such seemingly predictable products should want to have his workforce spending any of their working day being curious! But then, every success starts with a good idea and every idea starts with someone who is *curious*.

Scott Cook, one of the founders of Intuit, had the idea for Quicken software by watching his wife pay bills by cheque. eBay was started because one man was looking to buy a sweet dispenser (called a PEZ dispenser) for his wife and realized that there were probably many people who wanted something they could not find. That heartfelt desire to dig deeper is the beginning of *curiosity*. It allows people to bring flexibility and improvement to organizations that might be stale and think only in a structured way that follows the *latent instruction* set bred into the organizational psyche.

Encouraging people to become curious is not easy, particularly if it challenges cultural norms.

Judging the value of new knowledge is difficult until that knowledge is translated into a business advantage. Being alert to new opportunities and threats only becomes business-critical when the consequences of not doing so are fatal. Decisions based on poor information can ultimately be fatal to corporations. There are examples where large organizations have met their tsunami wave because they simply weren't looking for early warning signs. Exxon is one case example in the public domain, an oil company that failed to consider the possible consequences of overstretching its supply lines. When the single-hulled Exxon Valdez ran aground and spilled 11 million gallons of oil into Alaska's most scenic waters it dealt a fatal blow to the business.

A fluid workforce increases the risk of failure through poor internal controls. It is not uncommon for a *business tsunami* to come from within, as was the case with Barings Bank when its share value collapsed on February 26, 1995. In this case, safeguards were not installed to check the activities of one trader, Nick Leeson, who lost the company $1.4 billion by speculating on the Singapore International Monetary Exchange.

It would be easy to think that, in an agilized enterprise, workers all become star gazers and nobody is working on the necessary day-to-day processes that *make the money*. This is far from the truth. Though agilized enterprises are highly customer value-focused, they are nevertheless efficient enterprises to begin with. The fact that the enterprise needs to be more alert to change does not mean that it will always employ internal resources to do the looking. It is likely that a wide variety of duties will be outsourced to networks of individuals engaged in providing specific services such as insight capture, research, user-centred design analysis and improvement.

Understanding HOW to support curiosity

For decades, the word *knowledge* in the world of corporations has been hijacked by academics, technologists and management consultants keen to help organizations leverage information but not really understanding *why* and therefore *how*. The better informed people are, the better will be the decisions they make – so the argument goes. It is difficult to place a measure on the value attributed to systems that promise better quality of information and improved basis-of-decision, accepting that:

1. It might still result in someone making a bad decision.
2. The information might itself encourage the wrong course of action (have you ever trusted a radio traffic announcement that tells you the road ahead is blocked only to find out later it wasn't?)
3. You might adopt systems to identify market opportunities but never come across any that are actually relevant to your organization!

Accepting these points, I take the view that I would rather managers have some useful information than *none at all*. Often, the information that people need to make more informed decisions is already somewhere in the organization. Therefore, the initial challenge is to share what is already known, not to find new information. Creating the environment to encourage individuals to become curious requires managers to involve their workforce in plans and strategies. How can individuals be expected to source new ideas and recommendations for process improvement if they don't understand what the organization does, how it delivers value to customers and how the things they do in their day job make a difference to the performance of the organization as a whole?

To become effective creators of new knowledge, workers must have a clear appreciation of how processes work and how their contributions influence corporate outcomes, and must be able to interpret the value of knowledge and innovation to the organization.

(2) Encouraging double-loop learning

There are two main outcomes of using knowledge:

1. **Doing things better** and finding ways to improve the way that things work now.
2. **Doing better things** and finding different approaches that help to achieve an outcome, even though the process might be totally different to how things are done today.

These two concepts are called single- and double-loop learning.

"Suppose an organization manufactures a product X. When the employees of that organization detect and attempt to correct error in order to manufacture the product X, that is single-loop learning; but when they begin to confront the question whether product X should be manufactured, that is double-loop learning, because they are now questioning underlying organization policies and objectives." Argyris, C. (1977). Double-loop learning in organizations. Harvard Business Review, 55(5), 115-125.

Whilst single-loop learning makes improvements possible, double-loop learning provides the opportunity for step-change which is a fundamental characteristic of the agilized enterprise. Double-loop learning demands human curiosity. Curiosity is a very human process. Innovation frequently comes as the result of personal experiences that are introduced by individuals who have encountered completely different life events. These circumstances might make no sense to a computer because we programme computers to rationalize behaviours rather than look for contradictions! The ability of the human brain to irrationally jump from one concept to the next is perhaps our greatest gift (other than the opposable thumb).

We all think differently and respond differently to the same stimuli. Have you ever played that rapid-fire word game where, in groups of 3 or 4, one person comes up with the first thing that jumps into their mind and the next person then has to think of the first thing it makes them think about? As a family, this game has often kept my children occupied for hours when travelling coast-to-coast by car. It makes you realise why it is that no-one holds the exclusive on bright ideas.

Effective double-loop learning takes all kinds of thinkers

I have noticed through my career that some people are naturally better at logical thought (i.e. taking one logical step after another, as you would want to work out a mathematical problem) whilst others are more adept at making big leaps that, when taken on face value, appear to be illogical and unstructured.

I describe these two thought process types as straight-line thinking (that's Nick Lawrie with his great gift of understanding how processes build and work) and curvy thinking (which is me), the sort of person that comes up with so many ideas that it takes a straight-line thinker to separate the truly ingenious ideas from the mulch of complete nonsense! Apply these two different thought process types to being curious and you quickly see how both approaches can deliver values to the organization.

When presented with 'new information':

- A straight-line thinker will be the first to spot a missing link or a step that is illogical or out of place – and ask WHY?
- A curvy-thinker will spot two or three obscure concepts and rapidly look for ways to build them together, even though they don't appear to fit together or have any relationship at all.

The great story behind 3M's invention of Post-it® Notes is perhaps one of the best reasons why human curiosity and innovation will always be a key ingredient in extracting the *value* from information.

No-one got the idea of Post-it® Notes and then stayed up at night to invent it. A man named Spencer Silver was working in the 3M research laboratories in 1970 trying to find a strong adhesive. Silver developed a new adhesive, but it was even weaker than what 3M already manufactured. It stuck to objects, but could easily be lifted off. It was super-weak instead of super-strong. No-one knew what to do with the stuff, but Silver didn't discard it. Then one Sunday four years later, another 3M scientist named Arthur Fry was singing in the choir of his local church. He used markers to keep his place in the hymnal, but they kept falling out of the book. Remembering Silver's adhesive, Fry used some to coat his markers. Success! With the

weak adhesive, the markers stayed in place, yet lifted off without damaging the pages. 3M began distributing Post-it® Notes nationwide in 1980 -- ten years after Silver developed the super-weak adhesive. Today they are one of the most popular office products available.

Until we have silicon chips implanted in our heads, human instinct and the inquisitiveness of the human spirit will remain an essential ingredient in the process of translating insight into new ideas!

To achieve double-loop learning, organizations must:

- Understand how knowledge is created or captured (i.e. market research, horizon scanning, dialogue management, etc.).

- Understand how knowledge can be routed to the right parts of the enterprise (information flow and social network analysis).

- Find mechanisms to translate insight into value by developing curiosity and innovation in the enterprise (i.e. behavioural value management, issue signature analysis, etc.).

- Expose members of staff to a compelling vision and strategy, and make clear how their role contributes to these outcomes.

- Ensure the workforce identifies with the organization's values and abilities – so they are able to spot weak signals of new threats and opportunities even though these might not reflect the 'here and now' reality of what the organization does and what it is capable of (i.e. how could Sony tell its workforce to test demand for a Walkman device when nobody had any concept of what a Walkman was?)

- Encourage a workforce culture that rewards innovation and creativity.

Even with all these factors embedded into operational behaviours, there is no guarantee that double-loop learning will happen. The unfortunate hit-and-miss nature of innovation is that there are no guarantees that there is anything 'out there' worth learning, or that if this insight did arrive on the door-step of the enterprise, the people on watch will recognise its value.

Alexander Linden, Research Director at Gartner is quoted as having said, "As computer technologies cannot understand human information needs, they are consequently only of limited help in filtering the flood of information available. However, it is easier for companies to implement technology rather than changing the principles and culture in a company to foster information flow. The question of where, in this rapidly changing business environment, a company can provide unique value to its customers has become a key concern for corporate leaders."

(3) Extracting value from knowledge

In Chapter 10 I introduce the concept of *anticipationomics*. Knowledge helps organizations to anticipate change. New technologies such as horizon scanning, thematic search systems and sophisticated self-organizing map data analysis tools can be employed to identify, make sense of, and therefore *anticipate* opportunities and plan for them faster than the competition.

To exploit the value of knowledge, the *usefulness* of knowledge needs to be well understood and its channels of use formalized.

It's not always obvious when data becomes information or information becomes knowledge. Subject matter that is irrelevant today can suddenly become relevant tomorrow due to related events. The value that comes from information is heavily influenced by timing, perspectives and events that one can rarely predict. Knowledge management requires more than acquiring and husbanding data. Organizations need to make sense of information and direct it to the right person, at the right place and at the right time. This requires a fundamental appreciation of the way that people think and how they catalogue information.

Concepts such as information flow ownership and topic maps are new to business people. In the years to come, I expect that business investments into knowledge will be directed less towards software and more towards understanding how to connect the pockets of information that exist in people's heads. Successful knowledge management is a question of balance – right information, right place, right time, right person, right depth of detail, right context, etc. One of the main reasons for poor utilization of knowledge resources in organizations lies in poor appreciation of how people use it:

- Who needs the knowledge? (And why?)
- Who has the knowledge?
- What would people do with information – even if they had it?

I'd like to thank Dr Martin Vasey, a thought-leader on the subject of knowledge value exploitation, for this remarkable story:

"I was involved in a 16,000 seat intranet deployment. We initially adopted a classic IT sledgehammer approach by building a platform for sharing knowledge using all of the latest software tools. Nobody used it. Then we realized that we were trying to 'do knowledge management to them' rather than focus on the value of knowledge and how it could work for them."

Martin's team realized by talking to prospective user groups that knowledge systems are only valuable when the users and work-teams can quickly recognise a return on the time they invest in sharing their own knowledge. They also learnt that the technology platform needed to enable workers to contribute information in 'one hit' as they were using it and not expect workers to start knowledge-sharing as a separate exercise at 7pm instead of going home or exiting for the pub! As a consequence of what they learnt by talking to prospective users and work-teams they re-developed the technology platform to support these needs. In one of the work-team induction meetings, one of the engineers shouted out "Tell you what, why don't you do a search for great crested newts!"

This created a few blank and surprised faces in the room but it turned out that the engineer had an immediate problem to overcome. He had an infestation of great crested newts at a site where major civil engineering was required to take place. The environmental order protecting the great crested newts that inhabited the site was halting a multi-million dollar project, a delay that was typically six weeks. By running a natural language search, the workshop leader identified that one of the engineers located in the office next door had ironically attended a newt handling course and was qualified to re-site the great crested newt community, which he could do in a day. This information appeared on the search results with the picture of the engineer in question on the front of the internal marketing newsletter (not an HR database!) proudly holding up his newt handling licence!

It transpired the engineer that needed these skills never knew what his colleague did or that he had these peculiar qualifications. The resulting system delivered time and again the right information, at the right place, at the right time and deservedly won Best Intranet of the Year 1999.

Knowledge management deployments fail because:

- Managers do not consider how knowledge can contribute to the performance of an organization.
- Technology becomes the focus, not business outcomes.
- Project scope places too much attention on managing content rather than extracting value from it.
- Either there is no clear commercial benefit to the corporation identified during the early stages of a project or there is no clear personal benefit to individual contributors – or both!
- Little thought is given to the role of key workers who volunteer time to act as mediators, systems architects and project advisors.
- Little or no attempt has been made to embed the use of customer and market information into product development, marketing and other corporate planning processes.

People share information naturally, it's SYSTEMS that don't.

It took over 20 years for experts in the knowledge management industry to identify what most of us already know – that people are selfish and do things for their own self-interest!

This is not 'new news' but it is the foundation of how knowledge works. If there is no vested interest for an individual in sharing knowledge, it doesn't get shared. The only reason people share knowledge is because they benefit in some way.

Early in my career I worked with a man who refused to share information about what he did and the business area he was exclusively responsible for. He was impossible to take phone messages for because I never knew whether he had returned calls or not. He would never tell me if he had. He thought that his job was more secure because he retained his expert knowledge. As the result he became a threat to the business. Within two years he was gone. I later found out that I was appointed to work with him to overcome this problem!

My experience is that most people will generally share information if it is no great effort to do so. It is often technology that inhibits knowledge-sharing. How many times have you heard the excuse, "Sorry, I can't help you because our computer system has gone down", or "Sorry, I don't have access to that database!" The following is one of those classic stories that went quickly from reality to myth and then to legend. I make my apologies in advance for possible inaccuracies. It is however a wonderful story!

An office equipment company that was making a fortune from its maintenance charging and saw it as a cash-cow decided to turn up the heat on its engineering team, members of whom were seen to be spending too much time in the office canteen! So they closed the canteen. This forced the engineers to go to a cafe over the road from their office where they would meet before and after service calls to share experiences and pass the time of day. Soon enough, one of the engineers had the idea of bringing in a blue book that they left at the cafe where they could make notes on some of the regular customer problems to make their lives a bit easier.

The blue book became an essential information source for the engineers. Then the customer base started to put pressure on the corporation about its unreasonable service charges. A

period ensued where tremendous downward pressure was exerted on maintenance renewals. To counter this, one of the middle managers recognised that what they needed to do was provide more visible reporting to customers on the organization's service performance. Managers identified that fix times varied across the organization. To capture best practice and create a higher standard of conformity, the manager suggested the development of a knowledge system where problems could be captured and shared amongst the engineers. To his surprise, one of the engineers replied, "We don't need one, we've got the blue book."

"The blue book?" replied the manager.

Further reading and resources

Information bridging – For materials on the subject of information bridging, visit the NDMC website at http://www.ndmc.uk.com.

Horizon scanning – George Guernsey has led innovation in this area on both sides of the Atlantic. George Guernsey is Chief Executive of Insight Mapping Ltd (www.insightmapping.com).

Checklist for **Curiosity**

	Qualification	Score
☹️ A working environment that discourages curiosity	Workers are not encouraged to invest time in curiosity. No formalized processes exist for managing and exploiting curiosity.	☐ ☐
☺️ Double-loop learning	The organization has formalized how knowledge is created or captured. It employs methods to route to the right parts of the enterprise It exposes members of staff to a compelling vision and strategy. It ensures the workforce identifies with the organization's values and capabilities. It encourages a workforce culture that rewards innovation.	☐ ☐ ☐ ☐ ☐
☺️ Extracting value from knowledge	The enterprise knows: What knowledge matters. Who needs knowledge and why. Who possesses knowledge. How knowledge can be applied.	 ☐ ☐ ☐ ☐

14

(P) People

The country is full of good coaches. What it takes to win is a bunch of interested players.

Don Coryell, ex-San Diego Chargers Coach

(1) The wrong workforce fit and poor productivity

The agilized enterprise requires a high performance workforce that is made up of empowered, emotionally mature and intellectually nimble individuals who can act on new opportunities. Faced with a more fluid workforce, agile organizations will need to invest holistically in the people they employ.

Should you ever get a dog from the Royal Society for Protection of Cruelty to Animals (RSPCA), they will tell you that over the lifetime of a dog, you can expect to pay £9,600. Imagine the true lifetime cost of employees – recruitment, salary, expenses, car, pension, computer, office space ... the list goes on!

Some managers appear to see the cost of a worker as being 'salary+car+benefits'. This crude thinking might apply to other forms of asset, but workers become a wasting asset unless sustained investment is made in personal development. Workforce investment should be seen as a constant and never-ending programme, where the process of putting time and money into find the right type of people is only the beginning. The decision to retain an individual on a full-time contract will be a much bigger decision tomorrow than it is today.

By 2020, an employee on a full-time direct employment contract is likely to look like a white elephant. It will represent a difficult career choice for any individual in a market where working for a single employer for any extended period of time suggests the individual is insufficiently hungry for new challenges and is happy to *go with the flow*, perhaps not confident enough in his or her own ability.

A high performance enterprise needs energized workers

To retain the levels of energy needed to sustain an environment facing near-constant change, the agilized enterprise must sustain a *Happy Mental Attitude*. Whatever the nature of the contractual relationship that exists between employer and employee, it is important that the enterprise sustains a positive mental attitude within its workforce to drive energy for the remodelling of business models and processes.

I prefer to use the term *happy* mental attitude. It's difficult to be positive if you're not happy and it's more human to want to be happy than to want to be positive.

Motivation is not a group issue. It comes down to every individual having the motivation to get out of bed in the morning.

Most people, at some point in their career, experience the apathy of a workplace that has a poor leader who manages to kill any motivation to succeed. As workers, we know that our first priority is to put food on the family table and invest whatever time we have left in friends and families. Sometimes it's easier to accept the reassuring thud of a regular pay cheque dropping through the post box every month than to find a better job, but this is a trap for the individual and the employer where both have to deal with sustained unhappiness. When you only get one chance at life, is this any way to live it?

It is a difficult life lesson to realise that feeling happy or sad has more to do with personal disposition than environment. People who emigrate in search of a new life sometimes find it, but more often than not find the grass isn't any greener. If you're determined, you really can wake up one day and simply say, "Today I'm going to make myself happy". I think deep down we all know this is not rocket science. It's about setting some personal goals, *thinking happy* and addressing the life issues that make you *unhappy*.

A work colleague told me, during one of those common pre-meeting coffee shop conversations, that he had remarried. He explained how he had come to leave his first wife. In a matter-of-fact way, he said that he had woken up on one particular morning to realise that he was unhappily married. His wife started the morning with a rant about how depressing he was to live with and she ended her torrent of words by asking him why he was always so miserable. He thought about this for a minute and said, "Quite frankly darling – it's YOU." He promptly packed his bags and left that morning never to return!

Organizations that under perform often place their workforce under the microscope first to look for areas of potential improvement. Obviously lack of performance has nothing to do with the management team! It will come as no surprise that the most common reasons for lack of workforce performance are to do with leadership where managers:

1. Accept mediocrity as being the norm.
2. Lack energy and motivation.
3. Fail to employ the right quality of talent.
4. Lose energy and ambition through:
    –   Trying to be too many things to too many people.
    –   Engaging in mergers or acquisitions that disenfranchise the workers.
    –   Defining markets too narrowly, making it too easy to achieve targets.
5. Fail to invest fully in people.

Mediocrity never feels much like a crisis

An enterprise that is not performing at its peak may be happy to live with mediocrity. After all, it's not likely that anything dramatic will happen quickly – is it?

If an enterprise finds itself at a comfortable level of performance, the underlying message of 'no worries' passes all of the way through to the *norms of behaviour* of its workforce.

Ultimately, enterprise growth originates from the performance of people and processes.

It's important to really understand what a PROCESS is. Simply put, a process is a regimented series of events that leads to an outcome. Therefore, *motivating a workforce* is itself a process. All organizations, even the big brands that you probably think must be close to perfect, are never as good as they could be. We all live in a 'not quite perfect' world. Opportunities for organizational improvement always exist by tweaking processes or introducing new ones. So why should any management team be worried? It's because poor performing processes are like mice. They go unnoticed until your cheese starts disappearing! Processes can be so poor that they put the enterprise at risk, or noticeably inhibit its growth performance. *Comfortable* management teams normally put little effort into process improvement or anticipating change. Here's one example of how an enterprise can be underperforming and not even know it:

Nick and I worked on a consulting project for a global electronics company. The project involved exploring how well they could respond to customer requests to customize their products. I met with marketing managers in their regional sales organizations and found that whilst there was a major requirement for customization and lots of business was being missed out on, the sales organizations were no longer making requests to headquarters for support because they had already been told by the central marketing operation that these requests could not be resourced. The result was nobody in the organization was complaining, so no-one in management identified there was a problem. Meanwhile, millions of euros of business was being lost on a daily basis to competitive peers.

It's not good enough to have an exceptional management team but underperforming middle management. Departmental managers, if not given clear direction, can build their own power bases that move operational focus away from corporate objectives. Often, the good of one department comes at the detriment of another. For workers nowadays, it's the journey that counts and they do not expect to be around when the enterprise eventually reaches its landfall. They are only there for the ride, so it's important that they enjoy it.

(2) A new adaptive workforce formula

The 21st century will see an employment market emerge where as workers we are all contractors of one type or another. We know as employees today that we're not expecting to stay with our employer for life, we're just passing through. We don't care too much about what will happen to the enterprise we work for in the future. We're not that emotionally tied. It's likely we'll not be around long enough to experience the full journey.

What we want is to be well paid, enjoy what we do, work in a nice environment, have the opportunity to learn and grow, get the support that we need when we need it and balance our work and family life. Individuals should always expect and anticipate change. Workers today retain a belief system formed around a *job for years*, if not a *'job for life'* expectation, where the concept of working for more than one organization in the same year is almost unimaginable. Most workers today place a strong emphasis on the dependency relationship between employer and employee. The emotional instinct is to believe that any change to their environment is potentially going to risk job enjoyment or security. So why would any employee see change as positive?

Labour markets are evolving. The workforce is starting to go through a painful change in its relationship with industry, where more and more people are becoming sole practitioners, passing between organizations on an as-and-when-needed basis. As workers, we cling to the ideals of a job for life when the reality is that future career paths will be defined by a series of short passages with different employers. During the course of the next two to three years, the knowledge-based economy will show its natural employment behaviour and NOT having a single employer will become the norm for most people.

Our belief systems are changing. In the near future, when executives refer to 'workforce' we will not interpret this to mean a workforce on full-time contracts. Instead we will take it to mean people employed on *any* form of contract, at any point in time. When procurement executives examine how many full-time employees a supplier employs, they will question the commercial sense of large numbers of employees, whereas today a large workforce infers a large and therefore secure and successful enterprise. Once this change has been absorbed into our belief system, as workers we will not feel the same bond to the enterprise that ultimately pays our salary as perhaps we once did.

In the film comedy *City Slickers*, actor Billy Crystal said, "Change is such hard work", and this quote has been worked to death ever since by change management consultants. Yes change is unsettling, but when the emotional umbilical chord that links employer and employee is cut, no longer will change within an enterprise be seen to threaten job security. It was never there in the first place.

The agility demanded of organizations to compete in rapidly changing 21st century markets means that today's commitment to recruiting full-time employees is not sustainable.

Organizations must dispel the myth that full-time employment is better. At one time, it provided a promise of security for both employers and employees. This model does not work in a meritocratic, highly fluid, knowledge economy. For **employers**, full-time employment contracts have become a straitjacket, an unhelpful link between organizational change and job security.

- Employers focus too much on how to make *best use of internal resources* before looking outward towards the open creative networks that exist 'outside' their own resource pool.

- Employers are compelled to *invest in training and career development* of employees rather than expecting employees to take accountability for their own learning and growth.

- In-house staff are less able to inject *cross-learning experience* because of their long-term employment with only one company (or their experience of only one role or one industry).

- In-house staff are *less able to inject ideas* and new ways of doing things because they are married to a way of thinking manifested in actions and behaviours.

- Employers find employees are *less productive* because they stretch projects to fill time, rather than working as a project performance-based workforce where the individual contractor absorbs the time and cost of the project overhead

- Employers with a higher proportion of full-time workers will find it *harder to compete* with more agile *virtual organizations* that exploit contracted staff and third party resources to supplement their creativity, skills, resources, customer value delivery, etc.

For **workers**, full-time employment will inhibit their ability to learn and profit from a broad range of learning experiences to develop their knowledge and skills.

- True knowledge workers will make more money from their expertise by retaining their individualism.

- As individuals, workers will take accountability for their personal life-long learning and career development. In the UK, central government already operates an economic model for university education that places responsibility on the individual (rather than the state or parents) to pay for their own education.

- There will not be an expectation for employers to provide a job for life.

- Workers will opt out of long-term full-time employment contracts that might infer that they are not confident in their own abilities or hungry for self-improvement.

The 21st century encourages individualism not just for consumers but also for employees. It is breeding a workforce of self-confident, self-employed workers – and the numerical growth of this community is both remarkable and unprecedented.

Whilst it is unrealistic to believe that all workers will become self-employed, the pendulum is swinging in this direction and the first community to be affected by this phenomenon are the highly skilled, high-performing knowledge workers whose expertise is worth more when it is shared across multiple organizations and when the ability to learn and apply new knowledge is enriched by more relationships. Eventually, this phenomenon will release employers and employees from the security blanket of full-time contracts. Organizational changes demanded by an enterprise will in future be disassociated from the workforce relationship and any potential impact on an individual's job security. Can you imagine a time where less than 60% of the enterprise workforce will be directly employed on full-time contracts? We're quickly moving in this direction today. There are organizations today in the public and private sector that have outsourced contact centres, production lines, printing facilities, logistics, IT data centres and shared service centres for finance and human resources. This trend is likely to increase and will be further exacerbated by a higher proportion of self-employed workers.

The agilized enterprise has a fluid workforce of individuals that:

- Operate within open networks as self-employed contractors.
- Are employed by HR contracting organizations.
- Work for specialist third party outsourced service providers.
- Contains a smaller minority that are on full-time contracts

Most *knowledge workers* will not expect to be retained by a single employer for more than two to three years. This will influence a number of factors surrounding the workforce relationship:

- The cost of acquiring the best staff will be absorbed by recruitment agents and new forms of 'people providing' organizations.

- Training will become the responsibility of the individual worker and a "learning for life' attitude will be more commonplace.

- The processes that support the full-time workforce of the 20th century enterprise – induction and appraisal, succession, incentives, etc. – will envelop both directly and indirectly employed workers.

- The provisioning of the working environment (including information technology (IT) systems) will support a fluid and mobile workforce.

- Information processes and operational practices including corporate governance will of necessity need to become more regimented.

In this new employment environment, employers will need to maintain a frugal approach to appointing staff on full-time contracts in order not to be disadvantaged by competitors adopting more fluid workforce contracts. Attitudes surrounding full-time, direct employment contracts will change. It is rare even now for workers to feel the same level of attachment to the success of their employer as they once did. When I started work with British United Shoe Machinery, it was like joining a club and many of my colleagues had their silver watch or cuff-links for 10 years of service to the company. It was true that people *cared* about the company.

It would be great if all organizations had a *heart* (and a heart beat) but in reality most do not. How important is workforce loyalty to an organization? According to a Gallup poll in 2004, disengaged employees cost the U.S. economy $300 billion a year in lost productivity costs. There have been a number of surveys done recently that point to a clear relationship between an engaged workforce (i.e. a workforce that cares about the organization it works for) and organizational success.

Japanese business culture recognizes workforce loyalty as important, which is why mutual loyalty between employer and employee is almost taken for granted in their culture. Should a Japanese corporation need to make adjustments to their business, they will not make employees redundant but will re-skill and redeploy them in different areas. In one case, a global electronics company retrained a production line that made computer hardware as software quality assurance engineers.

In contrast, American corporations are happy to cut headcount down in an instant if their figures don't make the quarterly targets. The dilemma facing employers is that a lower headcount and the ability to contract out non-core business disciplines is appealing in terms of creating greater agility, reducing operational overheads and bringing in fresh thinking and good practice from specialist providers, but at the same time these changes can deplete workforce moral and result in an organization that has an *uncommitted* workforce. Corporate leaders must choose between the inflexibilities of a direct workforce or accept the reality that indirect employment contracts can result in a workforce that doesn't understand what the organization is about and doesn't really care.

Are direct employees any more loyal than contracted staff these days?

Isn't it the case that most people go to work and want to do a job as well as they can? Nick Lawrie and I have worked on behalf of major corporations for over six years and I'd like to think that not only have we honoured the brand commitments of these organizations, but we have discharged our expertise probably in a better way than any internal employee could have done because we have the benefit of learning from our other clients and are constantly refining and improving on our specialization. When a client invests in our time, they benefit from inherent good practice partly paid for by other corporations.

Do YOU believe that employees repay the loyalty of employers that offer a job for life? Do YOU believe that employers repay the loyalty of a person that goes above and beyond the hours of work on their contract to do the right thing for the organization they serve? Whatever your view, I believe both sides run the risk of making a promise that they can't realistically keep.

- Employers adopting a policy of offering full-time employment contracts to staff as a matter of course will be disadvantaged when faced with the challenge of constantly revisiting their business model to compete. They will need to invest in costly redeployments and retraining. Compare this situation to that of more agile competitors who indirectly employ contractors of one kind or another and are able to turn on and off a skilled workforce as they please without incurring high costs.

- Employees that are retained for long contract periods with the same employer are unlikely to retain the drive and desire to bring maximum value to their employer. Neither do full-time employees have the opportunity to develop the experience and specialization that independent contractors do. Full-time employees might find themselves in a position where their loyalty to one employer puts their future career prospects at risk.

In the future, employers or employees will not be seen to be 'bad people' if they fail to honour the unhappy marriage that direct employment represents.

(3) Excellent workforce fit – and 'fit measurement'

Faced with a higher proportion of contracted staff and a more fluid workforce, employers in future will need to exert even more effort in ensuring that people have the right skills and attitude fit. Getting the right blend of people with the right skills and 'fit' for your organization has never been that easy and deservedly occupies significant management time. There is a plethora of tools and techniques around to help reduce the cost and risks associated with recruitment. Inevitably mistakes will be made.

Within any successful organization there are people who are encouraged by the opportunity that change represents. These individuals possess an attitude of *getting the job done*. They have a supercharged 'passion spring'. They put passion and energy into everything they do.

It gives these people seemingly boundless sources of energy. I call them the *doers* because they can be relied upon to get the job done, because they value the opportunity to learn from new experiences. We live in a world of lifelong learning, where the opportunity to learn is itself one of the most valued benefits of a good career.

There was a time when you needed as many plodders (i.e. people who are happy and suited to sustaining long periods of working on repetitive tasks) as you did *doers*. *Plodders* would be the administrators that would process accounts payable invoices day after day, they would be the sales people that always delivered a moderate sales income and they would be the warehouse administrators that made sure all stock was accounted for. In the digital age, the most mundane of these process tasks are automated. The cost of labour today means that organizations will only compete effectively against their competitive peers if they employ a small number of high-performing people, supported by as many technology-led productivity aids as possible. That means lots of *doers* and a smaller number of *plodders*.

Getting the job done comes as naturally to doers as swimming does to fish. They want to do SOMETHING NEW every day, and do it well. Doers simply aren't happy doing half a job. When they do, it feels a lot like failing themselves. They want responsibility and thrive on new challenges. From doers comes a natural talent pool of managers and leaders.

There are many names for the behaviours displayed by doers, people with initiative, tenacity, people who they never know when to stop and are full of energy. The wonderful thing about doers is that to be a doer does not require a brain the size of Saturn or membership of MENSA, it is an approach to life that lies within most of us. The rewards for being a doer do not always reflect the value brought to the organization they serve. Many remuneration schemes do not *reward* doer behaviour. Two individuals, one that always gets things done and one that does *just enough*, will regularly be found sitting next to one other on the same salary.

Like all subjects there are shades of grey. Some individuals COULD be doers but perhaps through peer pressure or educational conditioning, the native urge to want to rise to new challenges and get things done is somehow held back. Good managers know how to release it. Organizations need a doer attitude in their people more than any other qualification you can find on a CV – because without it nothing happens. Doers only need to be told what must be done (and why) and – rest assured – they will make it happen.

My mother is one of the best examples of a doer that I've ever had the pleasure to meet. When my father's business finally came to an end (ironically because of external market forces that he could not foresee), my mother had to find a new career. At her stage in life – having by this time raised two children – it wasn't going to be easy. So she went back to college and refreshed her typing and computer skills. Sure enough, she found a job in the typing pool of our local authority. It wasn't long before she gained promotion through the secretarial ranks and moved through a series of jobs before becoming responsible for the roll-out of a schools administration database for the council's education department.

At every stage of her career she has been a doer and managed the activities of many people her senior through her energy, ideas and well-guided recommendations. Everyone that came into contact with Patricia Tomlin always knew that the job would get done. She will always be a *doer* no matter what life throws at her.

How do you spot 'good attitude' in the interview process?

There is no single test but I often find a good indicator of the 'spark' of attitude that shines from doers can show itself through the hobbies and pastimes that individuals quote on their CV. Some people say, 'You are what you eat'. I tend to think that whatever people do in their free time while away from work is a good indication of drive and temperament. People with no family, no pets, no hobbies and no interests may lack the *get-up-and-go* and social skills that you're looking for.

Too much time is spent on finding workforce with the *right qualifications* and not enough emphasis is placed on finding people that have the *right attitudes and fit*. Formalized fit measurement techniques have now been translated into software-driven measurement systems (see www.matchQ.nl) that assess the core fit qualities and behaviour of executives and match these with a predetermined profile based on the fit characteristics that managers decide are demanded for the role.

These measurements need to balance *fit* qualities on three levels:

Strategic
: Which *fit qualities and behaviours*, in which parts of the organization, are needed to make the enterprise successful? The answer to this question provides a profile of a specific role or function.

Tactical
: Where within an organization are there *matches or mismatches* between the *profile* and the employee profile and what influence does this determination have on human resource planning? The answer to this question produces a view on areas of the organization where the fit profile runs out of step with the behavioural profile of individuals.

Operational
: What are the selection criteria employed by the organization for *fit qualities and behaviour of individuals* and how is this knowledge used to prime the matching of these with candidates? This will determine whether the fit profile meets the needs of the enterprise.

All organizations go through phases of growth, of rationalization, of harvesting business, etc. These economic modes have an inevitable impact on the fit of employee attitudes and behaviours. If a person has worked in a role for over 10 years and is then suddenly viewed by their supervisor as underperforming, is it the person who has changed, the negative influence of the supervisor, or a change in the economic mode of the enterprise that has changed the expectations placed on the role? These are complex balances. As organizations shift into new gears, new challenges set new expectations of workers. Not all will match up.

Fit profiling is not only useful when trying to balance new starters with roles or old hands with new economic modes. It is also a useful mechanism for steering career path development and formulating succession strategies (i.e. anticipating who will replace today's managers and supervisors in tomorrow's business).

The price of failure

If you get your selection of people wrong then the harsh reality says correcting the problem may be expensive and time-consuming. Employment tribunals will seek to protect the rights of the employee over employers that appear to flagrantly change their minds on the type of folk they're looking for. The simple answer is to make sure you don't get your selection wrong by spending more time examining the fit of people before you make a commitment to employ them!

Central to the in-built metabolism of a doer is the instinctive thought process that says, "Okay, so how do I get this done?" It may be that on the face of it, the path to getting a task accomplished is too difficult or unclear, but the difference between doers and other people is the willingness to believe a task can be done as long as personal human weakness doesn't fail you. Doers with good leadership and a vision to follow make an impossible team to beat.

(4) Guardian roles

Guardians are experts responsible for overseeing cross-organizational discipline areas that don't align themselves to standard value-chain areas of operation.

Through the 80s, 90s and now 2000s, organizations have become accustomed to introducing external consultants with specialist expertise. The introduction of guardians emerges as organizations recognise that some attributes of organizational behaviour and activity need to be constantly monitored and assessed. Guardian roles are likely to be contracted rather than offered as full-time roles because it is essential that guardians do not get subsumed by internal culture and protocols to become benign in their influence.

I mentioned previously that the agilized enterprise has a fluid workforce made up of short-term employment contracts and third party or independent contractors? Guardians have a key role to play and tremendous impact on the performance of an agilized enterprise that must fashion and manage the activities, performance and behaviours of a fluid workforce. Guardian roles demand creativity, constant learning and process improvement, which is the main reason why employing a third party expert is preferred. Organizations in the 21st century will have the challenge of managing distant and remote workforces, and the difficulty of retaining a corporate identity and presenting one face to the customer. Therefore, one of the most influential guardian roles in the agilized enterprise is that responsible for instilling workforce behaviour. Key to achieving fluidity and consistency within a workforce at the same time is the absolute need for shared values and behaviours, firstly at management level. Managers need to be managed and rewarded against a set of specific behaviours built around core values and leadership ability. Frontline managers who 'touch' customers should be measured and rewarded against specific behaviours around customer service and teamwork.

Positive workforce behaviours are the organizational *glue* that transcends operational silos to build a 'one team, one organization' approach. Key to breaking down the barriers between silos is the energy, commitment and resource applied by managers to embed new values and behaviours as a way of everyday life.

Jenny Turner says, "Guardians act as a conscience, actively challenging leaders on their own behaviours and actions first and then coaching them in the ways they encourage and challenge behaviours in their teams. It is through this process of measuring and developing behavioural performance that

organizations will ultimately deliver a consistent customer experience that becomes their competitive edge and the service profit chain is realized."

Leaders are beginning to recognize the value of external objectivity that comes from guardians who are distanced from the everyday politics and have a heightened awareness of *normed behaviours*, behaviours that to an outsider would seem strange or unacceptable but on the inside have become custom and practice: 'It's the way we do things around here'. To explain this point, I turn to Jane Ling of Ling Turner.

"In one organization we worked with, we were shocked that a senior male manager felt it acceptable to barge into the ladies' toilets and pull out a female colleague in order to get her immediate response to a customer complaint."

Jane adds, "We have worked with many leaders who at a workshop stage showed great levels of energy and commitment to adopting new values and behaviours, looking to implement these through new behavioural measurement systems. Typically though, six months into the newly created 'culture', this wave of intent has been diluted to a small band of champions, the rest merely falling by the wayside, having been consumed by the power of previously 'normed' behaviours. So much money, energy and time have been wasted over the years on these cultural change programmes. One organization who contacted us had just embarked on a customer service culture change for the third time in seven years!

"Where organizations limit themselves currently, in our opinion, is the extent to which they look to learn and develop the original thinking and activity beyond just the theories to the real application on site. It is our experience that once the theory is in place, there is a misconception that the transfer of learning will happen automatically, and yet this is probably the most critical stage that gets the least focus and investment. Guardians help to transfer the knowledge and skills to become a way of life."

The role of the guardian will be pivotal in ensuring that newly adopted values and behaviours are embedded. With such a diverse workforce, this becomes even more critical.

(5) Effective productivity measures and incentives

It probably goes without saying that workers are unlikely to achieve the desired strategic goals of the enterprise unless their remuneration and incentives encourage them to do so. Most organizational structures today are geared around departmental outcomes rather than individual contributions to strategic outcomes. This means that they are more likely to spend their time focusing on departmental issues, possibly at the cost of initiatives that could make a significant difference to the strategic priorities of the enterprise. I use the term 'contributors' because it is likely that many of the individuals and organizations that contribute to the achievement of organizational outcomes will be beyond the corporate firewall. All these individuals and agencies must be 'incentivized' to achieve the desired objectives or they won't happen. You could believe in some offices today that the performance of some people is measured by the number of emails and spreadsheets they produce.

In the agilized enterprise, performance is about the level of contribution individuals make to business processes, knowledge creation and customer value. I liken this change in perceptions of workforce performance to the way people think about photocopying today. It's an odd slant on office culture, but if you walk up to a water cooler and chat to another member of staff you're networking, but if you talk to another member of staff whilst you're photocopying a document, you're seen as being unproductive. The agilized enterprise measures the productivity of individual workers around the *visible contributions* they make towards ideas, innovation and activities that produce targeted outcomes. People that are seen to be spreadsheet jockeys or email addicts will no longer be considered to be useful or *productive*. According to the analyst firm Gartner, 30% of large companies will adopt systems that reliably apportion corporate performance outcomes to individual information-worker contributions by 2012. The effective measurement of workforce productivity can only be truly appreciated when the role of individuals within social networks and information flows is understood. To make this possible requires information worker productivity measurement, a subject I cover in Chapter 15. Furthermore, aligning incentives to corporate rather than departmental outcomes – the issue that I turn to next – can only be achieved when the contribution of each individual is measurable so that rewards can be set.

Checklist for **People**

	Qualification	Score
☹ **The wrong workforce fit and poor productivity**	Mediocrity is the norm.	☐
	The organization lacks energy and motivation in its workforce.	☐
	The organization fails to employ the right quality of talent in its workforce to fit its culture and behaviours.	☐
☺ **A new workforce formula**	The organization thinks about how its workforce can be encouraged to enjoy the journey.	☐
	It operates a fluid workforce and encourages individualism in its workforce .	☐
	It exposes members of staff to a compelling vision and strategy.	☐
☺ **Excellent workforce fit – and 'fit measurement'**	A method for determining workforce 'fit'.	☐
	The organization has established interviewing techniques that identify the 'fit' of personnel.	☐
☺ **Guardian role**	A guardian to take responsibility for 'positive norms of behaviour'.	☐
☺ **Effective productivity measures and incentives**	The organization measures the contributions of individual information workers.	☐
	The organization aligns incentives to corporate outcomes.	☐

15

(T) Technology

Regulation is driving information technology (IT) spend and this is stifling innovation. We are seeing 'vanilla IT'. Vanilla IT has become too prevalent in many large enterprises. The organization is preventing users having anywhere near the computing power they have at home.

James Bennet, Director of Technology, Communications and Entertainment at Ernst & Young

(1) IT systems are out of alignment with business needs and encourage information workers to adopt poor ways of working

Inflexible IT systems encourage operating silos to form

Organizations have invested millions of dollars on IT, yet they still fail to systematically deliver the right information to the right people at the right time – and systems don't adapt to change quickly enough.

The 'vanilla IT' mentioned in the quotation from James Bennet of Ernst & Young is oriented around departmental structures and historic transactional processes. IT is predominantly concerned about business continuity. The creative people charged with growth, improvement and innovation remain the unheard and unsupported community while the back-office systems they access are fragmented, serving the needs of functional silos above the needs of the organization.

Unified views of data are unavailable to most information workers who frequently must plead with IT team to access the data they need to discharge their roles.

True, IT systems ARE complicated, but the way they are implemented can foster even more complexity. This complexity creates inflexibility.

A survey of 163 companies that had implemented enterprise resource planning systems conducted by Accenture in the early 2000's found that the mean number of instances (separate and distinct implementations of the same software across regions or business units) was eight, with 32% having implemented from six to more than 20 distinct instances.

Such fragmented implementations result in disparate, disconnected sources of operational information. Large organizations operate enormous computer systems and do not always have the level of control over programs and systems they would like. Mainframe applications developed in the 1970s and 1980s can grow to a size where they become awkward to migrate to new platforms and so continue to operate on ageing database and operating systems that are no longer understood or well supported.

Another factor that creates inflexibility in IT systems is the way they're developed. In the heady days of IT dominance in boardrooms in the 1970s and 1980s, IT teams would adopt a waterfall development model for software application programming, where a specification was cascaded to a series of developers using different tools and possessing different skills. Tasks were performed in parallel and the resulting code blocks were eventually knitted together to form a software application. This off-line approach to software authoring limits the involvement of users; so many authored applications just don't work right. The end result of a big IT investment is often a sub-optimal system that information workers have to 'work around' and that does not marry with the needs of the business. This approach produces rigid, inflexible systems that are difficult to modify.

The trend towards buying shrink-wrapped software to address specific processes continues to form *siloed* data repositories and information systems. Every department will have their own mix of IT systems and none of them operate across the enterprise. As organizations change they find much of the data they need to access is held in these many different places across the enterprise and in many different formats. This is no way to run a business. All that IT does when deployed in this way is make it harder for people to work together and be creative.

Information workers face content overload

Information workers are experiencing information overload. By 2012, global companies will have to handle 30 times more data than they did in 2004. Organizations are exposing workers to a burgeoning flow of data. Business leaders are coming to realise that *information overload* is as detrimental and costly to business as *too little* information.

An IT analyst survey conducted in May 2002 found that 90% of companies believe they suffer from information overload and that their competitiveness is negatively impacted as a result. They say that over the last few years, Internet, intranet and similar developments have brought an unmanageable amount of information to the average employee.

Information, not content, is the lifeblood of business. Modern organizations have to expediently flow information through the enterprise to supply decision-makers at every level with the rich business insight they need. A conundrum of the 21st century is that, whilst most people say they receive too much information, management teams struggle to access the information they need to drive growth initiatives.

Middle managers spend more than a quarter of their time searching for information necessary to their jobs, and when they do find it, it is often wrong.

Source: Accenture Information Management Systems sponsored survey, January 2007.

Much of the information that workers manage and share is held and distributed in unstructured office file formats such as .DOC (MS Word), .XLS (MS Excel) and .PPT (MS PowerPoint) formats. Information is trapped inside these electronic documents and becomes invisible to the organization. This makes it difficult to find later without the use of sophisticated search tools.

This is a serious problem. NDMC's own research suggests that use of unstructured content and informal information processes cost organizations $17,000 per employee per year. Work this out for yourself. Consider how much time you spend every day hunting for information on your desktop, requesting information from departments, re-compiling or re-presenting information. If it works out to be around 15% of your work-day, I would say you're not untypical of most workers I talk to. Poor information access and use represents a huge drain on resources that can be better used to solve the 'innovation-inhibition' problem. This ignorance towards the information needs of creative thinkers has never made sense to me. Successful corporations of the 21st century depend on effective IT. I count myself as an IT enthusiast, but even my enthusiasm for IT dwindles when I see examples of wasted investments due to siloed approaches to the application and management of systems.

Workers lack effective tools to access and use information in a way that makes them as productive as they can be

The challenge to make information workers more productive has been around for a while. There have been many software technologies that have attempted to deliver workforce productivity improvements. Here I list some of them.

Desktop software tools like Microsoft Office were the first genre of technologies aimed at improving office worker productivity. In many ways, Microsoft Office took the way people worked with hard-copy documents in the pre-desktop computing world and made it electronic. They also gave individuals access to data management and analysis tools that hitherto had been the domain of data centre operatives. Instead of a set of green line reports, users could serve themselves. The net result was more information became accessible, communication was easier and faster. Most offices lost a tier of secretaries and office juniors (the sort of roles that school leavers used to enjoy to learn about the ways of business and get on the first rung of the ladder). True, the advent of the spreadsheet was a revelation to most of us in the 1980's and made a significant personal impact to the way we could make sense of (and share) data but that was a long time ago in 'software years' and I don't think anything since has made such a significant impact.

Use of office desktop software such as spreadsheet or word processor applications results in data being held inconsistently in different data formats that make information difficult to manage. Spreadsheets, for example, are used as the receptacle and carrier of information for applications such as performance management, budget reporting and compliance. When people enter data into spreadsheets they use spurious characters that databases don't like or understand. People tend to play with formatting and distort the data structures unless they are created as secure templates. Word processor document formats might also be used as the receptacles and carriers of information for applications such as departmental budgeting, complaints processes, competitive analysis and product releases, etc. Use of word processor documents can sometimes requires the recipient to aggregate and repurpose content probably by copying and pasting paragraphs or sections into new master documents which, as I know from personal experience, can take considerable time.

Has Microsoft Office made people more productive? I would say that it has removed a layer of administrators – but at the same time I'm not sure this will prove to be a good thing for our society. For 'knowledge workers' I find most people spend much too much time re-keying, searching for, editing or re-purposing content than they would want to. Are people being productive when they use a spreadsheet or a word processor? How do these activities contribute to corporate outcomes? It's difficult to measure.

The next wave of productivity enablement software came in the form of intranet and content management software. These systems store, share, and manage published documents to make this content available across a community. Lotus Notes was the first and arguably most complete of the intranet solutions. Company intranets have not in my experience made a huge difference to the productivity of information workers.

I visited a financial services company in 2001 to be told that their intranet was mainly used by staff to sell cars to one another. Inappropriate deployments of company intranets can mean workers effectively copy the contents of their laptop hard disk and publish it to the corporate 'black-hole' intranet, never see it again. Capturing and storing content alone (the mistake made by early document and content management solutions) does not make it useful. Unless care is taken, the attention of knowledge management projects quickly moves towards husbanding content rather than exploiting its value.

When email became popular in the 1990's I think many of us expected it to hold the *secret of success* for workforce productivity. But email has proven to be a poor person-to-person communications conduit for formal business information flows. When it comes to managing discussion threads on topics it really falls short and most email systems are hopeless at managing the data they create.

I don't know an organization that captures, tracks and measures the productivity of their workforce by analyzing email traffic. When email is used as a conduit to gather information it produces inconsistent responses and does not deliver a single record of the truth. Even as far back as 2004 global corporate email volumes exceeded 17 billion a day. They continue to grow. Email has become a business inhibitor that reduces the amount of thinking time information workers have and it constantly interrupts their working day. Ironically, 21st century workers are addicted to it. They feel a need to receive 50+ emails a day just to feel connected and important!

In the late 1990s, it was the turn of clever search engines to be the IT silver-bullet solution. These applications, that would often cost more than $100,000 to buy, promised to take the hard work out of finding knowledge for you. Then it was the turn of enterprise business intelligence tools.

By the 2000s, corporations had invested millions in software. These big IT budget hangovers led many CEOs to divorce themselves from the subject. Throwing all this technology at the problem of information worker productivity has done little to help people to work smarter. After decades of investment in software to bolster office workforce productivity, users are no better off.

If you're an information worker, it's still terribly difficult to get hold of the right information, at the right place, in the right context and at the right time, just as it was in the 1980s. Information workers STILL don't have useful software applications to support them in their roles. The IT industry is only now beginning to question how well today's software tools support what management guru Peter Drucker called 'knowledge workers'.

At some point down the long winding road of computing we took the wrong turn, lost our way and found ourselves the slaves rather than masters of IT. I think commerce has been held back over the last 25 years by believing that if IT could be any better, leading players like Microsoft and IBM would have developed it by now.

Office desktop tools that information workers have used for over three decades have done little to formalize human-centric information flows.

Anyone who has worked in an office environment for any length of time will appreciate the 'pain' caused by information processes that have no systematic IT support. Whether information workers are gathering data, compiling results or searching for business activity monitoring information, it's a 'given' that IT generally underperforms.

The default digital support is the spreadsheet, ably assisted by the word processor. Neither of these applications was designed for the gathering, carrying or discovery of information and its safe storage in robust databases. The spreadsheet was designed for mathematical modelling and analysis, and the word processor was intended to be a computer-based typewriter. It is a testament to their authors that these software applications have been so widely employed as information carriers. More organizational information is carried on MS Excel spreadsheets today than by any other 'system', however asking information workers to make-do with spreadsheets and word processor documents comes at a cost. A lot of time is absorbed into the mere process of information re-purposing and gathering – and the people that do it are often middle managers.

In my experience, the most useful knowledge that exists in organizations today passes between people – the users of information – within the people networks of the office environments. Much of this content is found in word processor documents and spreadsheets that experts believe have an average estimated life of three to five days.

Respondents to a recent IT industry analyst survey ranked informal information sources, such as personal networks (e.g. friends and close colleagues) and emails as more beneficial to their business decision-making than information available on company intranets and the Internet. In addition, they reported that their companies poorly supported informal networks.

I suspect, years from now, we will look back on how we work with information in office environments today and scratch our heads! Almost any corporate initiative aimed at engineering a competitive advantage –

acquiring new customers, building closer relations with existing customers, entering new alliance relationships, improving performance, harmonizing operations, etc. – demands supportive information technology. With all of the investment made in IT, I find it truly baffling that information workers still haven't got useful tools that support them in their roles by effectively capturing, managing and sharing information. People are not being empowered by appropriate supporting technology. They need this technology support in order that they can have more time to innovate, more time to increase the value of their function or the potential to decrease the cost of their function. Business people work with office desktop software not because this is the best way to capture, extract and share information, but because there are no better tools available to them.

What I believe the IT industry has missed is that most information and knowledge worker activities are not *ad hoc* but *repetitive*. There are hundreds – if not thousands – of human-centric information flows that permeate across the 'people networks' that individuals build and employ to get their work done. Formalizing these flows and supporting them with appropriate technology is essential for driving organizational improvement.

The absence of information flow-centric software tools means that hopes of achieving corporate outcomes, sharing knowledge, listening to customers and managing performance are doomed to failure before they begin. Without formalizing how information cascades through the organization content will continue to exist in silos, on hard drives and intranets but it will never deliver worker productivity improvements.

Workers are not equipped to exploit their 'people networks' to achieve outcomes

The majority of information worker tasks are collaborative in nature. How many information tasks do you complete utterly on your own? It's likely that – if you're banging out a letter to a client or creating a prospect list on a spreadsheet, putting the finishing touches to your budget plan or outlining the next product launch – all information worker tasks SHOULD involve other people. An easy way of considering the collaborative nature of office tasks is to review how many people receive the information you produce. If the only person that receives the information you publish is YOU then okay the task is not collaborative – it's probably an aide memoire!

The content we read, edit or author forms part of an information flow that crosses a 'people network' of some sort. Appreciating the value this content brings to the *information flow*, and the contributions that people make to it, provides managers with the data they need to understand the value of content and the value of people.

In the context of agilization, how to energize the pockets of innovation found in people networks I believe is the main challenge facing IT in future if we are to make workers more productive but we are only just beginning to appreciate the business context of our social networks.

(2) IT supports internal processes

The organization adopts federated IT systems aligned to the way it needs to think

Management information systems need to grow up to support the new processes of the agilized enterprise such as market horizon scanning, customer insight capture, provisioning of knowledge markets that inject innovation, the formation of people networks that spark creativity. Perhaps the most important aspect of business operation that information systems need to align to is identify opportunities for improvement of their *economic engine* – i.e. how they transform their customer value into money (or other rewards in the case of public service organizations such as grants or votes).

Organizations have had to change gear in the new century of business. When at one time they focused management capacity on honing their internal processes in order to achieve operational excellence, now in the post-mechanized wind-driven enterprise they must look to harness the new world of collaborative supply-chains, industry partnership frameworks and knowledge markets for their competitive advantage. They also have to contend with less control over their workforce and manage the complexities of loosely coupled people networks.

Businesses have to think in different ways. To support these new ways of thinking the focus of management information systems must ultimately reflect this re-focusing of priorities. Unfortunately in most organizations today they do not.

How is this *new thinking* initiated? In the next section I describe how agilized organizations will re-align management systems to achieve their strategic outcomes but the critical success factors are these:

- Organizations must recognise the new processes and tools of competitiveness such as people networks. knowledge markets, horizon scanning/anticipationomics, insight capture and learning systems (etc.) and adopt homogenous technology architectures to support them – and give workers access to back-office and web-based data sources without requiring 'IT department' intervention.
- Information should be aligned to the way the enterprise produces (or contributes) its customer value and turns it into cash or rewards.
- 'Liquid information flows' – that cascade through people networks – should be supported by self-service information platforms.
- Information platforms must support remote and mobile working behaviours of information workers. The formation of these new 'virtual workspace' environments should be largely automated (see below) and must ultimately provide measurement of worker contributions – even perhaps clocking in and clocking off tools!
- Business critical data should never leave secure data management environments. With advances in web-based platforms this is quite possible to achieve.
- Intellectual property should always be 'fire-walled' to protect the enterprise from investing in innovation it doesn't own.

The organization adopts IT to support human-centric workflows and manage the productivity of workers

Measuring the productivity of office workers is never easy but it is particularly difficult when workers are using desktop applications such as spreadsheets. How can managers hope to ascertain whether successive tasks are contributing to the good of the business or not? In the near future I believe organizations will insist on installing tools to measure the productivity of information workers not on how much time they spend at their desk, but by their contributions to processes and knowledge markets. This is essential if organizations are to become more virtualized.

Mark Raskino, Research Vice President for emerging technologies at Gartner Inc. states, "Businesses have poor understanding of the way information and knowledge work progresses and crude measures of the outputs and their value. During the next decade, several threads of work will come together to improve the measurement and valuation of information and knowledge.

The management science equations of 20th century car production lines simply won't do in a knowledge-based economy. This is creating a growing efficiency gap. We see large variations in knowledge work input costs between businesses, with no explanation of the reason except local management culture and perceived wisdom."

The agilized enterprise liberates its workforce with appropriate information systems that are always in tune with the needs of workers.

The first step to improving the ability of an organization to harvest the knowledge of its workers is to make sure that information flows are understood and contributions to them are well managed. I see information flows like water cascading across a landscape. Left unchecked the information will flow where it wants to. In any organization there are thousands of information flows that go unnoticed. Were you to track the passage of emails between people in a business you would start to reveal where these largely invisible and generally uncoordinated flows exist.

It's possible to identify many poorly formalized information flows just by sitting in a busy sales and marketing office. Consider for example what happens when a sales person is asked to respond to a tender opportunity. They might call on the assistance of some of their marketing and technical colleagues. They will probably start entering their response into a word processor, author content about what their company does and how their solutions comply with industry standards and deliver customer value etc. This is information that has no doubt been produced many times before in slightly different forms. Is this sales person going to make promises to the customer that the business can't keep? Does he know who he SHOULD speak to in order to get the right answers? It is far too difficult for workers today to author information systems that pool this knowledge, help colleagues know what others do and where to go to find out more. Organizations must formalize these 'liquid' human-centric information processes if they are to achieve greater agility. When workers have a clearer understanding of who is responsible for the flow of information and how they can contribute to it then less time is lost to re-keying data, duplicating effort and running parallel processes. Changes to processes are much easier to qualify and apply. How can you possibly hope to apply improvements to processes if you don't know how they work?

Information Worker Productivity (IWP) software improves the productivity of information workers. Microsoft's analysts suggest the global market for this segment of IT will be valued at over $117 billion by 2012. A number of vendors are developing software in this area including industry giants like Microsoft, Sun and IBM. A tiny aspect of this segment today is software used to formalize liquid information processes.

There are several technologies in the IT market today that could play a role in formalizing liquid information processes. They include light-weight *business process management* software like Cordys, light-weight *business intelligence* software like TIBCO's Spotfire and QlikView, and light-weight systems integrations software *sometimes called business mashup software) like Serena, Kapow and JackBe that help to bring data together and make sense of it. All of these products are designed for use by IT people and so don't take into account the new market reality and its impact on organizational structures and behaviours that is taking place within corporations. For this reason they don't help to example the genre of technology that fits the agilized enterprise. So in this chapter I'm using the software we've incubated at NDMC called Encanvas to example the new generation of software specifically designed to formalize liquid information processes and how they manage the productivity of information workers operating within loosely coupled 'people networks'.

To understand the role of this information flow software, it is important not to think of organizations as they operate today. When agilized, the organization is structured as loosely coupled networks of individuals that contribute to projects as contributors to loosely coupled work teams. With this fluid structure, individuals are not confined to a rigid departmental structure but instead contribute to parts of the business where they can bring value. This is not a free-for-all, the enterprise still has structure and form, but the organization is modelled more on a Jazz band rather than an orchestral model (see my comments on the need for a loosely-coupled structure in chapter 9).

The success of this agilized organization structure depends upon the organization of people who are given the responsibility to form 'people networks' and ensure that they deliver the corporate outcomes they are charged with. When a new *situation* emerges, an individual (the 'Process Manager' for want of a better term) will be made responsible for the actions that follow. This individual will create a collaborative workspace and invite others to join the project. In one form or another, this 'people network' will want to gather, cleanse, manage, analyze, interpret, share and publish information. It is likely the data they need is held in a variety of formats on different systems. The agilized enterprise must have an economic and effective means of authoring new applications that respond to these information management challenges.

It was IBM that came up with the term 'situational application' to describe applications that are created within a small group of users where they are used, sometimes by the users themselves.

Situational applications may be used and then discarded or can sustain to continue to channel information effectively through the business to boost workforce productivity. What makes this possible is a unique blend of economics and functionality that new 'point-and-click' software is able to provide. It means that corporations can rapidly build robust information management solutions and still afford to throw them away if their use turns out only to be temporary. Situational applications are essential to the agilized enterprise because they give information workers the tools to serve themselves with business applications that meet their situational needs for collaborative and analytic tools.

It is in this area of designing and publishing situational applications that the software technologies pioneered by IBM and tools like our own incubated software (called 'Encanvas') comes in.

Early in the 'how do we fix the problem of Information Worker Productivity' phase the good people at NDMC identified that the biggest problem was giving information workers the self-service ability to work with databases and create portals. These tasks have previously demanded IT skills. The solution was to come up with a single data file that contained absolutely *everything* to do with the creation of a new *situational application* in a single transportable data description file including the data, the definition of the application, the tools workers needed to manipulate and interrogate data and printed output and portal presentation.

This was how our 'Encanvas' software came into being. Encanvas is a self-contained data environment that *process managers* can self-author. It produces files that we call 'canvases'. Canvases formalize how information flows across people networks. They serve the information needs of small networks of people and also enable them to gather the information they need from databases, spreadsheets and other forms of data accessible on the enterprise network. I describe Encanvas to others as 'LEGO brick' technology because canvases are authored using ready-made building blocks of software code to remove the need for *process managers* to have IT knowledge or programming skills. These elements combine to facilitate the capture, management, analysis and sharing of information which means that process managers can create workspaces for their people networks that fit the way teams needs to work and interact.

The architecture of an Enterprise Network Canvas

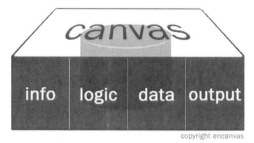

Canvases are made up of five layers of technology:

1. Interface   Employs building blocks – selected from a point-and-click menu to create user interfaces.

2. Logic   Designs the logic between the building blocks to decide how different elements work with one another.

3. Data   Describes the data management properties of the application, to access, integrate and build databases.

4. Output   Designs the formatted print or electronic output.

5. Properties Manages the user administration, version control, help scripts and other properties of the canvas.

Canvases capture and present information within structured templates to improve the consistency of data capture. Canvases example a new form of hybrid data management technology that:

- Combines data and business logic and applications within a self-contained and transportable file.
- Bridges across the various sources of information.
- Provides the components required to enable non-technical users to create their own formalized information flows.
- Links information workers with their informal social network through a collaborative workspace.
- Provides a means for managers to understand how information flows across their organization and measure the productivity of information workers.

Using technology like Encanvas to support the user formation of situational applications gives the agilized enterprise the ability to support its people networks with robust and secure data management technology. I believe in the future, this same technology will enable individuals to rapidly formalize the *liquid information processes* they need to implement to achieve corporate outcomes and create a framework to measure the productivity of contributing individuals to these processes.

(3) IT supports workforce productivity and innovation

The organization adopts 'Frictionless IT' and agile software systems that align IT to worker needs

The start-point for Information Worker Productivity is to give information workers access to the information they need within a robust and secure data management framework. To respond to new situations as they emerge, information workers need agile IT systems but to get these new tools, organizations will need to refocus their IT spending priorities.

Corporations today spend over 90% of their IT budget on 'vanilla' business continuity IT, the core of IT operations. This investment goes into securing the perpetual availability of information systems that sustain core business processes – managing transactions, governing the supply chain, protecting and leveraging customer information, etc. In contrast, less than 10% of IT spend is committed to business growth and market 'fit' technologies intended to support the information needs of high-performing individuals 'at the edge' of the organization.

Since the turn of the century however there has been new impetus from business people to reclaim their IT systems, demanding tools that provide them with the ability to be as productive as they know they can be. This change of attitudes is being called Business 2.0 in the IT industry and is closely associated with more agile Web technologies that serve business applications up to users like Encanvas does.

'Frictionless IT' describes a situation where the costs and constraints associated with aligning IT to emerging business needs are non-existent. This creates unrivalled AGILITY.

Technologies like Encanvas are the enablers to Frictionless IT. They provide the ability for communities of users to repeatedly develop information management platforms to support their information needs without incurring additional programming or software procurement costs.

Imagine the impact of a 20% shift in the allocation of IT budgets towards this new agile computing approach! Such a change would demand a reorientation of the risk averse, closed-box world of corporate computing.

Given the pressures on corporations to encourage business agility, I believe this is more likely to happen than not – but will take the courage of business leaders to make it happen.

The IT industry expects a shift to agile computing in the next 2-3 years

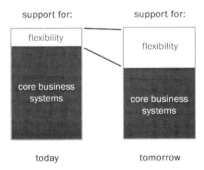

The organization adopts systems to manage workforce productivity

Measuring the productivity of worker has never easy – but it is particularly difficult in the case of office workers are using desktop applications such as spreadsheets. Sometimes, the time and cost associated with 'micro-management' of worker productivity can outweigh the advantages. There are also huge issues to do with civil liberties and the use of personal information that have to be considered. How do managers determine whether the activities of information workers are actually contributing to the good of the business or not?

I believe organizations will in future measure the productivity of workers not on how much time they spend at their desk, but by their individual contributions to processes and the development of knowledge. This is critical to organizations as they virtualize.

"Businesses have poor understanding of the way information and knowledge work progresses and crude measures of the outputs and their value. During the next decade, several threads of work will come together to improve the measurement and valuation of information and knowledge.

The management science equations of 20th century car production lines simply won't do in a knowledge-based economy. This is creating a growing efficiency gap. We see large variations in knowledge work input costs between businesses, with no explanation of the reason except local management culture and perceived wisdom." Mark Raskino, Research Vice President, Gartner Inc.

The organization understands and harnesses social networks

Monitoring the movement of information across social networks using database technologies means that, for the first time, organizations will be able to understand how information workers are contributing to knowledge and processes. Organizations will be able to use this knowledge to place a value on the contributions made by individual information workers.

Social networks are identifiable groups of individuals that communicate with one another on a reasonably frequent basis, sometimes because they have a common interest, other times because they have a common goal. Understanding social networks is important because it helps managers to understand how individuals contribute their knowledge to support business activities, even how individuals contribute to the achievement of processes. Social network analysis describes "the mapping and measuring of relationships and flows between people, groups, organizations, computers or other information and knowledge processing entities" (Valdis Krebs, 2002). It enables relationships between people to be mapped in order to identify knowledge flows and to understand who people seek knowledge from and who they share their information with.

The Corporate Leadership Council describes social networking as "the most accurate, systematic means to identify key value creators and informal knowledge communities that drive corporate core competencies." My example explores information flows associated with the focus area of customer service and complaints. Each line suggests a significant information flow. Thicker lines show larger flows.

Illustration of a social network

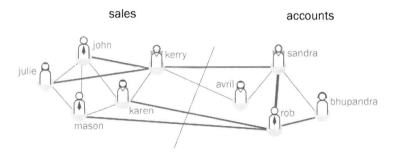

In this case we can see that Kerry, Rob and Sandra are major knowledge contributors. More sophisticated social network analysis models can specifically profile who is a contributor, who is receiving and which subject matter areas they specialize in. Often these knowledge areas are not made obvious through job titles or in published skills records. Access to social meta-words and phrases from email systems is perhaps the way ahead.

In contrast to organization charts that show formal relationships (who works where and who reports to whom), social network analysis charts show emotional relationships (who depends on who, who shares information with whom). They allow managers to visualize and understand the many relationships that can either facilitate or impede knowledge creation and sharing. Once these relationships and information flows are visible, they can be used to:

- Detect information bottlenecks.
- Highlight teams and individuals playing central roles
- Identify isolated teams or individuals.
- Manage the flow of insight across departmental boundaries.
- Improve the effectiveness of formal communication channels.

Visualizing these networks surfaces inter-relationships between individuals. The prominence of an individual within the network is characterized by the strength and centrality of links. Social network analysis identifies skills and capabilities of workers. It helps systems designers to direct insight to the most appropriate parts of the business and ensures that even global businesses can think and act as one organization.

The organization adopts systems to support increasingly virtual knowledge workers and PONDs

I've described earlier in the book how knowledge workers are becoming more mobile and independent. I've also introduced the subject of Primary Open Network Devices (PONDs) – the knowledge markets made up of seekers and solvers that become the primary means of innovation and creativity. IT systems have to meet these new challenges too although precisely how this works nobody knows!

What we are beginning to see is the emergence of CLOUD COMPUTING where the computer servers that information workers use to manage their data and run their business applications are not maintained by the organization itself but by independent service providers. Google and Microsoft already provide hosted applications and email services for individuals and in 2007 Google suggested that they woiuld offer a full suite of hosted services for a $10 annual fee. It is quite easy to imagine that the converged computer and telecommunications industry will in future operate a fully hosted information services model where the entire desktop environment is maintained by third party *telecomputer* companies. Are we entering an era where IT becomes someone else's problem?

(4) IT supports decision makers

The organization applies both active and reactive decision support systems

Decision makers have been poorly served by IT. Rarely do middle managers and senior executives to enjoy access to the business information they really need. Why is it so difficult to get right? Here's a clue:

During 2003 I invested some time to meet with Chief Executive Officers of Local Authorities in the UK to learn what information mattered to them. Over 30 interviews later I was in a meeting with a CEO who said, "Ian, let me tell you the 5 things that every CEO wants to know." I sat prone with my notebook open just waiting for his wisdom to hit. He said, "Ian, CEOs need to know

the 5 things that are going to keep them awake at night. The problem for you is that the list of 5 issues changes every week."

The nature of business is that management teams face new situations every month, week, sometimes day. Managers will make sense of what's happening and then install processes and management systems to monitor and resolve issues. Then a new situation emerges and the cycle occurs again. With the pace of change increasing so dramatically in the 21st century, managers need IT to help them to support this lifecycle.

Systems to support decision makers can be *reactive* – i.e. a new situation emerges and the decision maker needs to rapidly build knowledge of the subject in order to make a judgement, or they can be *proactive*, such as the anticipationomics systems that alert the decision maker to the liklihood of a new situation.

The agilized enterprise needs both and the characteristics of these systems are similar:

- An easy to learn and use human interface
- Tailored to the specific information needs of the user
- Enabling users to serve-themselves with information
- Accessing data 'from anywhere'
- Offering rich views and analysis tools to *drill into content*

The organization operates an Action Framework management information system

On page 121 I introduce the Action Framework: a holistic, corporate 'thinking and acting' system that unites and supports an organization faced with constantly changing internal processes and behaviours. I believe it will become an essential technology component for organizations living in a business climate where strategic plans might need to change at any moment.

The first time NDMC attempted to put together an Action Framework we found the project demanded such huge volumes of manual data re-keying that it became uneconomic. This overhead of data entry resulted from much of the data existing in unstructured wordprocessor document formats when it wasn't held in back-office systems that we were unable to integrate with. So in 2002 NDMC developed an Action Framework toolkit that incorporates data extraction, aggregation, data management, portal design. dashboarding and business activity management components. This toolkit overcomes the need for specialist IT people with database skills to aggregate and manage Action Framework data.

Technology moves on quickly and now there are many vendors that specialize in off-the-shelf yet highly configurable dashboarding software for performance management and business intelligence – Proto Software™, Spotfire™, Outlooksoft™, Business Objects® and Oracle Hyperion® to name just a few – that can be applied to build an Action Framework system.

However you build it, your organization needs an Action Framework 'system' and at the heart of it will be a relational database. Otherwise your business just won't have the management capacity to make sense of the complex web of relationships that associate actions to their ownership, learning, evaluation and outcome metrics.

Checklist for **Technology**

	Qualification	Score
☹ **IT systems are out of alignment with business needs /encourage information workers to adopt poor ways of working**	Inflexible IT systems encourage operating silos to form	☐
	Information workers face content overload	☐
	Workers lack effective tools to access and use information in a way they want and need to	☐
	Workers are not equipped to exploit their 'people networks' to achieve outcomes	☐
☺ **IT supports internal processes**	The organization adopts federated IT systems aligned to the way it needs to think	☐
	The organization adopt IT to support human-centric workflows and manage the productivity of workers	☐
	The organization adopts systems to support increasingly virtual knowledge workers and PONDs	☐
☺ **IT supports workforce productivity and innovation**	The organization adopts 'Frictionless IT' and agile software systems to support self-service computing	☐
	The organization adopts systems to manage workforce productivity	☐
	The organization adopts systems to create and support people networks	☐
☺ **IT supports decision makers**	The organization applies both active and reactive decision support systems	☐
	The organization operates an Action Framework management information system	☐

Section 3

THE AGILIZED WORLD

Learning is NOT compulsory, neither is survival!

W. Edwards Deming

Section Introduction

In the first section of this book 'THE NEXT INDUSTRIAL REVOLUTION' I overview the social and economic factors that are dramatically changing the world of business and the drivers that demand organizations revisit the way they think and act.

In the second section 'THE AGILIZED ORGANIZATION' I describe the 10 key subject areas likely to shape the ability of an organization to repeatedly adapt to always fit its most profitable markets.

In this final section 'THE AGILIZED WORLD' I aim to explain how an agilized enterprise turns its agility into profit. I have structured this section in the following order (overviews provided):

Chapter 16   The Innovation Factory

How the systems and capabilities of the agilized enterprise as highlighted in Section 2 come together to form an agilized enterprise.

Chapter 17   The Agilized Ecosystem

How organizations will operate in collaborative ecosystems.

Chapter 18   IT and the Information Worker

How IT will meet the challenge of supporting the needs of information workers.

Chapter 19   Tribal Business

How the agilized enterprise supports tribal business

Chapter 20   Final Thoughts

What is the value of agilization to corporations?

16

The Innovation Factory

This chapter brings together the components of agilization to show how the subject areas interlink to create a coherent way of working.

This is presented with a series of illustrations to make it easier to understand starting with figure 1 below that shows the core elements of strategic management –vision, strategy and learning – presented in the form of a FACTORY.

Figure 1.

THE INNOVATION FACTORY: A strategic framework for an agilized enterprise

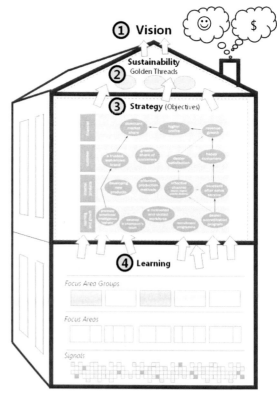

Above flies the Vision (see ❶ on the illustration) of where the organization is trying to reach. Inside the factory there are three floors:

1. **The Attic.** These 'golden threads' ❸ are identified as long-term priorities critical to the sustainability of the enterprise beyond the lifetime of the present management team that should be constantly used to positively influence the decisions made by the organization.

2. **The Upper Floor.** Home of the boardroom and the place where strategic decisions are made, articulated as a series of objectives on a strategy map ❷.

3. **The Lower Room.** Home of the engine room and the place where the organization learns what matters to its customers, what it must do differently to improve its products and how it can turn customer *wants* into customer *value* ❹.

Like a Victorian Flourmill of the industrial age, this is the production cycle of an agilized enterprise of the digital age mapped out as a building.

The *ideas* manufacturing process starts at the very bottom with the gathering of thousands of individual pieces of customer insights 'signals' that might be comments made during a telephone conversation, feedback from a customer survey, a research report, suggestions from retail or reseller partners, website tracking data and snippets from news-feeds.

These are filtered into focus areas and then focus area groups to align the incoming filters to the organizations contextual understanding of its processes and capabilities. These ideas flow through the organization and are used to challenge the current strategy and actions. Any changes to strategy that are considered in light of the organizations sustainability golden threads and whether these new thoughts will help the organization to achieve its vision. Unfortunately, at this scale it's not easy to read all of the detail but you can easily obtain electronic copies of all of these illustrations and other resources at http://www.agilization.com.

For organizations that must transform their organization to become agilized we have to consider how this strategic framework is formed in the first place. This is shown in figure 2 overleaf which shows the learning process in more detail.

Figure 2. The learning enterprise

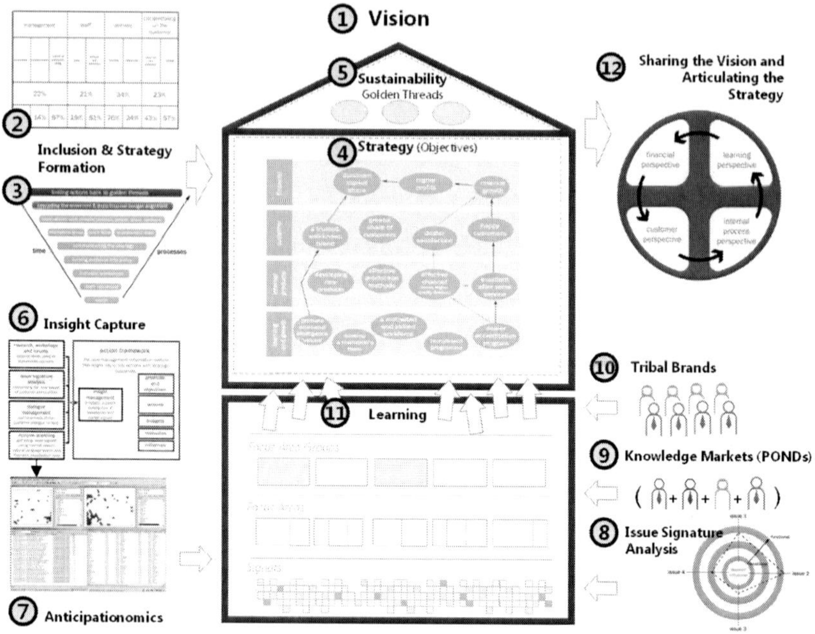

Our story starts as always with the organization's Vision (see ❶ on the illustration). This was the subject of chapter 6.

The management team conducts an inclusion programme ❷ to understand from its customers, staff and stakeholders what they think is important and what can be improved (see page 200).

A champions team is formed and they step through the implementation process ❸ I describe in chapter 8.

This activity results in the formation of a ❹ strategy map and balanced scorecard (see chapter 8).

The exercise to develop a small number of strategic objectives highlights a series of issues that are critical to the sustainability of the enterprise beyond the lifetime of the present management team. These 'golden threads' ❺ are identified as long-term priorities that should be constantly used to positively influence the decisions made by the organization.

The management team appreciates how rapidly demand can change for its products and so it establishes comprehensive systems to capture insight ❻ including the provision of a horizon scanning service ❼ to feed pre-vetted analysis of key issue topics against a series of pre-defined 'hot ' areas. This service scans web-sites and news-feeds for any new information on these topics and this data is presented to the relevant managers every month. A key component of its insight capture strategy is the dialogue management system that the organization employs to engage its customers. This system automatically captures conversations and highlights key interest topics identified using advanced natural language search tools.

The Issue Signature Analysis method is used to interpret customer priorities and to understand what they would be prepared to pay for.

Knowledge markets ❾ (PONDs) are frequently used by the enterprise to resource research and development projects and these experts are consulted for their suggestions on how the organization can improve its product and service offerings.

In addition to these known sources of insights, the organization is for the first time working with its tribal brands ❿ – who represent a significant number of target clients – to engage their communities in defining new product and service expectations

The resulting insights from these capture processes are entered into an Action Framework ⓫ system that contextualises and feeds 'signals' into the decision making processes of the organization.

Having established a strategy, the organization presents its objectives to staff, customers, shareholders and business partners in the form of a Steering Wheel ⓬ to effectively communicate its strategy.

So the organization is making good progress. It has developed the critical strategic framework that governs the business. It has got its staff and other stakeholders on-board and the strategy has been well communicated. The organization also knows that it has customers 'waiting' for its new products and services. The next step is to ensure that this enthusiasm does not get wasted on activities that are not focused towards the achievement of the agreed outcomes. This is where the next set of management techniques and tools come in. Figure 3 shows the process of turning strategy into action using the management information systems of the agilized enterprise.

Figure 3. Turning strategy into activities

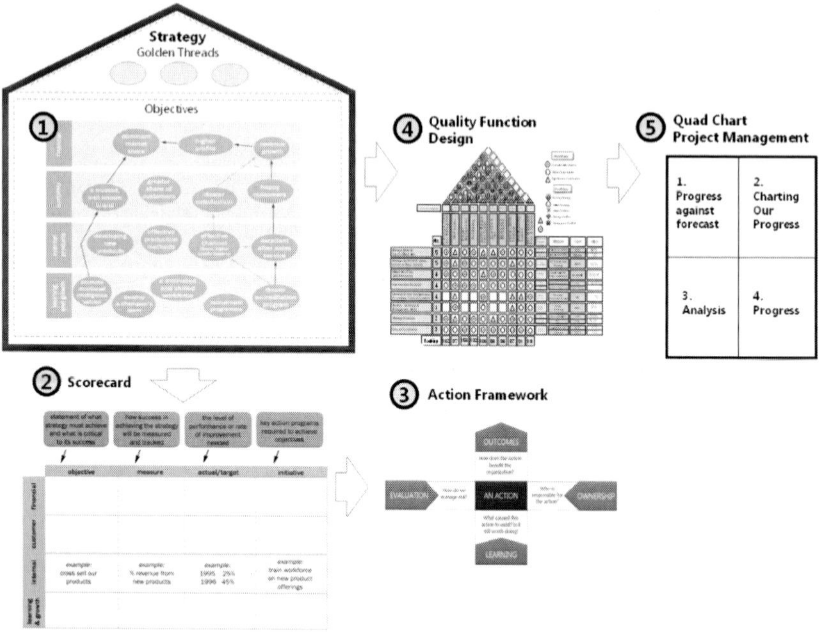

The organization takes from its strategy map ❶ the list of agreed objectives and determines how best to measure their achievement. Baseline data is captured on the current performance and targets are established. Individuals in the enterprise (and beyond it) are appointed as **Process Managers** and made accountable for delivering specific outcomes.

A balanced scorecard ❷ is developed and from this work a series of actions are agreed. Existing departmental plans are aligned to this plan to make sure there are no other activities taking place within the enterprise that would unnecessarily demand resources.

Process Managers employ an Action Framework ❸ to formalise their projects. These are signed off by the management team. Process Managers engage their 'people networks' and appoint a series of 'solvers' to work with them to deliver the process outcomes they have been tasked with (within budget guidelines).

To bring all of the project threads together the management team implements Quality Function Design ❹ to implement a holistic view of project activities. This includes a reporting regime every month. Because many of the Process Managers are remote, they need an effective way of communicating their progress on projects and so the organization adopts the use of Quad Charts❺ to enable its Process Managers to report on their progress on projects (see page 175).

Implementing this small set of management information systems is not painful and case studies show this approach can boost project performance by up to 140% – so why wouldn't organizations want to do it?

17

The Agilized Ecosystem

Few organizations in the 21st century will do business alone.

One of the major challenges that will face many organizations in coming years is the move towards economic collaboration where organizations discharge a role as part of a process that delivers customer value but they do not own the process. They become a cog – a very important cog of course – in a larger process.

I call this an *economic pathway* because normally there is a very obvious value chain that links each of the contributing process steps to its outcome. The challenge that faces all parties is that they must work together in an efficient and effective way to make sure their economic pathway is better than alternatives.

Figure 4. Illustration of an Economic Pathway

The above example comes from the UK's public sector in the area of traffic management. Highways authorities across the UK are responsible for managing road networks and they are encouraged by central government to do this well. Outside of London most people (70% on average) commute to work by car and about one third of commute trips are into an urban area. Towns and cities across the country are regularly gridlocked, with pollution levels reaching unacceptable levels all too frequently. The CBO calculates that congestion costs employers £20 billion a year.

The Network Management Duty placed on highways authorities means that they must as organizations work with industry colleagues to effectively manage their network – but also contribute to the improvement of networks that exist beyond their territory.

When drawn on a page, the key stages to this economic pathway (see Figure 4) reveal a simple value chain:

1. Monitor and evaluate the needs of the network.
2. Identify network demand – what is causing demand and how it is likely to change; how can it be managed?
3. Improve the road network
4. Mange road network
5. Maintain the road network
6. ...and, when discharging these functions, make sure that any changes are enhancing the local community

No single organization can claim to own this economic pathway but all organizations have a vested interest to ensure the pathway is efficient and effective in delivering customer value. Organizations become collaborators in an economic ecosystem they contribute to but do not control.

This type of multi-organization economic pathway is becoming common. Utilities companies today work hand-in-hand with their sub-contractors to keep assets maintained, civil engineering contractors work hand-in-hand with their clients to oversee vast building projects, healthcare professionals speak in terms of patient care pathways, social workers protect children with care pathways, insurance companies must work with web broker sites to reach the majority of their customers....the list goes on.

What it means to organizations is that management information processes and systems have to mature to support an holistic view of performance and project activity aligned to how they bring customer value as a group of contributors – where the focus of the 'system' falls on the unit of value that is produced. Determining what should be measured in such circumstances can itself be complex.

Figure 5 overleaf illustrates how the agilized organization operates within this context.

Figure 5. How an agilized enterprise operates within its workspace

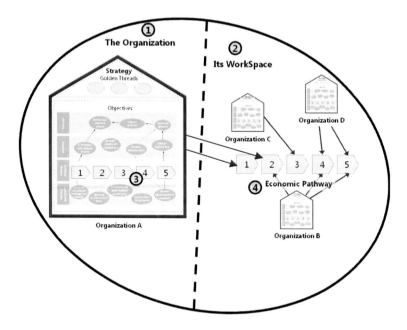

We see the familiar FACTORY structure of the agilized enterprise (which I have simplified to the basic strategy map and golden threads) which is displayed within its own space ❶that now contributes to a 'WorkSpace'❷.

Notice how the internal processes of the organization are displayed as a value chain❸. Many organizations will continue to 'own' the full pathway that produces their customer value for some time to come. But in this more complex market-place, we now see an economic engine formed within a workspace ❹ where other organizations (B, C and D) are also contributing to the pathway and have become critical to the success of 'Organization A'.

It might be that Organization A in this case is a manufacturer or provider of raw materials and that it contributes therefore to process steps 1 and 2 in eth economic pathway, but steps 3 to 5 are left to others to fulfil. In this situation, no doubt all of these organizations will want to know how well the economic pathway is performing, but most industries do not have the dexterity of management systems to robustly show this perspective.

Within an agilized enterprise we also have to realize that many of the resources and sources of innovation are themselves not owned by the enterprise. This model therefore becomes ever more complex as illustrated below in Figure 6.

Figure 6. How an agilized enterprise accesses its resources

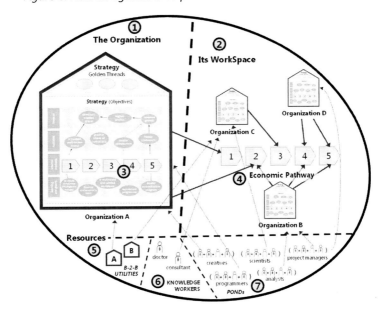

Organization A ❶ is shown adopting resources from other business to business outsourced service organizations ❺, knowledge experts ❻ and open networks ❼. Other organizations within the same WorkSpace ❹ are also exploiting these competencies and skills. This is understandable because industries tend to acquire communities of skilled workers that move from one business to the next to exploit their knowledge and capabilities.

As more of these highly skilled individuals become economically independent, it is likely that they will ally themselves with associated knowledge networks that serve the industry.

18

IT and the Information Worker

Chapter 15 describes the critical role information technology will play in supporting the processes of the agilized enterprise. What I have yet to do is explain how information technology architectures are maturing to support knowledge worker and organizations.

Cloud computing is a term you will hear a great deal about over the next few years. It describes...

> **"...a computing platform where data and applications are hosted by vendors on web-servers – where cloud is a metaphor for the Internet because it brings access to systems wherever a user wants to work."**

Cloud computing brings an 'in the office' work experience to users wherever they might be. All they need is a device that connects to the Internet. The portfolio tools that information workers need to discharge their daily roles, engage with their knowledge networks, collaborate on projects and meet with colleagues are served to them by their cloud computing provider. This means in the next few years individuals will be able to access a level of richness of business applications and tele-communications tools that today global corporations can not afford to deliver. Technology companies like Google, Microsoft, IBM and Yahoo are investing billions of dollars to meet the demand for Cloud Computing.

Cloud computing is set to grow exponentially over the next 5 years. Over the next five years, IT market analysts, IDC, expects spending on IT cloud services to grow almost threefold, reaching $42 billion by 2012. It is forecast to capture 25% of IT spending growth in 2012 and nearly a third of growth in 2013.

Demand for Cloud Computing comes from:

- Worker demands for 'always-n-the-net' communications.
- Flexible worker trends and growth in numbers of economically independent knowledge workers
- Globalization and need for information workers to collaborate on projects whilst working apart in different geographic locations
- Organizations seeking to reduce their IT costs associated with managing and operating internal applications for their businesses
- IT departments seeking to improve their ability to handle demand volatility for computing resources

There are a number of contributing technologies that are converging to make this possible now that I will briefly summarize. These include:

- Broadband and mobile technologies
- Service Oriented Architecture
- Cloud integration tools
- Web 2.0
- Mashups and widgets (the democratization of IT)
- Security of web based computing

Broadband and mobile technologies

The idea of always being online is today becoming a reality. Tele-communications companies have done well out of broadband and their broadband service propositions are moving towards more comprehensive forms of broadband service contracts that are agnostic of connection or device type. To you or me and others in the Western world this means that someday soon we will always be able to access the Internet from our mobile device or browser.

Service Oriented Architecture

A service oriented architecture (SOA) is a protocol adopted in modern computer systems architecture to present data from database systems in a structure that makes it accessible to new processes 'as a service'. SOA architectures make database-centric systems – that have previously locked information away from workers – more open and accessible. In the context of cloud computing SOA means that information services can be made available to information workers in their cloud workspace whilst still remaining secure and robustly managed.

Cloud integration tools

Software applications like Encanvas, Boomi, SnapLogic and Cast Iron give IT people the easy-to-use tools they need to build bridges between pockets of information held in different systems to create new information processes *in the cloud*. These technologies provide a migration path to port incumbent business applications to a cloud computing platform. All of these systems support SOA to provide compliance with a set of protocols that everyone is coming to understand.

Web 2.0

The technologies and tools people use to create web-based business are improving radically. At one time, presenting information to computer users via a web browser was very limiting. Browsers worked in very different ways and would display information inconsistently. This meant that programmers would need to use downloadable components to manipulate and present data. Harmonisation of standards (mainly driven by user demands) is leading to greater conformity in the way browsers present data which means that developers have much more control over the way screens are presented.

A limitation of browsers when used to display applications was found in the way browsers would refresh the entire page users saw. This meant large volumes of data had to be served to the browser any time a minor change occurred. This meant the quality of user experience was diminished when compared to traditional resident software applications. But now the computing industry has introduced methods of changing only *active* parts of screens that users are interested in. This reduces the volume of data being updated and means developers can produce richer user experiences that compare favourably with resident software that runs on a PC.

Mashups and widgets (the democratization of IT)

Technologies are emerging to empower information workers to serve themselves with new ways of working with data. With these tools they are able to build composite applications for themselves provided that IT departments provide them with access to data. Two forms of building block technology making this possible are Mashups and Widgets.

Mashup software enables users to take information services and application building blocks provided by third parties and bring them together in creative ways. An example of a building block is GoogleMaps which people can use to present data on digital maps. Mashups permit users to create new ways of using information without IT skills. Encanvas is type of mashup software. Other examples include Kapow, JackBe and Serena Mashups. Growth in mashup software has been enormous over the last year and will continue to grow.

Widgets are another 'technology glue' that people can use to create composite applications of their own making. They are created using web scripting languages – Hypertext Markup Language (HTML), Cascading Style Sheets (CSS) and JavaScript – which means that web developers already have the necessary skills to build them.

The opportunity for mashups and widgets is that, instead of organizations having to develop new programmes or purchase shrink-wrapped software applications, information workers can 'serve themselves' by creating their own applications *in the cloud* by mashing together ready-made technology building blocks. This is the first step on the road to Frictionless IT. Widgets democratize IT by giving anyone – not just programmers – the ability to create new applications that use information in a way that individuals or groups want to use it. Mashups and widgets today are lightweight tools that focus on the consumer market or people who might use them to improve a blog or build a social networking website but their application in business will grow as cloud computing becomes more commonplace. We are in the very early stages of a new industry.

Security of web based computing

The corporate market for IT has been very cautious of Web 2.0 technologies and the progression of business applications to web platforms. The major concern has been the threat of data and networks becoming exposed to attack (the IT managers' first priority is business continuity). Technologies are emerging however that make web based applications very secure and these innovations are likely to fan the flames of cloud computing adoption levels. I expect in the next 5 years the computer industry will completely transform itself towards a cloud computing model. The level of investment going into innovations in data and network security (fuelled by the promised revenues attached to cloud computing) will surely resolve any lingering security doubts.

What cloud computing looks like

The sum of all of the technology innovations occurring at a time when information workers are demanding always online access to information and the ability to serve themselves with applications – is Cloud Computing.

Figure 7. The information systems architecture of an agilized enterprise

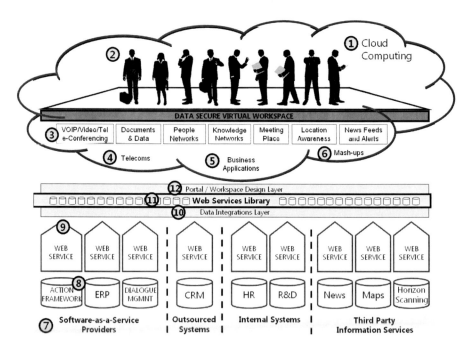

Over the next few years information workers will expect to log into a single information environment to access their telecommunications and business applications. The user experience will attempt to replicate the experience of working in an office today. The only big differences will be that meetings and conferences will be 'virtual' and applications and data will be served up via the cloud. This is the reason why IT companies are battling to achieve the critical mass of useful solutions to meet these needs. This is the cloud ❶ where knowledge workers and the majority of flexible workers (who spend a proportion of their time away from the office) ❷ will work and make their money. This environment will encourage innovation in various tools ❸ that knowledge workers need including:

- Tele and video conferencing, desktop sharing etc.
- Secure access to documents and files (personal or shared amongst a community). These may be authored individually or together.
- Access to 'people networks'; both social and business networks
- Tools to contribute towards or create knowledge markets and team-spaces to support collaboration and the formation of PONDs.
- Virtual meeting places where people can come together.
- Location aware applications that connect people to people, resources and facilities in their locality.
- News feeds and knowledge alert services (offered by brokers)

We can expect ❹ telecommunications technologies and architectures to combine with computing platforms to provide 'access-anywhere'. The majority of ❺ business applications information workers need to work collaboratively in knowledge markets will be 'self-serviced' from within the Cloud Computing environment. Frequently used light-weight composite applications will be authored using ❻ mashup and widget components.

The way back-office systems present their data will be rationalized by Service Oriented Architectures and web services. Software companies ❼ that used to sell software will move to offering their tools as a service. Outsourcers that today 'look after IT' are in a prime position to run server farms to serve up their clients' data. Internal IT teams will employ middleware tools (a ❿ data integrations layer) to migrate their platforms and combine data sourced from different systems into more usable structures. Other information services will be offered by third parties. Some will broker personalized information services that contextualize information.

All of these information silos will present their information in a common to all ❽ web services architecture based on SOA which is today the adopted standard. This means that organizations will manage large ❶ Web Services Libraries providing a data access layer for information workers to use in the knowledge that the data is robustly managed and secure. Systems administrators will have access to application design and administrative tools in a ❷ portal workspace design layer to manage interface presentation styles, rules, user privileges etc.

Cloud computing and organizational structures

The opportunity for Cloud Computing is to have a profound influence on how society works and how we share information with others. It provides the telecommunications, information sources, connections, collaborative tools and virtual office environment at a very low cost of entry (Google speak in terms of the $10 per person computing environment). It will change our world in a number of ways:

- I firmly believe that Cloud Computing will encourage organizations to try new loosely-coupled organization structures forged around the *jazz band* model of small groups of information workers collaborating in small 'situational networks' to solve specific issues. This will ultimately lead to innovation and transformations in this area of the way organizations think and act.

- IT will move IT from being a specialist subject that a small number of people understand to a utility (like electricity or water) that everyone will expect to be able to access.

- This accessibility will enable more people (see Alter-preneurs, page 132) to seek economic independence and work beyond the enterprise. These people will form the backbone of creativity and innovation for organizations where specialist knowledge or skills are occasionally required to achieve specific outcomes.

- Knowledge networks (PONDs) tribal brands will form more easily because individuals will be able to find each other based on their interests, values, skills, knowledge, geography etc.

Together, cloud computing and sensor networks will inflict an unimaginable change in society and business.

19

Tribal Business

Chapter 3 introduces tribal brands and their likely impact on consumer markets. So how will the agilized enterprise operate within 21st century tribal markets made up of individuals formed into potentially hundreds if not thousands of loosely coupled buying communities?

To recap; *tribal brands* form when individuals come together through the use of participative (always-on) digital networking technologies and find they have 'sticky values' in common. First examples are likely to result from the efforts of social entrepreneurs employing creative capitalism to do good whilst making their profits.

These social networks evolve to assert their sticky values on suppliers of products and services as buying communities under a tribal brand. The consequence on markets is that instead of selling products and services directly to end users, suppliers approach tribal brands to tailor their offerings to appeal to communities with common buying interests and preferences.

Figure 8 overleaf illustrates the complex web of relationships in tribal markets. Individuals surfing the web ❶ and using other participative technologies come together by finding other people who share their ❷ sticky values. This coming together of individuals will be made much easier in the next 5 years as social networks become better at managing interests and grouping individuals together (already in business social networking products like LinkedIn® and Plaxo® we are seeing intelligence being introduced that highlights potential people that users might be interested in connecting with).

Tribal brands ❸ are formed to harness buying interests of individuals who come together around their sticky values.

Figure 8. The tribal market

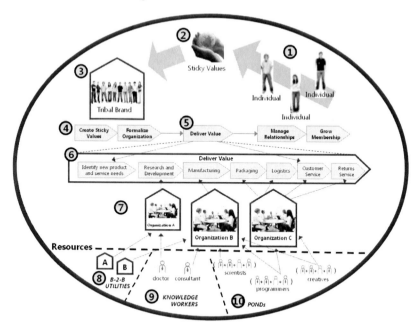

The economic pathway of a tribal brand ❹ includes the process of creating sticky values, formalizing the agilized organization and its processes, delivering value in the supply of products and services, to manage relationships supported by advocacy-led customer support and grow its membership. Expanding the 'delivering value' ❻ process reveals the contributions made by other ❼ agilized organizations. These organizations call on a portfolio of external resources including ❽ outsourced utilities and service organizations.

As outlined in the previous chapter, agilized organizations call on the resources of ❾ knowledge workers and ❿ open networks to support their creativity and enrich their internal resources.

Tribal markets are likely to increase the pace of change in industries still more. They will reduce the barriers to entry for new organizations to enter the market either as tribal brands or niche product and service providers. The mighty corporations are those at the base of the pyramid who must operate with huge asset resources to support common core processes.

20

Final Thoughts

Institutionally, the ability to be agile enough is the gut issue in leading an organization today.

James McNerney, CEO, Boeing

What is the value of agilization to corporations?

The agilized enterprise is exceptional at listening to customers and possesses the skills and capabilities to rapidly translate this learning into products and services that they want to buy.

Peter Drucker said, 'there is only one valid definition of business purpose: to create a customer.' When your organization is able to repeatedly listen, apply and act on customer insight to deliver customer value you have a competitive edge. Any good business should want to understand what matters to their customers and work like billio to satisfy that demand. I'm sure it's always been that way. But the consistent trickle of profits year after year can dampened the desire of *mediocre* corporations to innovate, to understand what their customers want and make efforts to get products and services right. Apathy can soon set in. For me, the great thing about the digital age is there is no place for management apathy anymore in business. Increased levels of competition expose poor leaders who take no interest in their customers or staff. That has to be a good thing. A friend of mine said to me recently that good companies are those that grow in a recession. I'm sure that's true. Business does demand a competitive streak!

Agilization helps to turn great product and service ideas into things that customers want to buy. There are many great ideas out there but most of them don't make it the last mile to customers that want to buy them because business people have missed the big message, namely, it doesn't matter what *you say*, it matters what they, the customers, *hear*. It's hard when you're passionate about your business to peel back the layers and get down to the thing that customers are interested in.

Sometimes it's not the exciting new design or the great features you've added to improve serviceability or usability. It can be heart-breaking to find when you've put thousands of R&D hours into a product that customers elect to buy the cheaper model from the competition because it's slightly cheaper. These lessons point to a very important piece of insight (and it's not that customers are always right, or that they have the best ideas, because neither statement is true); that customers will buy what they *understand*, not necessarily what they *want*. Customers in the 21st century can buy their products and services from practically anywhere. They can afford to be discerning and demand products and services as they like them. To constantly re-visit how products and services are designed and presented to meet these demands requires a different *kind* of enterprise, evidenced by the broad range of vocabulary I've used in this book, summarized in the diagram below.

Figure 9. The language of agilization

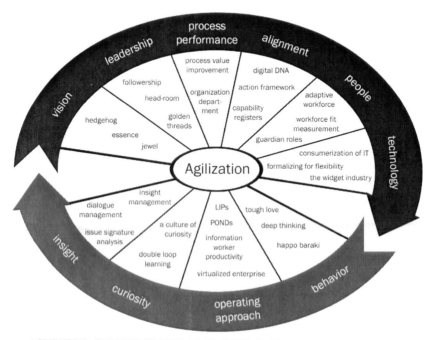

The mechanized versus agilized enterprise

Nick Lawrie posed the question to me early in the writing stages of Agilization, 'If you were a businessman contrasting the mechanization enterprise logic with the wind driven enterprise, how would you tell them apart?' My initial reaction was 'WHERE DO I BEGIN?' but fortunately I had time to reflect on my response. Below is the answer I came up with.

The differences between how an agilized organization thinks and acts compared to a mechanized organization is best described by slicing 'the corporate onion' to reveal four layers of the agilization model:

The upper area of the chart covers the topic areas that business books tend to focus on because they are tangible aspects of how an enterprise acts. The lower area of the chart (titles in the lighter grey) cover subjects that are less tangible and more to do with enterprise logic (the way it thinks). Corporations who have lost touch with their customers and entrepreneurial innovation need to improve their capabilities in these more thoughtful subject areas if they are to regenerate their competitiveness.

1. The *first layer* of the agilized organization is its **externalized perspective**. It looks outward more than it looks inward. It looks at tomorrow and thinks about what it needs to do to reshape its capabilities to fit new markets, to meet new challenges. It constantly seeks to find new opportunities (and threats) and continues to look outward to source the delivery of the knowledge and resources it needs to deliver customer value.

2. The *second layer* lies in its **leadership approach**. Its leadership drives improvement and always aims to better itself. The leadership believes passionately in achieving a vision that is commonly shared by its workforce and constantly reviews its strategy in the light of an ever-changing commercial landscape.

3. The *third layer* is the **operational model** that aims to achieve operational excellence by engineering the alignment of its resources to ensure they are fully trained on the attainment of strategic outcomes.

4. The *fourth layer* describes **capability factors** – i,e. how the organization maintains the appropriate supportive environment for its workforce (and contributors) that encourages positive norms of behaviour needed to create its customer value and embrace a culture of constant change.

From this thought process I produced an illustration that you will see overleaf to pictorially illustrate how this jigsaw puzzle piece of the agilized enterprise engineers itself to always fit its most profitable markets.

Figure 10. The agilization enterprise logic model

Agilization refers to an organization that is always willing and able to 'fit' its most profitable markets by gathering insight and using it to adapt and develop new business models

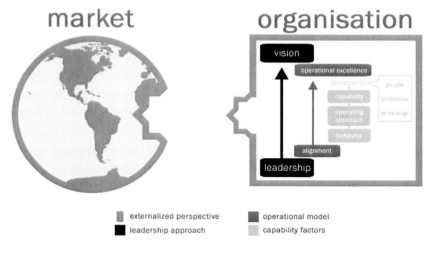

There were some other points that I jotted down to this question:

Agile organizations are intensely curious and always looking ahead for new opportunities. This thirst for insight leads to the development of mature processes to gather and interpret customer and market information. They want to be the first to see an opportunity and are prepared to invest time and resources to identify weak signals that suggest the slightest aspect of market change.

Contrast this view of the world (and management logic) to corporations of the last century that have thrived on operational excellence alone. It is an alien world to most leaders of the 20th century that have survived and thrived without really needing to do any different from one year to the next! One must feel a twinge of sympathy for management teams that have attended the same office for perhaps several decades, to check the dials and tweak the processes before switching off the lights and heading for home.

We live in a very different world now.

The *process* of being agile

On to the next question: 'Is agilization itself a process and if so what does it look like?'

To me Agilization is an *outcome*. No doubt others would identify it as the process of producing an enterprise that always fits its markets. The *process* of agilization could be described as the steps employed to enable an organization to sense, apply and act on its insights. An agilized enterprise knows that it is more likely to sustain its growth and achieve its vision, not by re-enacting a single business model year after year, but by constantly evaluating its strategy, business model and enterprise logic so this belief in constant change is fundamental to the culture of the agilized enterprise.

In this way it becomes adept at rapidly translating threats and opportunities and formulating new business models that respond to the changing balance of stakeholder needs and expectations. There are five core steps attached to agilization that cause the enterprise to be always consciously fitting its market opportunity.

I call these the five pillars (see overleaf).

Figure 12. Diagram to illustrate the five pillars of agilization

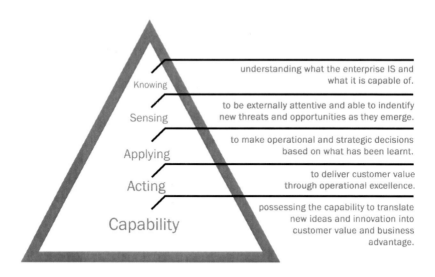

Knowing — understanding what the enterprise IS and what it is capable of.

Sensing — to be externally attentive and able to indentify new threats and opportunities as they emerge.

Applying — to make operational and strategic decisions based on what has been learnt.

Acting — to deliver customer value through operational excellence.

Capability — possessing the capability to translate new ideas and innovation into customer value and business advantage.

The five pillars are:

Knowing   Making decisions based on a deep appreciation of what the enterprise is, its values, place in the supply-chain, brand reach, skills and assets – and what it is capable of.

Sensing   Sensing emerging threats and opportunities.

Applying   Making decisions on new business models and management approaches based on new insight.

Acting   Delivering meaningful, targeted customer value through operational excellence and fit.

Capability   To build a capability to make all these things happen.

This top level view of 'being agile' shows the principle processes of turning customer wants into customer value – which is great if your organization is already *good* – but for organizations that are not energized and tuned-in to doing this, a process of modifying the *norms of behaviour* from *mechanization* to *agilization* will be needed that will touch on:

- The **operational excellence** of the enterprise – i.e. how good it is at discharging appropriate processes that fit its business needs today (and tomorrow).

- The ability of the enterprise to learn and develop new skills, approaches and capabilities (what I call **'learning and growth'**).

An organization that is excellent at delivery alone (i.e. very good in terms of its operational excellence) can no longer assume that it will sustain its success, due to the rapid fluctuations in market structures and customer demand. However, its ability to repeatedly fit market opportunity is heavily influenced by the way it *thinks* and *acts* on a day-to-day basis. Therefore, operational excellence remains critical to enterprise agility. The driving force behind agility remains the ability of leaders to build shared values across the enterprise and thrust towards a vision that is both qualitative and ambitious. Without this strong, passionate DRIVE, the process I describe has little chance of making a difference.

Much of the new thinking I describe in this book has to do with the key areas managers must focus on to reset the latent instruction set that says "This is the way organizations work." However, it is important not to forget the basic rules of good business management and housekeeping and the recognition that 'process excellence' remains the essential *jump-off point*.

Agilization underpins the growth sustainability of an enterprise, but it does this by encouraging deep thinking management behaviour and a culture of curiosity. Leaders can regenerate their competitiveness by thinking more about the way they are structured, what their latent instruction set actually looks like, their innovation process. This book hopefully kick-starts that deep thinking process.

Agilization examples

If we look at some of the successful corporations that exist today, there are signs of *early stage* agilization emerging. Companies exampled in this book such as Tesco, Apple, Nintendo, Rackspace and Pret A Manger provide snapshots of how organizations will think and operate in future.

None of these offers a complete example. Each succeeds in selective aspects of agilization but fails in other areas. The truest test of agilization is evidenced by corporations that can always appear to meet market demand as it emerges. So if these corporations were to be rated, I suspect that Tesco, Nintendo and Apple would be top of our list so far. But just because these organizations are today's benchmark does not mean they will always be the top players. I expect we will see a new list of brands emerge over the next few years that will transform the market view of what an agilized enterprise can achieve!

I'm thinking of course about the **tribal brands**. The customer's choice. The *trusted* brands. This new genre of organization will be the first place to go when people want to find something new. Something different. These new mammoth brands will benefit from low operating costs and high profits. How will traditional corporations compete with an advocacy-led customer champion brand? I don't think they will. Sensible manufacturing and service corporations will embrace this new brand culture because they will be the sales and marketing engines that remove the need for offline market research or the need to manage customer information. Some organizations like Apple and Google are rapidly moving towards this democratization of brand. They are feeding it, encouraging it, diving in as willing participants. Becoming followers. Will tribal brands displace the Internet-based broker sites that have emerged over recent years? I suspect not completely, as some of the better web comparison brands still have a few years yet to cement their customer and supplier relationships. They have time before the emergence of tribal brands to invest their profits in new contracts with suppliers that will guarantee their market position for at least a decade.

Smaller companies have *agilization* built in

Some leaders and managers will automatically agilize their organizations – without needing this book to help them – because they THINK this way. This is particularly true of smaller organizations. Take this story as an example:

> **In April 1999, the Sydney area of Australia suffered one of its worst-ever hail storms. Hail stones the size of small bricks were literally coming through the ceilings of houses and occupants were crowding under tables for cover. There was considerable property damage. Cars were overturned, trees torn from their**

roots. One of the consequences was that many houses suffered roof damage. A large number of them were under heritage conservation orders and this meant occupants had to replace rather than refurbish. One astute businessman was quick to recognise that all the slate tiles would need replacing. He explored the various sources of slate tiles. The biggest source was the Welsh quarry industry. He contacted the Welsh slate quarries and bought up supplies of their slate. When the Australian insurance industry kicked into gear following the storms, they found suddenly that the market price of replacement Welsh quarry tiles had shot through the roof (apologies for the pun!). What happened? Well, if the stories surrounding the aftermath of this event are true, an entrepreneur on the lookout for emerging customer demand realized that the storm would result in a consequence that would change demand within a particular market. He saw his opportunity to service this demand before others did, and had the confidence and resources to act on that knowledge.

Was this good entrepreneurial endeavour or true agilization? Does it matter? I would say, if it was one individual that did this, they would classify as an *entrepreneur*, but if it was a corporation, the enterprise would have needed to be agilized in order to achieve this outcome.

How many large organizations do you know that could have pulled off this *fleet-of-foot* response to leverage this opportunity? Yet with the resources available to a corporation, they would probably be better placed to organize such a response. And why didn't any of the insurance companies work out what their requirements might be and get there first by securing the likely stocks of slate tiles that they would need?

The Size and Shape of the Challenge

For many corporations, agilization will be painful. It will demand a widespread change to the way businesses secure and manage their innovation, resources and assets. As I have described in this book the rules of management practice are evolving and this will require new skills and a more thoughtful management approach.

There is a risk that management teams will *throw the baby out with the bath water* when transitioning from one economic engine to the next and may come to realize only too late that the people and the skills they needed to succeed were always accessible to them. Some will fail to properly appreciate what their organization is good at. They will misread what matters to their customers because they have not listened hard enough. They might also fail to harness the knowledge that exists within consultants and industry partners that they work with. These are all common mistakes I see happening in the businesses I work with.

There is no IT silver-bullet solution sitting in the wings to simplify the management task of becoming a wind-driven enterprise. 21st century organizations cannot presume that they will fit customer demands. They must constantly assess and re-assess their market opportunity. Businesses will need to invest in their IT systems to develop a holistic view of what their organization is capable of. These new systems will be needed to ensure the enterprise CAN react in a positive and timely manner when the light breezes of customer and market demand grow into gales. These methods and tools are not the secret of agilization, but they are necessary enablers. Management Information Systems must be reshaped to fit the new reality of business.

To regenerate their competitiveness, leaders of Western world corporations will have to prioritize agility over mechanization. To release management time, they will need to automate monitoring and supervisory tasks wherever possible; and to do this they will need to encourage *followership* – not just because that is what is needed to attract the best creative staff, but because they won't have the time to micro-manage.

Clearing out the 'in tray' of inward-looking management tasks means that leaders will be able to give more time to thinking creatively about how they can exploit their organizational competencies and abilities to their advantage. Leaders must think about what strengths they have to fit customer demands better than their competitors. This is an extremely creative process. More than ever before, the new leaders of corporations will need a team of highly motivated, creative thinkers. Where will they come from? How will the organization ensure that they fit?

The innovation organizations must nurture to *always fit* their market rarely comes from *within*. Corporations are likely to depend on a much broader community of innovators. Innovation is likely to be sourced from independent knowledge workers and new market *organisms* such as tribal brands. Organizations must learn how to harness these resources and break down their closed-wall approach to encourage a business behaviour that flourishes without walls.

No longer is it a simple question of coming up with the world's greatest technology or solution. Even that may not be enough! Remember that the technology behind the iPod was nothing revolutionary. It took the market-aware visionaries of Apple to transform customer value into a marketable product through design and the appreciation of what mattered most to young people, connecting into the psyche of the techno-savvy, mobile, participative generation – to find the right fit. Knowing what *fit* looks like will demand that customer insight management becomes a fundamental internal process within most businesses. Creating formalized information flows and systems to harness customer feedback, both online and offline, will introduce new skills and methods that will shift the balance in boardrooms towards customer-centric skills and roles.

My biggest fear is that organizations will become obsessed about how to capture and process customer insight and master agilization to the point that they spend EVEN MORE TIME looking inwardly at how they can mechanize these new processes.

My creativity soapbox

"Why," you ask, "isn't creativity one of the 10 agilization topics that I cover in this book?"

Creativity is integral to many of the topic areas – but creativity today is fighting against the latent instruction set of the enterprise, of behaviours and embedded, seemingly immovable processes. The harsh reality is that in many organizations, optimal processes and the ideology of mechanization are favoured above innovation, which smells a little of too much risk and arty people with lots of tattoos, body-piercing and bling.

To harness creativity, loosely-coupled organization structures and greater formalization of information flows is needed. But I'm not talking about those deeply-embedded business processes that grind out the deliverables of an economic engine day after day. I'm referring to those invisible flows of information across social networks that are the invisible bond between people and knowledge, talent and invention, customer service and brand confidence. This deeper appreciation of who does what, why and how enables the organization to capture insight, make sense of it, direct it to parts of the enterprise that need to make decisions, husband and mature great ideas and, in doing so, helps to deliver what matters most to customers time and again.

Considering how important creativity is to organizations today, it still takes my breath away when I see creativity being stifled by leaders and managers because they listen too much to protocol; because creative thinking is not encouraged; because poor IT tools mean that people who really can make the difference in the 'pockets' of the enterprise simply don't have the information they need to be empowered to do their jobs properly; because leaders do not make decisions or engender *followership*; because HR departments don't spend enough time thinking about the fit of their employees or practise tough love; because the organization is poorly aligned and wastes the time and energy of committed people who really want to make a difference and do a good job if only they knew how; because the organization shuts out its customers, cocoons its managers from outside markets, and stops listening; because the enterprise carries on thinking and behaving the same way as it has since the 1900s because it hasn't tackled the latent instruction set that exists that is creating the negative norms of behaviour; because the leadership team hasn't thought deeply enough about why it is doing what it has set out to do; because the enterprise has lost its ambition; because there aren't enough doers and the passion has long since died, switched off the light and shut the door.

If you are employed by an organization that resembles this description I sincerely hope you will have the drive and self confidence to move on.

What will cause the corporate push towards agilization?

There have been many books and articles over recent years that have sought to identify the tipping point that will create the next dramatic turn in social behaviour and the business environment that will necessitate the shift to agilization.

In this book I argue that that the tipping point has come and gone unnoticed but as a consequence the constancy of demand no longer exists as it did in the infancy of capitalism. Consumers are less prepared to settle for the 'standard Model-T Ford' and poor quality customer service. They want attractive designs, nice smells, tactility – they want to be different. 'Individualism' has emerged in the past decade as a term to describe a psychological self-determination among new generations to make life choices without interference. These values will be encouraged and enabled by emerging technologies but I believe *individualism* will ultimately show itself to be the biggest change in the way society and capitalism work.

Getting a head start on the competition

The reality today is most organizations are not agilized. The majority of corporations are unlikely to take action and change the way they think and work until they experience some sort of cataclysmic market event to produce a tipping point. This is the nature of change; a small amount of innovators are at the door when opportunity knocks and others wait in the wings to see what happens. Why wait? Why not take the lead?

Understanding how to engineer an organization to give it the ability to always fit its most profitable market is a sure way of stacking the odds in your favour and to achieve sustainable profitability. Whatever happens to our world in the future, individualism, participative technologies and tribal brands will be a part of it. So too with agilized organizations.

Go for it.

Index and Glossary

Advertising (23,39,43-46,58,148,188) describes a communication (usually paid for) intended to persuade a third party to invest in a product, service or idea, normally through various media.

Activity (111-116,163,167) describes something that could be done in an enterprise.

Action (70,88,89,110-126) describes something to be done in an enterprise.

Action framework (110-126) describes the data model that manages the relationships between day-to-day actions, organizational outcomes and insight that supports the processes of a wind-driven organization.

Agilized enterprise (15,62,68,72,78,123,145,146,160,162,174,180). An agilized enterprise demonstrates an ability to change tactics or direction quickly, i.e. to anticipate, adapt and react decisively to events in its business environment so that it may always fit its most profitable markets.

Agilization (3,20,53,57,63,68,71-77,97,123,160,256,267-281). The process of change from the traditional 'mechanized' and inward looking enterprise logic to a new externally focused enterprise logic that is characterized by successful corporations of the 21st century.

Anticipationomics (169,209). The process of anticipating changes to market conditions commonly supported by advanced search and self-organizing map technology.

Balanced scorecard (99.102.108,114,203). A model of business performance evaluation that balances measures of (1) financial performance, (2) what matters to customers, (3) internal processes and (4) innovation.

Blog (5,24,30,34,37,38,44,280) is short for weblog. A weblog is a journal that is frequently updated and intended for general public consumption. Blogs generally represent the personality of the author or website. See my blog (www.agilization.blogspot.com) for an example.

Bloggers (34) are people who blog (see above).

Brands (14,19,23,24,33,41-50). The name given to a product, service or idea that comes to represent its value and differentiation.

Business model (16,69,72,79,147,161,162,232). A business model describes the mechanism the enterprise plans to use to make money comprising an organization's value proposition, market segment strategy, value chain positioning, revenue generation model and cost structure. It is common for an enterprise to operate more than one business model.

Business intelligence (117,124,243,245,245). Business intelligence (BI) is a broad category of application programs and technologies for gathering, storing, analyzing, and providing access to data to help enterprise users make better business decisions.

Canvas, enterprise network (252). An information agent used by process managers to author formalized ways of gathering, sharing and managing information.

Capability (Enterprise) (69,70) describes the enterprise assets, skills and resources that will be employed within the strategy to deliver outcomes that will guide towards its vision.

Capitalism (29,30,58,60,268) describes a market system of private investment and industry with little governmental control.

Carlyle, Thomas (60). A truly gifted social commentator who reported on the consequences of the Industrial Revolution in the early 20th century

Challenges, corporate (113,116,122,127,139,154-157). A feature of an action framework operational model that introduces activities to test the usefulness and exhaustiveness of processes to meet stakeholder outcomes.

Cocooned enterprise (173). An enterprise that builds cultural and behavioural barriers that prevent managers from learning from customers and markets.

Code-free software (256) describes a software application for authoring information systems that negates the need for code-based programming.

Companies Act of England and Wales of 1844 (57,59) formalized the incorporation of joint-stock businesses and made it safer for individuals to invest their money in commercial enterprise.

Consumerism (58,59). The theory that a progressively greater consumption of goods is economically beneficial (closely linked to materialism – "the theory or doctrine that physical well-being and worldly possessions constitute the greatest good and highest value in life").

Content management, enterprise (245,248) describes a computerized system to manage the digital information assets of an organization. Content management systems were initially introduced to manage the content used in websites but have subsequently taken on a broader role to manage and track the location of, and relationships among, an organization's content at an element level in a repository.

Corporate challenge (154) is a process that asks the organization to respond to questions regarding its operational behaviour and performance.

Creative Capitalism/Capitalists (111) **Creative Capitalism** is a term popularized by American entrepreneur and Microsoft chairman Bill Gates at the 2008 World Economic Forum. The ideology calls for a new form of capitalism that works both to generate profits and solve the world's inequities, using market forces to better address the needs of the poor.

Customer Relationship Management – abbreviated to 'CRM' (177,179,181) refers to the methodologies and tools that help businesses manage customer relationships in an organized way, characterized today by computerized applications software systems that manage customer information and theme customer behaviours to facilitate marketing campaign programming.

Culture of curiosity (134,215). An enterprise behaviour that encourages employees to invest time in asking 'why?'

Database (35,43,110-119,123,124,138-143,154,173,180-183,200-202, 221,222,234,241-248.252-255.262) describes an organized body of related information normally today associated with computerized systems.

Database, relational (112,113,118,119,123,124,140,141,154,202). A database system in which the database is organized and accessed according to the relationships between data items without the need for any consideration of physical orientation and relationship. Relationships between data items are expressed by means of tables.

Dialogue management (134,179-188) describes a method and computing platform used to manage the two-way dialogue between businesses and their customers.

eBay (45,184) is The World's Online Marketplace®, enabling trade on a local, national and international basis. With a diverse and passionate community of individuals and small businesses, eBay offers an online platform where millions of items are traded each day.

Encanvas (143,251,258). Business agility software used to formalize the flow of information across and beyond the enterprise.

Enterprise action framework (110-126). See Action framework

Essence (69,75,78-83,164,169,182,258) also called organizational essence. Describes the emotional values that are established by leaders to determine the vision, strategy and operational behaviours of the enterprise.

Enterprise logic (96,97,115,119,158,160,169,287) describes the way an organization has been programmed to think and act; a blend of operating culture and procedure.

Enterprise network canvas (252). An IT system for gathering and sharing information using relational databases to theme and catalogue information that can be authored without programming code by process managers.

Enterprise resource planning – abbreviated to 'ERP' (245). An industry term for the broad set of activities supported by application software that helps a manufacturer or other business manage the important parts of its business, including product planning, parts purchasing, maintaining inventories, interacting with suppliers, providing customer service and tracking orders.

Faulkner, William (86) was a prolific American writer and Nobel Prize-winning novelist (1897-1962)

Focus area (114,196,206,262). An aspect of enterprise logic that catalogues stakeholder signals (comments) into interest themes that align insight to the way the organization thinks.

Focus area group (206). An aspect of enterprise logic that catalogues interest or themes into higher level groupings for analysis and interpretation purposes.

Followership (206). The ability of leaders to encourage people to want to make an *emotional commitment* to a *project*.

'Frictionless IT' (258) describes a progressive information management approach where costs and constraints associated with aligning IT to emerging business needs are non-existent. This creates unrivalled AGILITY. As organizations experience change, groups of users find themselves faced with situations that demand new information management applications. These key worker teams – the pockets of innovation in your business – need information systems that respond to their needs.

Gallwey, Tim (282). Wrote a good book about how to play tennis.

Golden threads (88-90,111,114,116,121,124). Strategic management initiatives that deliver stakeholder outcomes and cut across operating silos.

Hedgehog concept (84). A concept of strategic defence authored by Jim Collins in his book *Built to Last*. Collins studied the most consistently successful companies and found they had an objective understanding of (1) what the organization can be best in the world at (2) what drives the economic engine and (3) what the organization is deeply passionate about.

Hindenburg (60) was the name of a great airship built in the early 1900s that people thought at the time would revolutionize inter-continental travel. It blew up and consequently didn't.

IEEE (38). A non-profit-making organization, the world's leading professional association for the advancement of technology. The full name of the IEEE is the Institute of Electrical and Electronics Engineers, Inc.,

IEEE 802.15.3™ and IEEE 802.15.4™ (38). In January 2006, the IEEE Standards Association (IEEE-SA) published new high-rate and low-rate personal area network (PAN) standards, IEEE 802.15.3™ and IEEE 802.15.4™

for low-rate wireless personal area networks. In its technical materials, IEEE-SA suggested that the markets likely to be affected by the standard include consumer electronics, personal healthcare, toys, games, and home automation and security.

Inclusion programme (109,204,205). A key step in the formulation and articulation of strategy. This is a method used to gather the thoughts and ideas of stakeholders whilst at the same time breaking down cultural walls and understanding how stakeholders can contribute to delivery.

Indicators, performance (117,119,124,177). Describe the level of attainment. Also see Lead indicators, Lag indicators.

Individualism (5,19,20,23-31,41,46,48,50,132,179,183,229,230,268) The emergence of a social condition where individuals achieve a higher level of self-determination in making life choices and move away from paternalistic social structures that prescribe how the individual should act, how he should think and what he should be.

Industrial Revolution (23,59,60,259). A period of dramatic social change that began in England around the mid-1800s. People went from making goods in their own homes with simple tools to making them in large-scale factories with complicated machinery. As a result, many rural regions became more urban as cities grew rapidly around the new industrial activity.

Information flow (112,126,137,140-143,202,213,219-221,250-255). Management of the movement of information across social networks, organizational departments and operational silos.

Information flow software (140) describes a genre of applications software used to manage the movement of information across organizational silos.

Information process manager (140-142) describes a role responsible for overseeing the movement of information within a given operational process.

Information technology (33,75,119,129,210,231,241,247). All matters concerned with the furtherance of computer science and technology and with the design, development, installation, and implementation of information systems and applications.

Insight (173) describes a clear or deep perception of a situation. Chapter 12 describes insight capture mechanisms.

Issue signature analysis (178,193,196). An analysis system used to gather and interpret insight on what matters most to stakeholders for the purpose of aligning the external view of the organization with the incumbent enterprise logic (thereby creating an always learning organization).

Key performance indicator – abbreviated to 'KPI' (103) is a term that describes a reference point against which success can be evaluated prior to an activity being completed.

Knowledge workers (136,146,229,230,272). Peter Drucker used this term to describe a person who works primarily with information or a person who develops and uses knowledge in the workplace.

Lag indicator (103) – See also Key performance indicator – A generic term that describes a reference point against which success can be evaluated after an activity has happened.

Lead indicator (103) describes a reference point against which other things can be evaluated.

Ling Turner (7,92,95,236). A company specializing in delivering the service-profit value chain.

M&A (70,111,122,124,201,227) Mergers and acquisitions – refers to the aspect of corporate finance strategy and management dealing with the merging and acquiring of different companies as well as assets. Many mergers have failed to add significantly to shareholder value.

McKinsey Quarterly (52) a quarterly electronic newsletter published by the management consultancy firm and targeted at business leaders.

Mesh networks (35). A local area network (LAN) that employs one of two connection arrangements, full mesh or partial mesh topology. In the full mesh topology, each node (workstation or other device) is connected directly to each of the others. In the partial mesh topology, some nodes are connected to all the others, but some of the nodes are connected only to those other nodes with which they exchange the most data. The idea of mesh networks has been around for some time but it's only recently that the technology has been used in wireless communications.

Mission statement (81) describes the organization's "reason for being" – or at least it should do! Most are empty gestures that few staff know of or understand. To have meaning they must relate to the organizational essence.

Microsoft (52,118,180,242,250) is a global software corporation.

Multi-hop packet radio networks (38). An adaptive communication system that uses opportunistic peak-mode transmissions to transmit data between originating and destination stations via one or more intermediate stations. Each station monitors the activity of other stations in the network, storing connectivity information for use in subsequent transmissions. Each station also sends out probe signals from time to time to establish which other stations are in range. Messages are then sent across the network from station to station, with confirmation data being transmitted back to the originating station, until the destination station is reached. Old messages, which would otherwise clog the network, are timed out and deleted.

NDMC (6,83,87,118,129,175,196,199,202,209,213,242,251,252) is the management consulting business founded by Ian Tomlin and Nick Lawrie.

Objective (51,86-90,97-122,131,142,155,164,168,205-206,217,238). A goal to be attained (and which is believed to be attainable).

Outcome (15,19,53-59,62,69,70,75,81-99,100,123-126,221-276) describes the result of an action's being achieved.

Performance management (103,117,122,154,177) describes managing the process of doing something successfully.

Portfolio holder (88,115). in the context of an action framework, this describes a person responsible for a collection of objectives.

Priorities (88-90,98,99107-109,113,114,119,124,174,175,193,237). In the context of an action framework, these represent the areas of policy for focused attention during a given term.

Processes (128-145,151-155). A series of activities that transform an input into a desired output.

Quad-Charting (128,-145,151-155,154,167-169,271) – A method for managing projects on a single page authored by Mike Clargo of Tesseracts Ltd.

QFD (128,-145,151-155,154,167-169,271) – quality function deployment – a method of business activity management formed around a matrix that aligns business objectives with performance measures and delivery mechanisms (e.g. function, unit, department or process).

Responsibility (20,44,53,88,115,128,135,142,148,230-233,249,251) in the context of an action framework describes a person or organizational tier (e.g. a department) responsible for delivering a collection of actions.

Roosevelt, Franklin D. (94) – American president.

Scorecarding (98,99,103-107) – See Balanced scorecard.

Service profit chain (167,236) – (J.Heskett, W. E. Sasser, L. Schlesinger) – is a management model that identifies the link between profit/growth and loyalty, satisfaction and value.

Signal (17,57,61-72,74,106,114,119,121,134,169,173,174,196-199,205-219,254) describes an item of information that calls on the organization to act.

Stakeholders (105-107,110-112,123,134,140,144,202,205,209,210,249) is a term that describes a broad grouping of an individual, group or organization with an interest in the activities of an organization.

Steering wheel (87,103). An approach adopted by Tesco Stores Ltd that helps to make strategy something all stakeholders can understand.

Sticky Values (87,103). Values individuals share that lead them to come together to share experiences and common interests.

Strategy (19,37,69,81-129,197-203) describes an elaborate and systematic plan of action.

Titanic (60,290) was a ship that people believed couldn't be sunk because humankind had reached a stage in its innovative use of technology where it could even overcome the powers of nature. It sank.

Tribal brand (41-50). A brand created to identify a community developed 'organically' as the result of individuals wanting to share common values that results in a translation of these values into buying power.

Vision (78-83) describes the 'future wanted state' of the enterprise as determined by the board of directors.

Widget (259-261). Technology components that can be 'glued' together to enable non-programmers to link to, or create, composite applications of their own making authored using web-scripting languages – Hypertext Markup Language (HTML), Cascading Style Sheets (CSS) and JavaScript.

Wireless networking (38). Provision of an ability to connect to the Internet using a wireless (no cables) computer or mobile device.

Wedgwood, Josiah (57,58,259). Pioneered production management techniques during the Industrial Revolution.

Welch, Jack C. (79,173) was the man who led the rapid expansion of General Electric Company in the mid-20th century.

References

1. Robert S. Kaplan, David P. Norton, "The Balanced Scorecard", Harvard Business School Press.

2. The Revd. Dr Michael Moynagh and Richard Worsley "The Tomorrow Project, GLIMPSES of tomorrow", http://www.tomorrowproject.net.

3. Shoshana Zuboff and James Maxmin, "The Support Economy", Allen Lane, The Penguin Press.

4. Martin Lindstrom with Patricia B Seybold, "Brand Child", Kogan-Page.

5. "The rise and rise of the UK home worker", http://www.flexibility.co.uk /flexwork/location/Homeworkers2005.htm, 2005.

6. HM Government, "Changes to self-employment in the UK: 2002 to 2003", www.statistics.gov.uk/articles/labour_market_trends.

7. Gabriel Brown, "The Business of Fixed/Mobile Convergence", June 2006.

8. East of England Development Agency, "Report on Norfolk Open Link."

9. James C. Collins and Jerry I. Porras, "Built to last", HarperBusiness.

10. "Environment Report 2004/5", published by The Waste & Resources Action Programme (WRAP).

11. Joseph Boyett and Jimmy Boyett, "The Guru Guide", John Wiley and Sons.

12. Ethan M. Rasiel, "The McKinsey Way", Magraw-Hill.

13. Michael Clargo, "Managing by Design, Using QFD to Transform Management Performance."

14. Argyris, C. "Double-loop learning in organizations", Harvard Business Review 1977, 55(5), 115-125.

15. HM Government, "Modernising Government White Paper" published March 30, 1999.

16. David W. McCoy, Daryl C. Plummer, "Defining, Cultivating and Measuring Enterprise Agility". Gartner Inc.

17. Janelle Hill and Michael Melenovsky, "Achieving Agility: BPM Delivers Business Agility through New Management Practices". Gartner Inc.

18. David McCoy and Jim Sinur, "Achieving Agility: The Agile Power of Business Rules". Gartner Inc.

19. Bern Elliot, Steve Blood and Bob Hafner "Achieving Agility through Communication-Enabled Business Processes". Gartner Inc.

20. Lowell L. Bryan and Claudia Joyce, "The 21st Century Organization", McKinsey & Co. Quarterly, June 2006.

21. Personnel Today, "Does the HR Department have Oomph?" 2007.

22. Press release, "Managers Say the Majority of Information Obtained for Their Work Is Useless", Accenture Information Management Services (AIMS), January 2006.

23. Thomas J. Peters and Robert H. Waterman Jr. "In Search of Excellence", Harper and Row.

24. A. Reader, "Strategic Human Resource Management", The Open University Business School, Sage Publications.

25. Lowell L. Bryan, Eric Matson, and Leigh M. Weiss, Harnessing the power of informal employee networks, McKinsey & Co. 2007.

26. Joanna Barsh interview with Gary Hamel and Lowell Bryan, "Innovative management: Forward-looking executives must respond to the growing need for a new managerial model." January 2008.

27. Stephen Watt, "Mashups -- The evolution of the SOA, Part 2: Situational applications and the mashup ecosystem", IBM, November 2007.

28. Don Peppers and Martha Rogers, P.H.D. "The One to one Future", First Currency Paperback, 1997.

29. Alan Mitchell, "Right Side Up", Harper Collins Business, 2002.

30. Fred Wiersema, "The New Market Leaders", Free Press Business, 2001.

31. Walter Goldsmith and David Clutterbuck, "The Winning Streak", Penguin Business.

32. Peter B. B. Turney, "Common Cents, The ABC Peformance Breakthrough," Cost Technology.

33. Computer Business Review, "Mashups open up business Web 2.0 opportunities", Saturday, December 1, 2007

34. Phil Wainwright, "Enterprise Mashups, A lesson from history", Jan 2006.

35. L. Cherbakov, A. Bravery, B. D. Goodman, A. Pandya, J. Baggett, "Changing the corporate IT development model: Tapping the power of grassroots computing", IBM SYSTEMS JOURNAL, VOL 46, NO 4, 2007.

36. L. Cherbakov, Andy J. F. Bravery, Aroop Pandya, "SOA meets situational applications, Part 1: Changing computing in the enterprise", IBM, August 2007.

37. Martin LaMonica, "Start-up makes electric power from motion", November 2007.

38. David Cearley, "Wake up to mashups", Gartner, November 2006.

39. Helen D'Antoni, "IT Investments Drive Worker Output", InformationWeek, 2002.

40. Sandra Rogers and Rob Halstone, "Assessing the TCO of composite application approaches", IDC Report, September 2003.

41. Jackie Fenn, "Gartner Hype Trends 2006", Gartner Inc.

Information Contributors

I would like to thank the following contributors for their ideas, thoughts and experiences:

Dr Alpheus Bingham. Dr. Bingham is Founder and Board Member of Innocentive, the first online forum that allows world-class scientists and science-based companies to collaborate in a global scientific community to achieve innovative solutions to complex challenges. In 2005, Dr Bingham won "The Business Processes Award" category at the fourth annual Innovation Summit and Awards event, sponsored by The Economist magazine. (www.InnoCentive.com).

Nick Dodds, CEO of CWP Consultants Ltd. A well-respected innovator in the area of workspace consulting.

Mike Clargo, CEO of Tesseracts Ltd. Mike is a prolific management consultant and arguably the leading international business experts on the subject of how to achieve operational effectiveness.   His company Tesseracts Ltd promotes the adoption of the Quality Function Design model included in this book. To find out more visit (www.tesseracts.co.uk).

Peter Franklin, CEO of enstra consulting with specialist knowledge of business practises in the Energy and Utilities sector. Enstra enables teams to come to a common view of the best way forward when facing complexity and uncertainty using consulting methods developed in house. (http://www.enstra.com)

George Guernsey, CEO of Insight Mapping Ltd (www.insightmapping.com).

Bob Kiley. Leadership guru, practitioner and advisor on transport issues.

David Kingham. A prolific supporter of entrepreneurs. Amongst his many successful projects, David has established one of the largest and most successful chains of innovation centres across the South of England. David is CEO of Oxford Innovations Ltd (www.oxin.com).

Jane Ling and Jenny Turner have authored certificated training programmes to create positive norms of behaviour. Jane and Jenny are Directors of Ling Turner Ltd (www.lingturner.co.uk).

Guus Mannaerts has authored a new methodology, supported by technology, to help executives create a recruitment process that matches the attitudes of workforce to the behavioural and motivational needs of the organization. Guus is a director of MatchQ (www.matchQ.nl).

Dr Martin Vasey. A pragmatic thought leader in the area of extracting value from knowledge. Dr Vasey led a team at British Gas to design and deploy a successful 16,000 seat global knowledge portal that resulted in the team's winning an International Information Industry Award for 'Best Intranet of the Year' in 1999.

Judith Wainwright is managing director of Beeagile Ltd, a management consultancy specializing in the subject of this book. Beeagile help corporations to follow good practice, work in alignment to ensure agility and make sure that management teams are encouraging the right mindset. (www.beeagile.co.uk)